SUCCESS WITH LISTINGS

D1599070

PUBLISHING

AUSTIN, TEXAS
512-872-3843

www.SuccessWithListings.com

For more information contact info@SuccessWithListings.com or call 512-872-3843.

ISBN 978-0-9895872-2-8

Available at Amazon and other online retailers

www.SuccessWithListings.com

SUCCESS WITH LISTINGS

HOW TO FIND, SECURE AND SELL MORE LISTINGS

KNOLLY WILLIAMS

*To Josefina Saldaña Williams aka "Peet"
my best friend and life companion.*

SECTION 1:
Launching Your Listing Business

SECTION 3

Securing the Listing

11. Pre-Listing Questionnaire and Research 193

SECTION 4

Selling the Listing

14. Preparing Your Listing for Success

.... 293

15. Systematize and Automate Your Listing for Success 317

SECTION 5

Growing Your Listing Business

Section

I

Launching Your
Listing Business

CHAPTER 1

Becoming a Listing Specialist

Hi there! So you want to begin focusing on listings, eh? Great decision. I firmly believe that if you want to survive and thrive in the real estate game, listings are where it is at.

Whether you are a brand-new agent or a seasoned veteran, this book will help you focus on listings and streamline your listing system so that you will be able to help more sellers, work fewer hours and earn more income.

Before I got my real estate license in 2003, I had the good fortune of meeting Linda Ramsey and Mary Ann Nations, two outstanding leaders at Keller Williams Realty in Austin, TX. They both gave me sound advice about launching my career in real estate and Linda gave me a copy of *The Millionaire Real Estate Agent* by Gary Keller. I read through the book several times, and was fascinated by the wisdom I found on its pages. Six months later I began my real estate career with the firm decision that I was going to focus on listings.

I ordered my first batch of business cards and guess what my title was? Instead of just going with the traditional title of REALTOR® or Real Estate Agent, I chose LISTING SPECIALIST. I had never shown a home to a buyer nor had I yet worked with a seller, nevertheless I determined in my mind that I was going to focus on listings and be a Listing Specialist from the very beginning of my career.

The decision paid off, and I went on to take more than 1,000 listings within my first 10 years in the business. I was able to succeed where others were failing primarily by utilizing just one simple strategy: *I learned what top Listing Specialists were doing to achieve success in their business and I duplicated those 'best practices' in my own practice.* In the process, I amalgamated a streamlined system that many of my students have found is easy to duplicate and implement in their own business.

This book is designed to help you shortcut a path to becoming a top Listing Specialist in your market. As I was coming up, many mentors, agents and coaches helped me along the way, and now I am blessed to be able to pay it forward and give back by sharing this knowledge with you.

Truthfully, Success with Listings begins in the mind. You have to be absolutely convinced that you *are* a top Listing Specialist before you actually become one. I believe that success in the real estate game (or any business endeavor) is more than 90% mental.

We will get to the mental stuff in Chapter 3 (and then carry it throughout the book), but for now I would like to share with you the specific activities that take place during the listing lifecycle and what a day in the life of a successful Listing Specialist looks like.

The Listing Lifecycle

The volume of activities that go into a successful listing practice can seem overwhelming. My good friend and mentor Rand Smith has actually identified 256 specific activities that take place for each listing he takes!

In my simplified listing system, I have identified the 46 major activities that must take place during the listing lifecycle. When you further break each of these down you would probably come up with Rand's several hundred activities, but I'm going to keep it simple for you.

If you are new to the listings game, or just getting reacquainted with taking listings, just reading through the list of activities involved can make becoming a successful Listing Specialist seem like a daunting feat. Please don't be overwhelmed. In this guide I will serve as your *Success Coach*, and my intention is to help you grow your practice to the point where you are only handling just one, two or three of the 46 activities involved. Granted, you will probably want to handle most of these activities initially (so that you can learn each step in-depth), however in time you can hand most of these tasks off to others. In my own case, I took more than 21 listings during my first 74 days in the business and within eight months of obtaining my real estate license I hired and trained my first Admin. The decision allowed me to delegate the majority of my daily tasks so that I could focus on generating more listing appointments and building my listing inventory.

Let's go ahead and take a cursory chronological look at the 46 core activities you will be performing on each and every listing you take. Here I am going to simply give you a brief overview and synopsis of the 46 activities. In Chapters 6 through 19 I will be expounding on each of these specific tasks, and I will provide you with step-by-step details about each activity while showing you exactly how to purposefully implement each step into your successful listing business.

Note that there are five distinct listing phases that these activities fall under:

1. Pre-Listing
2. Listing Setup
3. Listing Servicing
4. Contract-to-Close
5. Post-Closing

Knolly's 46 Step Listing System

PRE-LISTING

- **Step 1. Generate Seller Prospect.**

  Generating each successful listing begins with prospecting for seller leads (lead generation). In chapters 6 through 10 I will show you how to generate all the leads you will possibly need from what I call the

3 Lead Buckets. Don't skip ahead! Chapters 1-5 lay the foundation for a thriving listing career. If you skip these fundamental chapters you will be building your house on sinking sand.

- **Step 2. Initial Phone Consultation with Seller Questionnaire.**

  On this brief initial call with your seller prospect, you will obtain the basic details about the property (so that you can do your research) and you will set a specific *call back* time to discuss the seller's needs and wants in greater detail. This step can be handled by either you or your Admin. I will teach you the specific scripts and questions to ask that will lead to success.

- **Step 3. Send Seller Prospect Your Follow-up Email.**

  Immediately after your initial phone conversation with your seller prospect you will send your follow-up email setting the expectation for a return call from you at a mutually agreed upon time. Your email will also contain a link to your pre-listing package (or an attachment). I'll give you the specific email script to use and show you how to create a winning pre-listing package.

- **Step 4. Input the Prospect into Your Database.**

  Before you move on to the next steps, you will want to immediately add the seller prospect to your database, so that you and your team can access their information quickly, and begin incubating them. I'll show you how.

- **Step 5. Do Comparative Market Analysis (CMA) and Research.**

  Your next step is to complete a thorough market analysis on the property. Here I will show you how to streamline your CMA in a way that makes the data leap off the page, and I'll show you how to allow the market to speak for itself. I'll also walk you through some simple ways to conduct the preliminary research thoroughly and efficiently so that you sound like the neighborhood expert, and gain the respect and trust of your seller prospects.

- **Step 6. Phone Consultation with Seller Prospect and Set the Listing Appointment.**

  Now that you have done your thorough research (due diligence), you are ready to conduct your phone consultation and set the listing appointment. People do business with people they know, like and trust. Here I will teach you how to build strong rapport and how to get the seller prospect to know, like and trust you before the call concludes. I will also show you how to lock in a solid listing appointment that the seller won't want to cancel or reschedule.

- **Step 7. Send Seller Prospect a Follow-up Email.**

  Now you will send your seller prospect a follow-up email which will be crafted to help solidify YOU as their agent of choice. In addition to further *building rapport,* this email also signifies to your client that you are a professional and that you are here to help them.

- **Step 8. Drop off Your Pre-Listing Package.**

  You will want to drop off a physical copy of your pre-listing package with your seller prospect as soon as possible. Here I will show you how to sneak in a quick 3 minute face-to-face with the seller to further your rapport and have them strongly anticipating your upcoming meeting together.

- **Step 9. Draw up the Listing Docs.**

  Now it's time to prepare the listing paperwork and put your listing presentation folder together. How you draw up the listing docs will most certainly help determine the size of your paycheck. I'll show you several fool-proof tactics that will help you net your full commission on every listing you take.

- **Step 10. Confirm the Listing Appointment and Request that the Seller Homework Be Filled Out Ahead of Time.**

  On this call you will not only confirm the appointment, but you will also request that the *Seller Homework* be filled out ahead of time. In Chapter 5 I'll show you how to put together a winning seller homework packet as part of your pre-listing package.

- **Step 11. Conduct the Listing Appointment and Secure the Listing.**

  During the previous steps you have gone a long way to build rapport with your soon-to-be seller. Now it's time to bag the listing so you can achieve success for your client. I will share with you an incredible listing presentation, presentation scripts and numerous tips and tricks that will make sellers want to list with YOU. You will learn exactly what to do and what to say to secure the listing. Since price sells homes, I'll also give you the 10 specific scripts that will help you get the listing at the right price.

LISTING SETUP

- **Step 12. Collect Property Survey.**

  If your seller has a copy of the property survey you'll want to collect this from them as early on as possible. I'll give you a simple email script to help the seller locate this important document.

- **Step 13. Prepare the House for Sale.**

  At the listing appointment, you gave the seller your *"Preparing Your House for Sale"* Checklist and now it's time to do a final walk-through to ensure that the house is ready for the market. This handy checklist will help you sell each listing faster, obtain success for you client sooner, and help you achieve the highest price possible for the listing, which means more money for your client and for you.

- **Step 14. Set Up the Property.**

  Now that you have insured that the listing is ready for the market it's time to place your sign and lockbox! Here we will talk about systems that will help you generate additional listings from every listing you take.

- **Step 15. Order Professional Photography.**

  The property is sparkling and ready for its glamour shots! According to NAR *(National Association of REALTORS®)*, 92% of buyers begin their home search online. Next to pricing, great photos can generate showings faster than any other aspect of the listing. I'll show you how to get fantastic photos every time. We will also discuss the role of virtual tours and video tours.

- **Step 16. Write the Property Description.**

  Writing a killer property description is critical for boosting showing activity. I'll show you how to create an accurate and compelling property description that will generate more showings.

- **Step 17. Input the Listing to MLS.**

  Since 92% of all home searches begin online, inputting accurate and complete information into all of the most critical data fields available on the MLS will ensure that you and your sellers receive the maximum amount of traffic. In chapter 5 I show you how to implement a 2 page Property Description checklist that you, a team member or the seller can fill out, so that nothing is overlooked.

- **Step 18. Upload Docs to MLS.**

  Upload key documents to the MLS to help streamline your interactions with buyer agents. I'll show you which time-saving documents to upload, resulting in fewer dialogues with agents prior to receiving offers on your listings.

- **Step 19. Upload Photos to the MLS.**

  Pick the best photos and upload them to the MLS before making the listing active.

- **Step 20. Review the Listing and Make it Active (GO LIVE!).**

  I'll provide you with a quick and easy checklist to implement prior to making the listing active.

LISTING SERVICING

- **Step 21. Set Up the Listing in Your Database and Start the Transaction.**

  At this point, you will input the listing and upload the documents into your online database. Using the Transaction Manager feature of your database, I will show you how to initiate the transaction so you can easily document all of the activities from listing through closing.

- **Step 22. Initiate and Invite Seller to the Online Transaction.**

  Since sellers don't often directly see the volume of behind-the-scenes tasks going into the successful sale of their house, they can sometimes get the idea that you are simply earning easy money. Using your online database, I will show you how to invite your clients to login to their listing transaction so they can see what is happening with the sale of their house in real time. When logged into their online seller portal, clients can easily view all of the tasks performed, notes, uploaded documents, and important dates. This helps sellers clearly see that you have handily earned your paycheck.

- **Step 23. Set Up an Action Plan for Your Listing**

  I will teach you how to relate to each new listing as a *project*. Your action plan serves as a project task manager (checklist) and helps you and your client keep track of which steps you have completed and where you are in the process. This system will eliminate all guesswork and streamline your listing business.

- **Step 24. Initiate Marketing Plan for Your Listing.**

  Now it's also time to pull the trigger on your listing marketing. An effectively marketed listing can generate at least one additional listing lead and two solid buyer leads. I'll show you a quick, effective and low-cost marketing plan that you can easily implement on each listing to spread the word, satisfy the seller and create more business.

- **Step 25. Set Up Electronic Showing Feedback.**

  Sellers want to know what prospective buyers are saying about their property. Using an electronic showing feedback system is critical to getting your listings sold faster and for the top dollar. I'll show you what showing survey questions to ask, and how to implement a low-cost system.

- **Step 26. Set Up "Weekly Update" Email Drip Campaign to Seller with Link to Your CRM.**

  One of the biggest complaints sellers have is not knowing what is going on with their property sale.

Without good communication, sellers can feel in the dark, which can lead to a bad rapport. Busy Listing Specialists get too involved with prospecting, negotiating contracts and listing appointments to effectively keep sellers in the loop. Using your online database, I will show you how to completely automate your seller updates by implementing an easy 5 minute system that will send weekly automated "project updates" to the seller. This system eliminates countless phone calls from your schedule and keeps your sellers happy.

- **Step 27. Make Periodic Price Adjustments.**

  Since price is the single most important factor in the sale of real estate, I will show you how to quickly calibrate and correct the pricing of each listing during the listing process, and how to save even more time by building automatic price adjustments into every listing you take.

- **Step 28. Receive and Negotiate Offers.**

  As you begin to receive offers on the property, you will see that emotions for both the buyer and seller are running at an all-time high, and adversarial tensions can arise. I'll show you how to master your own emotions, and how to use artful and skillful negotiation to obtain the best possible price for the seller, while helping the buyer realize they are getting a fair shake.

CONTRACT TO CLOSE

- **Step 29. Update MLS Status to *Pending*.**

  Congratulations! You are now officially under contract! Once the offer is executed by all parties, you will need to update the MLS status to Pending or Pending Taking Backups. I'll show you some easy tips to maximize the effect of this momentous occasion and show you some great ways to use each new pending sale as an occasion to generate even more listing referrals!

- **Step 30. Initiate *Closing* Action Plan.**

  Now that the listing is under contract, I'll walk you through how to initiate your Contract-to-Close Action Plan in your CRM.

- **Step 31. Congratulatory Call and Email to Seller.**

  Now it's time to officially congratulate the seller. I'll give you an effective email and phone script and show you how to use this momentous occasion to generate more listing leads from your seller.

- **Step 32. Send Executed Contract to Seller.**

  Once the offer is signed by all parties you will send a copy of the fully executed contract to the seller. I'll give you an effective email script and show you how to clearly and effectively generate more listing leads from your seller.

- **Step 33. Negotiate Any Post-Inspection Items.**

  The property inspection report can be one of the most ruinous aspects of the transaction. I'll show you how to set the seller's expectation and how to utilize artful and skillful negotiation techniques to navigate through this volatile period.

- **Step 34. Send *Client Information Sheet* to Escrow Office.**

  At this juncture you will want to provide all of the seller's contact information to the title company or law firm in charge of closing escrow on the transaction. I'll show you how to get the Escrow Officer on board with your expectations in order to achieve a trouble-free closing.

- **Step 35. Weekly Contact and Updates to Seller.**

  You will want to continue providing your seller with weekly updates on the status of the transaction. I'll show you how to save time by using your CRM to provide *automated* updates.

- **Step 36. Submit All Documents to Your Compliance Department.**

  Your office or broker will have a checklist of items that you need to submit in order to remain in compliance, mitigate future legal liability and get paid on the transaction. I'll show you how to gather these documents early in the game and alleviate last-minute pressure.

- **Step 37. Send DA and DI to Escrow Office.**

  Once your DA (Disbursement Authorization) is created by your office, I'll show you how to create and send your custom DI (Disbursement Instructions) so that you can get paid quickly.

- **Step 38. Handle All Closing Details.**

  Here I will show you how to conduct a final review of your file so that you can quickly handle any last-minute closing items and details in order to ensure a smooth closing.

- **Step 39. Review *HUD-1 Settlement Statement* with Seller.**

  Before you show up to the closing table, you will want to review the HUD-1 Settlement Statement with your seller. I'll give you a simple formula and script for reviewing this document with your seller so that you can avoid any surprises at the closing table.

- **Step 40. Attend Closing.**

  Create a final bond with your client by attending the closing and providing your congratulations in person. I'll show you how to piggyback the close of escrow with a script that will help you generate more listing referrals from your sellers.

POST-CLOSING

- **Step 41. Send Post-Closing Gifts to Seller and Buyer.**

  I'll show you how to incorporate some post-closing gifts for your seller (and the buyer), to ensure their future loyalty and generate referrals.

- **Step 42. Send *Homeowner's Tip Guide* to Buyer.**

  I'll show you how to create your Homeowner's Tip Guide and use it to build rapport and generate more future business.

- **Step 43. Update the Transaction in Your CRM.**

  At this juncture I'll show you how to update your CRM by changing the property status to *Closed*, halting any drip campaigns and closing out the transaction.

- **Step 44. Add Buyer to Your CRM.**

  I'll show you how to build your database (and future business) by adding the purchasers of your listings to your CRM. Over time you can convert them into loyal clients.

- **Step 45. Send Seller Your *Post-Closing Seller Survey* via Email.**

  I'll provide you with a quick and easy survey to send to your seller clients so that you can identify any necessary tweaks to the various components of your listing system. I'll also show you how to generate a great testimonial from your seller that you can use to generate even more listings.

- **Step 46. Pick Up Your Sign and Lockbox.**

  Finally you'll need to run by the property for the last time to pick up your goodies. I'll show you some great ways to use this opportunity to offer a final congratulations to the buyer and offer your "*Love it or Leave it Guarantee*" and *Resale Coupon* which will greatly increase the likelihood of you relisting the property in the future.

So there it is! These 46 steps are the core of a solid listing system that will allow you to achieve success on each and every listing you take. As I train you on each step, I'll be showing you how to generate even more listings throughout the lifecycle of every active listing, and how to build loyal clients for life.

Again, please don't feel overwhelmed. You can and you will master this. The really cool news is that the larger your business grows, the less you will *personally* have to do. In chapters 19 through 23 I will show you how to build a successful listing team to whom you can delegate roughly 93% of the aforementioned activities. That's when things can really get exciting! Once you have your team in place, this training manual will double as a guidebook for each of your team members.

Now that we've completed our cursory overview of your listing system, let's take a look at *A Day in the Life of a Successful Listing Specialist.*

A Day in the Life of a Successful Listing Specialist

Have you ever wanted to *shadow* a successful Listing Specialist? You know, be a fly on the wall or tag along with her during a typical day in her life. Well, let's do that now. Journey with me as we take a look at a Day in the Life of a Successful Listing Specialist.

6-7am | Personal Growth (meditation, reading, prayer).

Successful Listing Specialists are always expending positive energy. It is critical that you take time for yourself to refuel the inner man so that you don't run dry and burn out. Personal growth time allows you to fill back up and ignites your motivation by reminding you of your purpose.

7am - 8:30 am | Prepare for Success.

Exercise, personal care, healthy breakfast, dress for success and off to your lead generation bunker! Now it's time to build up the outer man. Preparing for success equips you with the physical energy to make it through the day.

9 am – Noon | Lead Generation and Prospecting to Set Listings Appointments.

The successful Listing Specialist is first and foremost in the lead generation business. As a Listing Specialist, prospecting will consume the first part of your work day. During this critical time, you will be focused on 3 activities: 1) generating listing leads from your listing lead buckets (chapters 6-10), 2) following up on leads received and 3) developing your marketing strategies.

Noon | Eat a Healthy Lunch.

For the successful Listing Specialist, it is critical to take a scheduled break to decompress and refuel from the fun yet demanding prospecting activities you've been doing all morning.

1pm – 5pm | Go on Listing Appointments.

Successful Listing Specialists spend their afternoon performing listing appointments and obtaining listing agreements. In between appointments you can check in with your team, check email, etc.

5-6pm | Wrap Up and Prep for Next Work Day.

Review your goals and numbers for the day/week and set up your schedule for the next work day. This final daily review allows you to compare your results with your goals and calibrate for success, keeping you on track.

Most successful Listing Specialists work a typical Monday through Friday schedule with the majority of nights and weekends off. Top Listing Specialists focus on only two core activities: 1) generating listing leads and 2) securing listing contracts. They delegate all other activities to others.

Deciding to become a Listing Specialist is first and foremost a mental process. You have to be absolutely convinced that you can and will succeed, even when your mind tries to get in the way of your success. You can't afford to let anyone or anything derail you from success. In chapters 3 and 4 we will take a good look at exactly what success is. To thrive at listings you should either be preparing for success (chapters 1-5), achieving success (chapters 6-18) or growing your success (chapters 19-23). This guide was written to help you during every phase and at every juncture in your journey.

OK – so are you ready to become a Listing Specialist? Are you ready to generate the kind of business you've always wanted? Are you ready to create the lifestyle that you've promised to yourself and your family? Are you ready to make an impactful difference in the lives of others? If so, let's move on to the next chapter where we will take a deeper look at why listings are king of the real estate jungle.

Chapter 1 Homework:

☐ Download my *46 Step Listing System* from www.SuccessWithLisings.com. This one page doc bullets my complete system.

☐ Review this list over and over again so that it becomes part of you!

☐ Decide which items you will do yourself and which items you will delegate

Chapter 2

Why Focus on Listings?

If you really want to build your real estate business to its highest possible potential, you will focus on seller listings. I see too many agents who launch their career with the idea that they will begin with buyers and someday graduate to sellers. This is the wrong approach. Even if you are new to the business, I want you to really take to heart the idea of becoming a Listing Specialist, now. Don't worry – if you've already been in the business for a while and you aren't currently seller-centric, this book will act as your transition guide to gearing your entire operation toward working with sellers.

To help you better visualize the stark contrast in the opportunity between a Buyer Specialist and a Listing Specialist, I have outlined 10 reasons why you should strongly consider focusing your business on seller listings.

On my top 10 list, the first 6 come straight from *The Millionaire Real Estate Agent*. I can't thank Gary Keller, Dave

Jenks and Jay Papasan enough for having the fortitude and foresight to pen that phenomenal and life changing book.

TOP 10 Reasons You Should Focus on Listings

Reason #1: Seller Listings Mean More Marketing Opportunities - Branding!

1. You get to put your sign in the front yard.
2. You get to market the listing through your database, direct mail, email, social media, etc.
3. You get to advertise via internet, print, etc.

All of this exposure shines the spotlight squarely on you and your expertise as a Listing Specialist. In this way, the more listings you get, the more listings you get. That's because listings beget listings. When working with buyers, there exists no such opportunity, because there is no prominently positioned signage that announces to the world that you are working with that buyer client. Nor can you market a current buyer in hopes of generating another.

Listings come already prepackaged with multiple promotional vehicles that continue to work on your behalf until the property is no longer on the market. Even the simple act of placing your yard sign in the yard and putting the property on MLS opens up a stream of marketing channels that showcase you and your listing. Each listing you have essentially assists you in generating more business.

Your yard sign tells the surrounding neighborhood that "The Smiths are trusting me with the sale of their house, and you should too!" Every time someone in the neighborhood drives or walks by your sign, you are making another impression and furthering your brand. As you build your reputation through farming (chapter 8) it will be easier for you to convert the homeowners in the surrounding neighborhoods to active clients whenever the time comes for them to sell. They have already seen you and they have witnessed your work.

I can honestly tell you that few things will bring you greater excitement and fulfillment than seeing your signs in yards across the areas where you serve. In this way you should consider each sign akin to a free neighborhood marketing billboard – working to further your brand and generate more business (buyers and sellers) for you and your team.

Reason # 2: You Get More Control of Your Time.

Buyers can be frantic and frazzled. They want to find the best deal and get it before a competing buyer does. And who can blame them for that? In the process they drag you along (sometimes by the ear).

Most sellers take a completely different approach. Sellers realize that the house is going "on the market" and they will need to sit tight until the right buyer comes along. Sure, sellers get impatient when you don't set the right expectations. But if you do your job correctly up front (pricing, home prep, setting expectations for the selling timeframe, etc) you will rarely have an issue. Becoming a Listing Specialist inducts you into a completely different side of the game.

When folks who are not familiar with our industry try to visualize what the work life of a real estate agent looks like, they envision us working nights and weekends and spending the majority of our time driving around and showing potential buyers properties. While this vantage point may be commensurate with how an overwhelming majority of agents conduct their daily real estate practice, it simply doesn't accurately depict the lifestyle of a successful Listing Specialist. As we saw in chapter one, the typical day in the life of a successful Listing Specialist revolves around a 9 to 5 schedule with most nights and weekends off. Unless you choose to work during your off time (as some overachievers will), working outside of this regimented schedule is seldom necessary.

One of the especially nice things about being a Listing Specialist is your ability to control your schedule, and take at least four 7-10 day vacations a year. Even if you are not the type of person to appreciate or desire a vacation, your mind and body will greatly appreciate (and reward you) when you begin to take regularly scheduled (and much deserved) hiatuses from the game. Best of all, once a year you can confidently sit down and plan out your vacations for the next 12 months and simply fix them to your schedule.

Now let me ask you a question – suppose you were a buyer specialist and you decided to go on vacation. This time you and your family are headed out on a wonderful cruise and you will be gone for 10 days. You made the plans for this vacation nearly three months ago, but little did you know how busy you would be when the time came to set sail! Now it's just two weeks before the big day and you are currently working with 12 active buyers (yikes!) who all want to find a property right now – like today! They are all eager to get into a new home right away. Perhaps having 12 active and motivated (ready to buy now) buyers is a good thing, but do you think you will be leaving on that cruise? Not likely. You better unpack your bags. As a dedicated buyer specialist, your clients will demand your personal time and attention.

Contrast the former scenario with the lifestyle of a successful Listing Specialist. Instead of 12 buyers, you have 12 active sellers (active listings). Would you be going on that vacation? Absolutely! All you would have to do is find a colleague in your office that you can hand your inventory list to, call your sellers and let them know who will be handling their file while you are gone, pack your bags and shove off! Bon voyage!

As we saw in Chapter 1, when working with sellers you can maximize control of your time and work a schedule that is almost the opposite of a buyer agent's schedule. Listing Specialists typically work weekdays, 5 days a week. Top buyer agents typically work nights and weekends, 7 days a week.

Think about it – when is the best time for a buyer to see a property? Nights, weekends, after hours, or "right now!" The best time for a buyer is generally when it's least convenient for you. That usually means lots of nights and weekends.

Sellers on the other hand are highly respectful of your time, once they are trained appropriately. Focusing on listings will allow you to work "regular business hours" throughout your real estate career, with nights and weekends off while taking at least four vacations each year. If that's the life you want, then focusing on listings is the key.

Reason # 3: Seller Listings Maximize Your Per-Hour Compensation.

Once you become highly leveraged with your systems and marketing in place, it will take you far less time to obtain a seller listing than it will for you to work a buyer transaction. When working with a buyer you may need to show 6 to 12 or more homes, do multiple market analysis on their different options, spend lots of time advising them of the area amenities, school rankings and resale feasibility, work with them through inspections, coordinate with their lender, perhaps compete with multiple offers and a myriad of other duties and aspects before closing on a transaction. Worse, you could end up working with a buyer for six months (or more than a year) before they actually buy, or they could simply decide not to buy at all.

With a seller, on the other hand, you only need to look at ONE house and do ONE market analysis. Once you list the property and place it on the MLS you can rely on your local army of MLS members to go to work bringing forth a good buyer and a solid offer. When you add up the time that it takes to work just one buyer vs one seller, you can easily see that you can work perhaps 3-4 times as many sellers as you can buyers, in a commensurate amount of time.

Reason #4: Volume, Volume, Volume.

With the right models and systems in place, you could easily go on as many as 15 to 25 seller listing appointments each month – and keep up the pace. You would be hard-pressed to work seven or eight new buyers per month and continue doing so over a long period of time.

Working with buyers can be fun… but work with too many buyers at a time and you may find yourself on the road to burnout. There is a limit to how many you can effectively and personally service at a time.

As a Listing Specialist, you can easily maintain an inventory of 20+ listings at a time. Now try to imagine working with 20 buyers at the same time. In my listing career, I have had as many as 127 listings at one time. I don't even want to begin to think about what it would be like to have 20 active buyers let alone more than 100! With the right leverage – working almost any number of listings can seem effortless.

Reason #5: Increased Market Awareness.

With seller listings you are on the front end of pricing, which translates to an immediate knowledge of the market. Therefore, the more listings you get the more knowledgeable you become about the current market.

Every time you sit down to work up a CMA, you are studying the local market in your area and becoming more of an expert. In time, this translates into a sense of pricing confidence that cannot be taught in any other way that I know of. You also get to actively participate in the front end of pricing trends as you watch demand ebb and flow in your target market areas.

Reason #6: Listings Bring You More Business (Both Buyers and Sellers).

When you market your listings effectively you will generate more business. I have found that on average one well marketed listing can generate at least two serious buyers and one new listing (not counting client referrals). That's 3 pieces of new business from every listing you take. Put another way, every listing you take has the potential of burgeoning into 4 closings. Without counting client referrals, how many closings do you think you could expect from each buyer client? Just one.

One of the biggest reasons that I've found for why real estate agents don't want to shift their business to focusing on sellers is because they really enjoy the buyer side of the business. I can certainly understand that, because looking at houses, showing property in nice neighborhoods and living the "real estate agent life" is appealing. The downside is that it leads to an unbalanced life and an unpredictable schedule while promising a much smaller potential income.

"But Knolly!" you say, *"I really, really like working with buyers and I'm not prepared to give them up!"* Well then,

what is the number one way to generate more buyer leads? Through having more listings! The truth is, the more listings you have, the more buyers you will attract! That's great news for agents who like working buyers, because you can cherry pick the buyers you want to work with and easily leverage out the rest to a great Buyer Specialist on your team, thereby creating a distinct and separate revenue stream.

The bottom line is this: Listings lead to more listings, more buyers, more closing and thus more paychecks!

Reason #7: If A Deal Falls, You Simply Pop It Back Active!

Real estate transactions fall out of contract for almost any number of reasons. Sometimes the deal just doesn't work out. What to do when a deal falls flat? Well, that depends on which side of the transaction you are on.

If you are the buyer agent on the transaction, you have no doubt already spent many hours on the deal, just to have it crumble at your feet. What's next? Well, (sigh) unfortunately for you it's back to the drawing board. Assuming that your client is still in a mindset to buy, and assuming that they still have confidence in you, then you have to hit that grind again, piling on many additional hours of your time, driving around town, pumping gas into your vehicle, showing more homes, spending more hours on narrowing down the buyer's short list, walking them through the inspection, holding their hand, warming their feet (when they get cold) spending hours as a consultant, delaying your upcoming vacations, etc.

Now then, if you are the listing agent on the transaction, the outlook is much more pleasant. If the deal falls you simply pop it back on the market! It's a simple keystroke! You simply log into MLS, change the status from *Pending* to *Active* and wait for a new agent to bring a new buyer. Plus, you are now armed with fresh and helpful information about the property (inspection reports, property condition information, etc) which will actually make it easier to sell the property the next time around, because you can provide full disclosure to the new buyer, reducing the chances of any surprises that could derail the next transaction. You have it made in the shade, and your vacation plans are still on!

Reason # 8. Run Your Business From Anywhere.

Once you have the "tools of the trade" (Chapter 5) you can run your highly leveraged listing empire from anywhere in the world. That's great news for agents who like to travel and love to be mobile. I'll show you exactly how to do this in chapters 22 and 23. For example, you can still conduct the phone consultation (step 6) while your Team Listing Specialist conducts the listing appointment (step 11).

Try running a buyer-centric real estate business from a beach in Maui. It's not as easy. Even if you had a team of Buyer Specialists working all of your buyer business for you (chapter 21), you would still want to run a thriving listing practice as your primary focus. Buyers are simply the gravy on top of the mashed potatoes.

Reason #9: You Get to Adopt the Buyer.

Once the real estate transaction is consummated, you can add the buyer to your database. Interestingly, buyers usually see the listing agent as the one who "sold" the house in the first place – so it's often easy to convert them to a seller client down the road.

I can't even begin to tell you how many times we've received a phone call from a buyer of one of our listings – looking to list their house with us. We don't even aggressively market to these folks – we just add them to our database and drip on them with our monthly e-newsletter and regular mailings. Of course they can opt-out at any time – but most of them don't. Meanwhile most of these buyers never hear from their previous real estate agent again. They end up orphaned, and we are happy to adopt them! Since you are staying in touch and you are already intimately familiar with their house, it's easy for you to earn their trust over time.

This means that for every listing you take, you are gaining another rather warm future listing prospect in your database.

Reason #10: Seller Listings Are Highly Leveraged.

As we discussed in the Chapter 1, I have identified some 46 tasks associated with a listing, from the time the lead is generated to after the transaction is closed. The good news here is that, in time, you will only personally have to handle (at most) 2 to 3 of these tasks.

If you care to grow your practice into a thriving team you will typically have to generate the lead and conduct a phone consultation with the seller prospect (setting the listing appointment). Occasionally you will actually go on the listing appointment. Your team can handle everything else. If you want to take it a step further, and exit the daily business completely, you can simply be the rain maker, spending 100% of your time doing nothing but lead generation. That means you are handling just one step in the 46 step process!

In chapters 19-23 I will show you how to grow your listing practice to its highest potential through the implementation of high-capacity leverage.

My Final Thoughts

There you have it – the Top 10 (or at least my top 10) reasons why you should focus on listings! Hopefully I've done a good job stating my case. I believe that every real estate agent should focus on listings as their primary business source. Of course you already know how important it is to focus on listings, or you wouldn't be reading this book – duh! Nevertheless it is so important to reinforce your decision to focus on listings, from time to time. Whenever the distraction of a busy buyer business waves its white flag in your face – don't give in! Simply come back and review this chapter!

If you are truly committed to Success with Listings, then all of your marketing, advertising, systems and models should be geared toward obtaining seller listings.

Well what are you waiting for? Let's move on to setting and reaching your goals!

Chapter 2 Homework:

☐ Write up a list of the Top 10 Reasons to Focus on Listings and pin that list prominently where you will be able to see it daily. This will help keep you focused.

Chapter 3
Setting and Reaching Your Goals

Do you want to be successful?

For almost everyone that I train the answer to this question is an emphatic "Yes!" So then, what is success? The title of this book is *Success with Listings*, so I think it behooves us to take a good look at exactly what success is.

Achieving success is 90% mental. Your mindset will determine whether or not you win or lose at the game of listings. This chapter provides you with the foundation for success. 90% of your success will be achieved if you can snap into the concepts in this chapter alone. Once your mind is on board, the rest will simply be learning what to do and what to say. The journey will begin with the renewing of your mind. You have to be willing to do *whatever it takes*. If you really believe that you can succeed, you can achieve success.

What is Success?

Most would say that success is reaching your goals. I would agree with that. And in order to reach your goals, you have to first know what you want. Once you know what you want you can set your goals and then go about reaching them. Once you reach a goal, you will have succeeded in that endeavor. Therefore, I define success as *having what you want* or better yet, *getting what you want*. In other words, if you have what you want, you are successful. But here is where it gets tricky, because knowing what you want is not as easy as one might think.

Learning to Swim Like a Salmon

From the time we are born we are influenced by many external and internal influences. These factors act as a raging white water rapid, pulling us in like driftwood, clutching us tightly and causing us to give up the fight and go with the flow.

Research shows us that the majority of the world live a life that is unfulfilling and outside of their true purpose. Those who truly want to succeed in life have to learn to swim like salmon.

In the wild, salmon live an average of 8 to 13 years depending on their species. Salmon spend their early lives in rivers, and then swim out to sea where they live their adult lives and gain most of their body mass. When they have matured, they return to the rivers to spawn.

The return to the river is known as a salmon run, and this once-in-a-lifetime event is the time when salmon, which have migrated from the ocean, swim to the upper reaches of rivers where they spawn on gravel beds. After spawning, all Pacific salmon and most Atlantic salmon die, and the salmon lifecycle starts over again with a new generation.

On their run, these poor salmon have it rough, but they are absolutely determined to fulfil their life's mission. Indeed, if you have ever watched a documentary of salmon on one of these runs, you will see that reaching their destination is an extremely difficult feat. It actually looks impossible, but it is what they have to do in order to succeed, and quitting is not an option.

For example, Sockeye Salmon from central Idaho must travel 1900 miles and climb nearly 7,000 feet to reach their spawning ground. It is a treacherous journey. The salmon have to swim upstream, fighting against the arduous rapids. They navigate waterfalls and rapids by leaping or jumping as high as 12 feet per jump. Along the journey they have to deal with skilled predators such as bears, bald eagles, sea lions and fisherman. Amid the chaos and treachery, they are drawn by an insatiable innate desire to fulfill their life's mission. They will succeed or die trying.

If we are to succeed in life, we must learn to swim like salmon. Going against the flow is a constant (and seemingly treacherous) uphill battle. Therefore many settle for the easy road of mediocrity. They become clones who operate like drones.

We all have an army of outward and inward forces battling both for and against us. Among other things, our peers, our friends, our family, our beliefs, our culture, our mindset, our faith, our feelings, our upbringing, our society, our leaders, our idols, our heroes and our enemies all shape our reality and create our desires. These internal and external drivers can be so powerful that many never step out of the whirlwind long enough to focus on themselves and discover their true purpose. They never connect with exactly what makes them happy and fulfilled.

This to me is a tragedy.

What is your mission in life? Why are you here? The salmon in the sea know exactly what they want, and they risk their lives to go after it.

What Do You Want?

Finding your life's passion and purpose is a topic that I love teaching on. I really like knowing what makes people tick, so "*what* do you want?" is a question that I often ask folks in casual conversation. And I generally ask it just that way: "What do you want?" Most people just look at me as if it were a trick question. It's not.

The question is simple enough but the answer can be elusive. That's because most people have never taken the time to really get to know themselves and understand exactly what creates deep, lasting and optimal happiness for them.

In most goal-setting exercises, the majority of my students begin answering the question of what they want by throwing out a monetary figure. Some will answer the question thusly *"I want to earn $100,000 a year."* Others might say *"I want to list and sell 40 houses a year."* While both of the preceding answers are worthy and attainable objectives, true goal setting begins at a much deeper level.

Recently I was casually loafing around in my living room with a close friend. He began telling me in great detail about how much he hated his job, how unfair his supervisors were and how little he was paid for the enormous amount of responsibility that he shouldered. Rather than weigh in on his pity party fueled by a victim mindset, I simply popped the question: *"What do you want?"* Silence. My friend looked back at me with a blank stare. It's the same stare that I have seen on many occasions when I've asked that seemingly simple question. In this instance, my friend was completely taken aback by the question. As I listened to him passionately speak about everything he did not want, I simply had to know, "what *do* you want?" Although he could speak for several minutes straight about all the things that he did not want in life, this simple question seemed to completely stump him.

As with any noble mission or grand objective, Success with Listings begins with setting your goals. In order to set accurate goals, you have to know exactly what you want.

The truth is most people do not know what they want – thus they will never achieve their true desires in life. Knowing what you want is where goal-setting all begins, and it is the first and most logical step toward achieving your goals.

The Four Groups of People

What does success look like? If I showed you a man with $500 Million in the bank, would you think he was a success? What if I showed you a woman that lived day-to-day with no money in the bank, would you think she was a success?

I have come to understand that, generally speaking, there are four different groups of people:

- Group 1. Those who don't know what they want.

- Group 2. Those who know what they want but are afraid to pursue it.

- Group 3. Those who think they know what they want but really don't.

- Group 4. Those who really know what they want and pursue it.

Group 1. Those Who Don't Know What They Want.

This group includes the vast army of individuals who have never taken the time to become self-aware. These people often busy themselves with trying to please others or trying to be like others. They don't really know where they fit in, so they just go with the flow. They fall into the cracks.

Group 2. Those Who Know What They Want But Are Afraid to Pursue It.

In my opinion this group is worse than the first. They actually have (or once had) a dream and a purpose, but alas they are afraid to go after it. It is shameful to squander the

SETTING AND REACHING YOUR GOALS

one life we are given on the pursuit of anything other than our true purpose.

Group 3. Those Who Think They Know What They Want But Really Don't.

This group starts out delusional and ends up disillusioned. Yet because they do have goals and aspirations, they can oftentimes look extremely successful on the outside. They pursue a career that is not a good fit for them in exchange for fortune, fame, to please another, or for some equally worthless reason. In their life they can have all the stuff (castles and toys) and lots of fluff (accolades and titles), but no substance. On the outside they may look like a wild success while they are truly miserable failures because they are a train that is off track. They are a big beautiful ship navigating the wrong seas and charting the wrong course.

Group 4. Those Who Really Know What They Want and Pursue It.

These are the happy ones. On the outside they can look like a wild success, a miserable failure, or anywhere betwixt the two. Nevertheless, on the inside they are full and fulfilled. This group represents those who are truly successful.

Jesus teaches us that it is impossible to spot who is truly successful by looking merely at the outward appearance. In Mark 10:17-27, we read the story of the rich young ruler. This man had great wealth, yet he was unfulfilled. He did not have the one thing in life he truly wanted, eternal life. Remarkably, this man intrinsically understood that Jesus would know how he could get what he so desperately

43

wanted. Sure enough, Jesus did know the answer and he shared with the man what he must do to inherit eternal life. Jesus basically told the man that if he truly wanted to be successful, he needed to walk away from all the stuff that was standing in the way of his success, and follow Him. The Bible records that the man went away sorrowful. He was not willing to follow the path of true happiness. Essentially this young man had everything that life had to offer, but he did not have the one thing that he actually wanted. And since success is having what you want, he was essentially a miserable failure.

It's important to understand that, for those of us in Group 4, success looks different for each one, because what we want will be unique to us. Nevertheless we will be called to forsake the path we are on if it is not leading us where we want to be. You can be a billionaire and be successful and you can live like Mother Teresa (who took a vow of poverty) and be a success.

Jesus himself was definitely in Group 4. He knew what his purpose and passion was, and he fulfilled it.

Like many of his peers, my good friend fell into Group 1. At 38 years of age he still did not know what he wanted and almost everything in his life represented what he knew he did *not* want. Which group do you currently see yourself in?

Last year's *State of the American Workplace* study (polled by Gallup with over 150,000 people surveyed) found that 70% of workers either dislike or absolutely hate their jobs. 7 out of 10! My friend was definitely in this category

SETTING AND REACHING YOUR GOALS

and much closer to the *hate* side of the scale. I shared with him that I absolutely love what I do and I always have done what I love. I then shared with him that my biggest struggle in life is tearing away from my "work" and that when I am not working, I am usually either dreaming about work or wishing that I was working. My friend looked at me as if I were an alien from a foreign world. "Don't get me wrong," I confessed, "I know that this too can be unhealthy." In my case it just so happens that my purpose and my mission in life is channeled through my work. In other words, my work is a conduit for my purpose. But I also understand that there are other meaningful pursuits in life.

To help keep me balanced (or counterbalanced) I have to focus on all of the goal categories in my life (spiritual, personal, career and material). As they say, *"All work and no play makes Jack a dull boy"*. But when your work *is* your play, the line of demarcation can become hazy.

Becoming a Citizen of the Fourth Group.

I believe that every person can and should be part of the fourth group.

As for me, I am a teacher and an inventor. Teaching and creating are my passion, with the overlying goal of making a connection with someone. As a teacher I love to teach, train, write, speak and perform, with the ultimate-goal of connecting with others. Nothing brings me greater joy than to see the positive impact I am having on someone else's life. As an inventor, I love to think, create and develop products and systems. In this capacity nothing brings me greater joy than to see my inventions come to life and better the lives of those they touch.

I have also learned that in order to put out you've got to put in. What I mean is that your input fuels your output. Your input is learning coupled with practice, and your output is your passion. I love to learn and I am a lifelong learner, because learning provides the data and raw materials that fuel my passion. As a learner, I love to read, watch and discover.

What is your passion? What is your purpose? What do you want?

To get to the heart of what you really want, consider these questions:

- If you could do or be anything in the world, what would you do or be?
- What would you do for free (without pay)?
- If you had $10 Million in the bank and didn't have to work, what would you do?

Why Do I Want That?

Once you know exactly what you want ask yourself this important follow-up question "Why do I want that?" So again, the two-part question is "what do I want", and "why do I want that?" Asking why helps you to continue the self-discovery journey, and causes you to scrutinize your goals to see if they are in alignment with what you really want. Try to dig deep, getting to the true bottom of why you want what you say you want. Asking the why will get to the heart of what really makes you tick. It's all about becoming self-aware, and understanding your passion.

Write it Down!

Once you begin narrowing down what you want, you will need to WRITE DOWN YOUR GOALS. Sit down and think of what you want and what you hope to accomplish during your stay here on earth. Remember that tomorrow is not promised therefore you must make the most of TODAY.

When I was 18 years old, my Uncle Miles shared with me a strategy that helped me stay focused through the years, until my goals were accomplished. Here's what I recommend you do: Take out four sheets of notebook paper. At the top of your sheets, write down the following headers (one header on each sheet):

❖ SPIRITUAL GOALS

❖ PERSONAL GOALS

❖ CAREER GOALS

❖ MATERIAL GOALS

SPIRITUAL GOALS

On this sheet write out all the goals you hope to accomplish pertaining to your spiritual life, and by when you hope to accomplish each goal. This information should include things like where you plan to attend church, particular ministries you would like to be involved in, how much time you will dedicate each day to Bible study and prayer, etc. For me, my spiritual goals are the priority of the 4 goal categories.

MATERIAL GOALS

On this sheet line list all the goals you hope to accomplish pertaining to material goods, and by when you hope to accomplish each of these goals. Your material goals should include information such as where you will live, what type of house you will live in, what type of car you will drive, how you will dress, etc.

PERSONAL GOALS

On this sheet line list all the goals you hope to accomplish pertaining to your personal life, and by when you hope to accomplish each of these goals. These goals should include how often and on what days you intend to exercise per week, how often you will take vacations, how often you will visit relatives and friends, your desired weight, the image you hope to portray, etc.

CAREER GOALS

On this sheet write out all the goals you hope to accomplish pertaining to your career life, and by when you hope to accomplish each of these goals. This information should include how you will structure your business, where you see yourself in 5 years, 10 years and 20 years. You will also want to list the major career achievements you will fulfill, etc.

It is not important that you write your goals down in the order you wish each goal to happen. Write down the goals you have as they come to mind. For me, I shoot to keep my goals realistic; however, I realize that anything is possible and attainable with God, provided that it's within His will for my life. Remember that you can always tweak your goals later on, but you must have some specific goals to begin shooting for!

Try to keep most of your goals relatively short-term, i.e. within the next 3 to 5 years. You may write a few goals that are long range, but keep these somewhat vague.

Once you have taken the time to write out all of your goals in each category, ask yourself "why is this goal important to me?" In other words "why do I want this?"

Your Personal Measuring Stick

You really never know where your real estate career (or life) will sweep you, however by having written goals, you will be able to gauge whether or not you are on or off track. Goal-setting acts as a measuring stick. Think about it – if you don't know where you are going, how will you know when you've arrived? How will you know when you've veered off the road? As Lewis Carroll put it, *"If you don't know where you're going, then any road will lead you there."*

All of these goals can be altered as you go along, however, they still must be written out as a foundation to begin shooting for. If a marksman begins shooting without a target, how will he know when he has hit the bull's-eye? When goals are written or typed out, and perhaps pinned on the wall or on your desk, they serve as a constant reminder to the direction in which you are headed. The most successful people in the world write down their goals. Also, setting your goals will activate your subconscious mind, and it too will begin to work on helping you accomplish your goals (even while you sleep).

Most importantly, I want you to completely understand that **You Must Be Absolutely Convinced About the Goal You Set**. If you are not convinced about your goals, then your mind will never get on board to help you achieve them.

Your Worst Enemy and Your Best Friend

I had an agent come to work for me once, and I asked him the question I ask anyone who is looking to join my team. "How much do you want to make a month?" He pondered the question for a few moments and then shyly retorted, *"$10,000 a month."* At this I reeled my head back, wrinkled my forehead in amazement and said with vigor, *"$10,000 a month!? That's a lot of money. Wouldn't $5,000 be all right?"* He looked at me and then looked away. He thought about it for about two seconds. Now guess what happened during that two second pause? Yep, he settled for less. *"Well,"* he responded, *"$5,000 wouldn't work, but $6,000 would be all right!"* He basically gave himself a $4,000 pay cut during a three sentence conversation. Two seconds was all it took for him to cut his pay by 40%. Mind you, I didn't give him a pay cut, he cut himself. All I did was sufficiently challenge him so that I could find out if his mind was on board with what he said he wanted. If your mind is not on board, you will never achieve your goals.

When it comes to getting what you want, who is your worst enemy? And who is your best friend and closest ally when it comes to achieving your goals? The obvious answer to both is YOU.

As you already know, when it comes to achieving what you want in life, you are your own worst enemy and you can be your own best friend. Blaming others for your lack of success is a futile undertaking. Your own mind will develop every scheme imaginable to derail you and to lead you to failure, and it generally doesn't need anyone else's help! You will sabotage your own success if you do not take the reins early on.

Eckhart Tolle put it correctly when he said that *"the mind is like a little child"*. That's why the Bible teaches that we must both tame the mind and renew it. You are the master of your mind, it is not the master of you.

Remember that the brain is lazy. It will always settle for the minimum standard. When the goals that you set seem arduous, you will look for ways to ease the burden, typically by lowering your standards (reducing your goals). However I have observed the flip side of this is also true. If you push past the pain you will achieve the pleasure. In other words, if you persevere even when the journey becomes unbearable, your mind will eventually get on board with your goals. Your mind will realize that this time you are quite serious about achieving your objectives. That is the point at which both heaven and earth will begin to move to assist you in reaching your objectives. Your mind will not only get on board with what you are doing, but it will invent clever and exciting ways to make your journey easier and more successful.

If you have ever gone on a new diet you have already seen this principle at work. Some years ago I became convinced (actually my wife Josie convinced me) that I needed to begin eating healthier. For me, that meant that I needed to incorporate fresh fruits and vegetables into my diet. But there was one big hurdle that I had to overcome: Alas, I don't like fruits and vegetables! I must shamefully admit that I generally crave cheeseburgers, pizza, tacos, pancakes, donuts and the like. So while my brain seems to crave the wrong kinds of fuel, I know that bad eating is detrimental to my health and wellbeing. Nevertheless the idea of sticking a leafy green substance into my mouth, having to chew repeatedly, and then having to swallow was not something I could fathom, so I came up with the clever solution of *blending*. I found that although I couldn't eat kale outright, I could blend it up and gulp it down almost before my tongue knew what hit it.

I developed an organic concoction of kale, spinach, celery, apple, carrot, walnuts, sprouts and blueberries, mixed with just enough water to make it drinkable. Pulverized by my BlendTec, the mixture has become my go-to formula for "eating" my daily supply of fruits and vegetables.

When I first started with the green drink, however, my mind really started playing tricks on me. It seems that my mind was hard at work engineering my downfall. My brain would tell me things like: *What in the heck are you doing now, son? Have you gone crazy? You know you want a cheeseburger!* Thankfully, I have learned not to allow my feelings to tell me how to feel. I found that I constantly had to check and correct my subconscious mind: *No, we are not doing a cheeseburger today, buddy! We are rollin' with that green drink!* As wild as it may seem, it felt like I was fighting against myself! This self-dialogue went on for many weeks. Every time I would begin putting my daily green drink together, my mind would challenge me thusly.

In time however my subconscious mind began to realize that I was quite serious about this new commitment. Eventually the dialogue from my subconscious mind began sound like this: *Wow dude, you're serious about this green thing, huh? Well I guess it's not that bad after all. I still would prefer some tacos, but I guess it could be worse.*

Fast forward six months after I began consistently blending. Guess what the dialogue from my subconscious mind had changed to? Now my mind was screaming: *Green drink, green drink!! Gotta have that green drink!!! Come on man... let's get that green drink already!* At which point I would glance down at my watch and gently and loving tell my mind *Dude, you need to chill. We still have another hour to go before you get your green drink. Calm down buddy – you'll get it soon enough!*

My journey with the green drink illustrates how the mind works. When you originally move forward in any endeavor, your mind will seemingly attempt to sabotage your efforts to achieve success. As you push forward and your mind ultimately becomes convinced that you are serious about succeeding this time, it will get on board with what you are doing. That's why you cannot allow your feelings to tell you how to feel.

Resistance, Acceptance, Assistance

I am no neuroscientist. Even those who study the mind on a daily basis have only scratched the surface of understanding the complexity of this incredible organ. I can, however, tell you what I have personally experienced after training tens of thousands of individuals, and what I have seen in my own life. The mind seems to follow a three phase pattern of resistance, acceptance and then assistance. You will generally see the pattern show up when you take on a new endeavor. During the initial *resistance phase*, the mind throws a fit, and it fights against you. Then, during the *acceptance phase* the mind reluctantly and begrudgingly goes along with your plan, typically murmuring the whole time. Finally, the mind moves on to the *assistance phase*, where it gets fully on board with your vison and empowers you to succeed. Just pay close attention to your mind the next time you begin to take on any new endeavor. It will generally follow this pattern.

The more you are aware of this process, the faster you can get through it. I have seen some agents get stuck in the acceptance phase for many years! Perhaps you got thrust into a real estate career out of necessity and haven't entirely embraced your profession. You aren't living up to your full potential. On the other hand, I know many agents who are in the assistance phase, and they seem to be listing magnets.

They have maximum positive energy, and listings just seem to magically float to them!

The truth is, the mind is resistant to change. Of course you are excited about focusing your business on listings and becoming a Listing Specialist, but perhaps you are also a bit apprehensive about what the future may hold. That's only natural. Soon your excitement will fade into the reality that you have got to start generating business and getting leads. Hard work follows, and your mind begins to throw you doubts: *Are you sure you want to commit to this? This is hard!* Your mind will try to talk you out of it, once it sees that big changes are on the horizon. As you continue to plug away toward success, your mind will reluctantly go along. *Oh well. I guess we have to make these dang calls to generate leads. Sheesh. Oh, well... let's get started.* Finally, when your actions become habits, your mind is pushing you out of bed... *Come on, let's go! It's time to prospect! Gotta set some appointments today!*

Mastery is achieved through time on the task over time. Sadly, many agents don't stay on task long enough to get past the resistance phase, so they don't reap the long-term rewards that come with having their mind fully on board and supportive of their endeavors. The assistance phase is the zone where success is possible. Tragically, many agents quit digging just 3 feet before they strike gold.

The Paycheck that You Will Never Spend

I was standing in the ridiculously long coffee line at a big annual real estate convention when an agent walked up to me and asked, *"Are you Knolly Williams?"* I glanced around and, said *"uh, yes, I am."* In my mind I was thinking: *Duh buddy, there 'ain't too many black cowboys here you know.* You see, I get a bit antsy (irritable and overexcited) at the big conventions and I hadn't had my coffee yet! *"Well, can I buy your coffee?"* he offered. *"Well... sure,"* I said, with a hint of *what's the catch* in my voice. As he stuck his hand out for and handshake and introduced himself, he went on to tell me *"You see, I've never met you, but I'd like to share with you how you've changed my life. About a year ago I was down to just one listing. I was on my way out of the business and I was at a crossroads. I was about to quit. Then I ran across a video you did with Tony DiCello on KW Connect. That video changed my life. You allowed me to see what was possible, and I have taken more than 60 listings in the year since then. Best of all, I am now able to consistently put food on the table for my family."*

Wow! What a testimonial! I was choked up and speechless. My simple act of service had changed someone else's life and helped provide for their family. A feeling of satisfaction, fulfillment and purpose enveloped me as I had the epiphany and reassurance that teaching, mentoring and giving back is what I was created to do.

That special sense of awareness that I received, and continue to receive are what I have come to know as the *paycheck that I will never spend.* I have earned millions of dollars in my lifetime. For the most part I can't tell you where the money went! But I will never spend the paycheck that my students give me when they share with me how my act of service has changed their lives.

Money cannot make you happy. You already know that. You also know that money is a very handy tool that can be used to accomplish much. You should also know that you don't have to exchange your passion and purpose for the pursuit of money. Proverbs 18:16 teaches us that *a person's gift opens doors for him, bringing him access to important people.* Therefore, if you focus on your purpose, the money will show up.

Indeed I have earned an amazing amount of income from listings. Yet over time I have come to understand that *it's not about the money.* For me it's about being happy, and I am happiest when I glorify the Creator by using the gifts He has endowed me with. Each and every day, I endeavor to put a smile on God's face. I know that He loves me no matter what I do. Yet I also know that He smiles, chuckles even, when He sees me busy about the purpose and passion for which He created me.

I want to make sure that you understand *that happiness is a byproduct of living your purpose.* Remember that in order to *have* what you want you must first *know* what you want. What you want in life should be in alignment with your purpose. In other words, living your purpose leads to true happiness.

I believe that the gift of this life is so precious that it should only be invested in that which fulfills your purpose and is in alignment with your goals.

Channeling Your Passion

The really cool thing I discovered along the way is that once you understand your purpose and your passion, you can channel it through almost anything you choose to do.

Every day I channel my passion, (teaching and inventing) through my real estate career and my training ministry. As a top Listing Specialist, I teach my clients the ins and outs of listing and selling their house for top dollar, and I create and implement for them the best systems, tools and tactics to help them succeed. As a trainer, I teach real estate agents how to succeed in real estate and create for them products, tools and systems to help them succeed faster.

Now suppose you were in a different industry. For example, suppose you were a flooring contractor, or an insurance agent, or city official. No matter the profession, your gifts could still be used to fulfill your purpose and passion. Likewise, no matter where your purpose and passion lies, your career in real estate can serve as the perfect conduit to fulfill your purpose.

One of my favorite examples of this principle comes from Frank Capra's 1946 film *It's a Wonderful Life*. This brilliant movie was adapted from a short story called *The*

Greatest Gift. The movie cleverly follows the story of George Bailey from childhood to early adulthood. From the time he was a little lad, George knew exactly what he wanted to be and what he wanted to do in life. At the age of 8 years old, if you asked him *"What do you want?"* he knew the answer. He wanted to leave his *crummy little town* and travel the world! He wanted to become a designer of modern cities, bridges, skyscrapers and the like. Due to one situation after another, and due to George's strong moral compass and constant self-sacrificing attitude of putting others before himself, his life dreams were put on hold. Finally everything came to a head when a major incident threated to devastate his already "ruined life".

It took George quite some time to understand that his passion and purpose could be truly realized exactly where he was, in the beautiful sleepy little town of Bedford Falls. George didn't have to go around the world to experience all the fullness that life had to offer.

With George Bailey, his situation didn't change but his *perspective* did. His mind was renewed. The Lord sent an angel to help George understand that he could still realize his passion and his purpose no matter where he lived and no matter what his chosen profession was. George had been living with the belief that he had been cheated out of the life he always wanted, but he came to understand that when you truly know your purpose, it can be a wonderful life after all.

Sadly, many go through their entire life and never come to understand this. For some, it is only on their death bed that they realize that they have squandered an entire life on the wrong pursuits. This will not be your fate.

How Are You Wired?

As I've discussed in this chapter, it is important to understand how you are wired, what your strengths and gifts are, where your talents lie and what you naturally enjoy. There are numerous resources available to help you do just that. Below are just a few.

Understanding your Personality and Behavioral Traits (DISC).

- Go to www.123test.com and click on the DISC Personality Test.

DISC is a behavior assessment tool based on the DISC theory of psychologist William Moulton Marston, which centers on four different behavioral traits: dominance, inducement, submission, and compliance. This theory was then developed into a behavioral assessment tool by industrial psychologist Walter Vernon Clarke.

Understanding Your Strengths.

- http://freestrengthstest.workuno.com/free-strengths-test.html.
- www.gallupstrengthscenter.com.

The Strengths Finder Test will help you discover your preferred way of thinking, feeling, and behaving.

BOOK RESOURCE: *Cure for the Common Life: Living in Your Sweet Spot.*

In the book *Cure for the Common Life,* author Max Lucado offers practical tools for exploring and identifying your own uniqueness and provides motivation to put your strengths to work. The book endeavors to help readers find and live in their "sweet spot".

Final Thoughts

Don't underestimate the importance of thoroughly understanding yourself. It is integral to your success. Take the time necessary to review this chapter, read the suggested books, and take the online assessments.

Once you have done this, you are ready to move on to your numbers.

Chapter 3 Homework:

☐ Take a look at the Four Groups of People and determine which Group you are currently in and which group you want to be in.

☐ Decide exactly *what* you want and *why* you want it.

☐ Write down your list of goals using the 4 Goal Categories (Spiritual, Material, Personal & Career)

☐ Take the online DISC Personality test and the Strengths Finder test

☐ Read *Cure for the Common Life* by Max Lucado

☐ Read *The Ultimate Secret to Getting Absolutely Everything You Want* by Mike Hernacki.

☐ Read *The Secret to Permanent Prosperity* by Mike Hernacki.

Chapter 4
Knowing Your Numbers

Now I would like you to focus on your numeric goals. Knowing your numbers is another critical component to your success as a Listing Specialist.

This chapter will guide you through a very simple exercise that will allow you to know all of the critical numbers in your listing business. As we mentioned, knowing where you should be will help keep you on track as the weeks progress.

How much income do you want to earn each year? This is going to be your starting point. We will call this your *net income*, the amount that will be paid to you, after your broker or team split.

Once you know what you want to make, you can proceed to determine how many listing appointments you will need to conduct each year in order to reach your income goal.

As you set your numeric goals, I want to let you in on a BIG yet simple secret that seems to evade most real estate agents: *Reaching your income goal in the real estate game simply boils down to how many appointments you go on.* That's the bottom line. Therefore the purpose of this chapter is to determine how many listing appointments you need to conduct each week, each month and each year.

To determine your listing appointment goal you will need to answer the following six questions:

1. What is Your Net Commission Income Goal? $ _____.

2. What is the Percentage Split Paid to You? _____ %.

3. What is Your Average Listing Commission Percentage? _____ %.

4. What is Your Average Sale Price? $ _____.

5. What is your Conversion Rate on Appointments Completed? _____ %.

6. What is Your Conversion Rate on Closings? _____ %.

Now let's go ahead and take a detailed look at each of these questions and the necessary mathematical formulas associated with them. Relax, even if you don't like math you will find this to be an easy exercise.

1. What is Your Net Commission Income Goal?

Your Net Commission Income is the annual amount of income you plan to earn (before taxes and expenses). This is the amount of money you are paid after deducting the split you pay your office or team. NOTE: This should not be confused with your Gross Commission Income (GCI). Your GCI is the amount you would earn before your office/team split, but for the purposes of our exercise, I want you to focus on what you are actually netting.

2. What is the Percentage Split Paid to You?

This is the percentage of the commission dollar amount earned (also called a split), that is paid to you on each transaction. For example, if you are paid 60% of the commission and your broker, team or office is paid 40%, then the *Percentage Split Paid to You* is 60%.

3. What is Your Average Listing Commission Percentage?

This is the average percentage that you earn on your listing transactions. For example, if you were to charge a six percent commission on a listing, and you paid the buyer agent half of that, then your commission earned on that transaction would be three percent.

To arrive at the most accurate figure for your average listing commission percentage, simply take the most recent 10 (or more) listings you took (x) and then add up the commission percentages (y). Then divide y by x.

In the following example we would take the total commission percentages (28%) and divide by the number of listings (10). The result is an Average Commission Earned of 2.8%.

	Address	Comm %
1	1807 Hickory Lane	3.00%
2	131 Newport Village Rd	3.00%
3	1603 Slyedale Rd	2.50%
4	2890 Hackberry Circle, #101	3.00%
5	505 Paxton Park	3.00%
6	101 Osborne St	3.00%
7	238 Circle S Dr	2.00%
8	138 Lewis Lane - Unit B	3.00%
9	438 Floyds Blvd	2.50%
10	1800 Tranqullity Path	3.00%
	Total	**28.0%**

4. What is Your Average Sale Price?

This is the average sale price of the homes that you list. To get this number, take your last 10 (or more) closed listings (x) and add up the closed/sold prices (y). Divide y by x.

To determine the Average Sale Price in the following example, we would take the total sum of all sale prices ($2,374,400) and divide by the number of listings (10). The result is an Average Sale Price of $237,440).

	Address	Comm %	Sale Price
1	1807 Hickory Lane	3.00%	$ 159,900
2	131 Newport Village Rd	3.00%	$ 302,000
3	1603 Slyedale Rd	2.50%	$ 286,500
4	2890 Hackberry Circle, #101	3.00%	$ 78,000
5	505 Paxton Park	3.00%	$ 240,000
6	101 Osborne St	3.00%	$ 372,000
7	238 Circle S Dr	2.00%	$ 148,000
8	138 Lewis Lane - Unit B	3.00%	$ 239,000
9	438 Floyds Blvd	2.50%	$ 149,000
10	1800 Tranqullity Path	3.00%	$ 400,000
	Total	28.0%	$ 2,374,400

5. What is Your Conversion Rate on Appointments Completed?

This is the percentage of houses that you successfully list out of the number of listing appointments you actually go on. For example if you go on 40 listing appointments (x) and obtain 31 listings (y) from those 40 appointments, then your conversion rate on appointments completed is 78%. The formula is y divided by x.

Appointments	40
Listings Taken	31
Appt Conv Rate	78%

6. What is Your Conversion Rate on Closings?

This is the percentage of homes that you list versus the percentage of homes that actually close. For example if you list 31 houses (x) and 25 of them successfully close (y) then your Conversion Rate on Closings is 81%. The formula is y divided by x.

Closings	
Listings Taken	31
Listings Closed	25
Closings Conv Rate	81%

How Can You Increase Your Numbers?

Throughout this book I will discuss some nifty ways for you to improve all of your numbers. For example, you can increase your average commission earned by using my escalating commission presentation (chapter 13). You can increase your average sale price by farming (chapter 8), focusing on Luxury listings (chapter 9) and simply staying active in the business. You can increase your conversion rate on appointments through the use of powerful tools (chapter 5) using proven scripts (chapters 5-19) and by mastering the listing consultation (chapter 13). You can increase your conversion rate on closings by getting the listing priced right initially (chapter 13) and regularly adjusting the list price throughout the term of the listing (chapter 15).

As your numbers improve you will need to go on fewer appointments in order to net the same amount of commission. As you move toward mastery, you will accomplish more with much less effort. Moving you toward mastery is the purpose of this book.

Your Numeric Goals Recap

In this chapter you learned that you have to set and track your numbers in order to experience the highest level of success. We looked at the six questions that you must answer in order to set your goals.

Let's take a final look at the six questions:

1. What is Your Net Commission Income Goal?

2. What is the Percentage Split Paid to You?

3. What is Your Average Listing Commission Percentage?

4. What is Your Average Sale Price?

5. What is your Conversion Rate on Appointments Completed?

6. What is Your Conversion Rate on Closings?

After answering these six questions you will know how many appointments you need to go on in order to reach your net income goal. We also learned that, in the listings game, reaching your income goal simply boils down to how many listing appointments you go on. As your skills improve, you will walk away from more and more appointments with signed listing agreements.

In the meantime, don't be concerned about how you will generate listing appointments. I cover that in chapters 6-10. For now you just need to know how many appointments you must conduct.

Knolly's Goals Calculator. For members of my *Group Coaching Club*, you can download a free copy of my *Goals Calculator* spreadsheet. This tool is an excel spreadsheet I put together that will help. When working with the goals calculator, you will simply input numbers 1-6 and the spreadsheet will automatically calculate your annual, monthly and weekly appointments goal (see the following example). Check it out at www.SuccessWithListings.com.

Your Economic Goals:		
Your Net Income Goal (GCI):	$ 100,000	1
% Paid to You from Team/Broker:	70%	2
Your Average Commission %:	2.80%	3
Your Average Sale Price:	$ 237,440	4
Your Average Gross Commission is:	$ 6,648	
Your Average Net Commission is:	$ 4,653.82	

Your Production Goals:		
Your Annual Listings Taken Goal:	26.5	
Your Monthly Listings Taken Goal:	2.2	
Your Annual Listings Closed Goal:	21	
Your Monthly Listings Closed Goal:	1.8	
Conversion Rate on **Appointments**:	78%	5
Conversion Rate on **Closings**:	81%	6
Annual Appointments Required:	34	
Monthly Appointments Required:	2.8	

Next, let's take a look at the power tools you will need to help you succeed.

Chapter 4 Homework

☐ Determine your listing appointments goal by completing your answers to the six questions.

☐ Login to Download my *Goals Calculator* at www.SuccessWithListings.com and input your data to determine your appointments goal.

Chapter 5

The Power Tools of a Successful Listing Specialist

After reading *The One Thing* by Gary Keller, I was prompted to ask agents I was training this important question: *What is the one thing you can do in order to GET MORE LISTINGS such that by doing it everything else will be easier or unnecessary?*

I often ask this question to the attendees at my seminars and the answers are usually the same. Some say *"Do more lead generation."* Others answer *"Stay in contact with my database."* Still others answer *"Hire the right people."* Of course all of these answers will help you do more business, yet if you could only pick ONE thing to do in order to increase your listing inventory, what one thing would you choose?

I have become convinced that the one thing that you can do to get more listings such that by doing it everything else will be easier or unnecessary is to *become famous*. It may sound a bit odd at first, but one of my principle goals with this book is to help make you a local celebrity.

Becoming a Local Celebrity

You should be well known in the areas you service, because notoriety can open more doors than anything else I know of. I believe this holds true for any profession. For example, suppose you owned a restaurant. What is the one thing you could do, to grow your restaurant, such that by doing it, everything else would be either easier or unnecessary? Serve better food? Of course having great food would really help! Unfortunately though, we all have seen restaurants with good food go out of business. Perhaps you can think of a restaurant in your town that continues to stay open, despite having a mediocre menu? So what is the one thing you could do? Have the best location? While this too would certainly help, I would say that becoming a *celebrity chef* is the one thing you could do that would make everything else you do either easier or unnecessary.

Becoming famous is not as difficult as you may think. In our present age, becoming known is actually easier than it has been in any other time in history.

It is true that if you do more lead generation, do a better job of staying in touch with your database and hire the right people, you will be more successful. However, if you are a celebrity agent in your area, all of these activities will become easier.

Becoming famous makes your prospecting easier. Think about it this way, does a famous person get their calls answered? Yes. Does a famous person get their calls returned promptly? Yes. Also–when we are in the presence of a well-known person, most of us are instinctively very conscious about time–and we don't want to take up too much of theirs. Because of this, a famous person can handle business transactions with more precision, speed and efficiency. Famous people can therefore handle a much higher volume of business and have an easier time attracting prospects. Even attracting top quality talent to work for your organization becomes easier as you become well known.

What if you were to become the mayor of your city or town? Would that help you increase your business? Of course it would. Part of my mission with this book is to help you become the *real estate mayor* in your hometown.

Becoming well known will make everything you do easier. Whether you are door-knocking, attending neighborhood meetings, marketing to your database, building a niche, farming, working with builders or simply networking, being known will open more doors.

When I discuss grooming you into a local celebrity, please don't get the idea that I am talking about becoming stuffy, haughty, arrogant or prideful. Being well-known does not require any of these traits. Like Jesus, you can adopt the spirit of service and humility and still have a significant influence over a very large audience.

Becoming well-known in your area does not happen by accident. Although a few stumble into fame and fortune, the rest of us have to be more strategic. This book will be your blueprint. My intention is to teach you how to be successful, productive and well known, with a focus on running a high volume listing business while working as few hours as possible.

Now it's time for you to begin getting groomed for the role. On your road to becoming a celebrity agent in your area, you will begin looking the part before you actually assume the role.

Now ask yourself this question. As a local celebrity, what will my listing business look like? Close your eyes and visualize it. Can you see it? Now think about the tools you are currently using to generate listings. Do they look like the tools a celebrity would use?

The Tools of a Listing Specialist

For thousands of years mankind has used tools to make life on planet earth successful and easier. As you venture into any new enterprise, you will need both skills and tools. Now suppose you were a professional flooring installer and you had all the skills and qualifications, but you didn't have the right tools. Will you get the job? Probably not. All the skill in the world won't help you if you don't have the tools necessary to get the job done right. If you have all the tools to lay carpet, yet the majority of your prospects want tile or wood flooring, you won't event get a chance to bid on the job. No matter how good you are at laying tile, you won't get the job if you don't have the tools.

Too many agents are showing up at the listing appointment with the wrong tools, or no tools at all. It's no wonder they are generating less than optimal success. If you are switching from a buyer focused business to focusing on more listings, you will need the right tools.

Here are the tools of a celebrity:

1. Your Book (this is your complete seller's guide).
2. Your Press Kit (this is your complete pre-listing package).
3. Your Movie (this is your virtual listing presentation).

In your listing business, you should implement these 3 essential tools: your book (most celebrities have one), your press kit (pre-listing package), and your movie (high quality pre-listing video). Of course you will supplement these 3 core tools with many of the other strategies you are already implementing like social media, blogging, YouTube videos, your website, etc.

TOOL # 1: Your Seller Book (Your Complete Guide for Sellers)

It is very common for a well-known person to have a book. Whenever I pass out my book to prospects, their reaction is the same "Wow! You have a book?!" I cannot tell you how many houses I have listed as a result of my Seller's Book alone!

Besides making an impression, your well-written book allows you to connect with sellers and leverage your time.

What if you actually had the time to divulge all of your wisdom and knowledge to a seller, and give them the full benefit of your acumen? What would you say? This is where your book comes in. Your book greatly leverages your time because it allows you to sit down with a potential seller and share with them the entire selling process from A-Z, without being physically present.

In addition to allowing you to immediately be viewed as a top expert in your area, your book also greatly leverages your time. Your book allows you to eliminate three or more hours of your time over the life of each listing. So if you plan to list 50 houses this year, your book should save you about 150 hours! How much is your time worth?

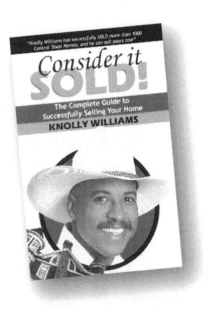

How to Write Your Book

You can write your seller book in just eight chapters. Your book should be filled with useful information along with photos and illustrations as necessary.

Your Seller Book Chapter 1 – *Deciding to Sell.*

Oftentimes the folks that you give a copy of your book to are just *thinking about selling.* The first chapter should be written to help them through the decision-making process. This chapter helps them to prepare mentally and emotionally for selling. It also aids them in examining their motives and reasons for selling – so that they make the best decision for themselves and their family.

We've all had would-be sellers who don't want to meet with us right away because they haven't made their mind up yet and they don't want us to "try to sell them". They don't want to feel pressured, or perhaps they just don't want to waste your valuable time. Now your answer to this put-off is quite simple:

You: You know Kelly – I can appreciate that you are just considering the idea of selling and aren't really sure at this time. Here's a copy of my book that I wrote to help my clients through the entire process.

Prospect: Wow! Well, thanks!

This approach will gain you more trust and win you more listings because you will be viewed as a dynamic (low pressure) consultant with their best interests at heart. Plus, you now have a great excuse to make periodic follow up calls to the prospect.

Your Seller Book Chapter 2 – *Marketing Your House for Sale*

You will use this chapter to outline your complete marketing plan. If you've done any number of listings, you know that sellers always want to know *"what are you going to do to market my house?"* This chapter outlines your complete plan for the successful sale of their property.

Your Seller Book Chapter 3 – *Pricing Your House.*

This chapter is written to show sellers everything that is involved in arriving at the correct price of their house. Everything from how price is determined, how to interpret a CMA, how the buyer's appraisal will affect price, and how pricing affects showings should be discussed here. This chapter saves you the time of having to explain these concepts at the listing appointment.

Your Seller Book Chapter 4 – *Getting Your House Ready for the Market.*

Getting their property ready for the market allows your clients to enjoy receiving the highest price possible for their property. This chapter explains the top 3 things they can do (declutter, clean and paint) and why these things are so important. This chapter should discuss staging as well, and you will want to include a complete checklist of things they can do to the exterior, interior, kitchen, bath and much more. This chapter should also contain a list of minor repairs that are typically recommended.

This chapter saves you tons of time because it allows the seller to walk through their own house at their leisure and make their own checklist of items that need to be addressed prior to you putting their house on the market.

Your Seller Book Chapter 5 – *Choosing the Right Agent.*

This chapter is dedicated to explaining to your prospects why YOU are the best agent for the job of getting their house sold. It is unfortunate that many sellers still believe that all agents are the same. This chapter serves to dispel that myth and makes the case for why they should hire YOU!

Your Seller Book Chapter 6 – *Handling Showings.*

This chapter of your book also leverages your time because it explains to your seller in detail how showings should be conducted. This chapter also consults your clients on how they should conduct showings of the property if it is rented (has tenants) and gives them a handy showing checklist.

Your Seller Book Chapter 7 – *Working with Offers.*

This chapter serves to enlighten your clients on how to review an offer. This chapter points out the most important paragraphs in the contract and gives your clients your best advice on how to interpret the information. Whenever you receive an offer on a client's house, you will simply call and use the following script:

You: Hi Samantha! Good News! We received an offer on your house!

Prospect: Great!

You: Now, Samantha - I'm going to email you the offer right now. I want you to go back and read chapter 7 of my book along with the offer and then let's discuss any questions you have.

Prospect: Sounds good!

Before using my book, I spent countless hours explaining to my sellers how financing works, earnest money, buyer closing costs, settlement expenses, the buyer's inspection process and on and on. I have completely eliminated these conversations with this one chapter.

Your Seller Book Chapter 8 – *Closing On the Sale.*

This chapter helps your clients understand everything that is involved with successfully closing their transaction. Here you will also discuss the buyer inspection process. You are preparing the seller by explaining how the process works so they won't have any surprises. The chapter also discusses what they need to bring to closing, how to prepare for the day of closing and should provide a handy moving checklist.

How Your Seller Book Leverages Your Time.

Your book not only makes you look like the rock star that you are, it also serves to shave at least 3 hours of your time off the life of every listing you take, and helps you generate more seller leads.

Your book will shave at least 30 minutes off your listing presentation time alone because the sellers you meet with are 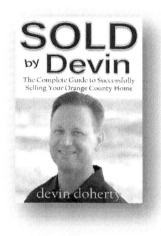 already educated on the process and what you can do for them. Your book can shave many weeks off the listing time on market, because it educates your sellers about pricing so that you can get it priced right at the beginning of the listing term. Your book helps convince your seller prospects that they absolutely should *list with you*. Your book helps your sellers make the right first impression and generate more offers by teaching them how to prepare their house for sale. Your book helps you save at least an hour during the offer negotiation stage because it helps your seller better understand the process and sets their expectation up front. Your book also helps to generate you more listing referrals.

Most of the real estate agents I train don't have a seller's book. Of the few that do, most of them have one that that is stapled, spiral bound or in a three-hole punched notebook. While there is nothing inherently wrong with that approach, it does not convey the look of a celebrity.

The seller book I wrote and use doesn't look like something that was created at a local copy shop or printed on a fancy laser printer. It's a real book. Your seller book should look and feel as professional as any book that your seller currently has on their bookshelf. You can have your book printed at a number of places for a cost of less than $3 each so it's not expensive at all. Plus, with book printers that offer *printing on demand*, you can print as few as 25 copies at a time. There is absolutely no excuse for you not to look your best.

TOOL #2: Your Press Kit (Pre-Listing Package)

In addition to your seller book, a complete pre-listing package is essential to Success with Listings because in today's competitive environment, you want to win the listing before you show up to the listing appointment. In other words, you want to influence your seller prospects to decide to list with you, before they ever sit down with you.

Think of your pre-listing package as your press kit. All famous people have one. Just imagine you were going after an important role in a movie. You would likely have to submit your press kit before being called in for an audition. Sure, if you are Russell Crowe you could probably skip this step, but if you are any of the other 29 actors in the film you had better send your press kit in advance! In your successful listing business your press kit serves the important role of convincing the decision makers to consider auditioning you for the job of selling their house.

Likewise, if you were going for an important job at any company, they would want to see your resume and qualifications before considering you as a candidate for the position. No one shows up at a job interview or a movie audition without first sending over their credentials. Yet I am still amazed at the many agents who will seek to have a prospect trust them with their *life-savings* without sending over their complete pre-listing package beforehand. Not doing this puts you at a disadvantage.

Perhaps you are already great at getting people to trust you. Perhaps you don't currently use a pre-listing package and don't see the need for one since you typically are able to walk away from the interview with the listing secured. Even so, if you don't have a pre-listing packet you are using a system that is outdated, less productive and inefficient. If you are good without a pre-listing packet, you will be on fire *with* one.

Along with your book, your pre-listing package will "toot your horn" for you so that you can spend far less time at each listing appointment. In fact, by the time you sit down with your prospect they should already be sold on you.

You want to make sure that your seller prospects receive a copy of our pre-listing package before you show up for the listing appointment. You, your Admin, a team member or a runner will hand-deliver it a day or two beforehand.

Here are several key ingredients to a winning pre-listing package:

- ☐ Cover Page.
- ☐ Cover Letter.
- ☐ Marketing Plan.

- ☐ Testimonials (Reviews/Results/Case Studies).
- ☐ Special Report: Top 4 Reasons Homes Don't Sell.
- ☐ Agent Interview Sheet.
- ☐ Top 10 Reasons to List With Me.
- ☐ Seller Homework: Why My Home is Special.
- ☐ Seller Homework: My Upgrades.
- ☐ Seller Homework: Property Information Sheet.
- ☐ Home Prep Tips.
- ☐ Top Tips on Showing Your Home.

☐ Cover Page

Colorful and impressive, the cover page is used to "wow" the client from the onset. You can have the cover page printed on thick stock - almost like a book cover.

☐ Cover Letter

The cover letter introduces you and briefly explains how you will meet their needs. It also serves as a table of contents.

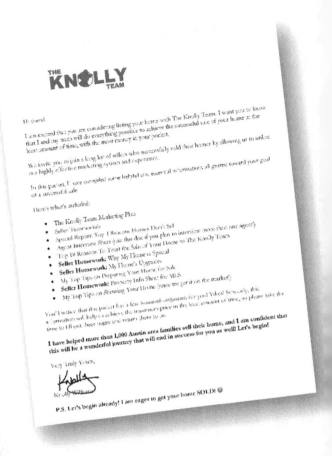

☐ Marketing Plan

Your marketing plan is essential. Although you already have this information in chapter 2 of your book, your one page marketing plan shows an easy-to-follow plan for getting their house sold. It sets you apart from other agents, because most don't have a written marketing plan. The marketing plan is written in a bulleted format and covers your strategy in the following areas:

1. Outdoor Advertising

2. Internet Advertising

3. Print Advertising

4. Premium Marketing

5. Industry Marketing

In chapter 13 we will discuss your marketing plan in full detail.

☐ Testimonials (Reviews/Results/Case Studies)

Your pre-listing package should include a page with 7 or more testimonials. Getting testimonials is an absolute must – even if you are new to the business. I've usually found it more effective to write the testimonials on behalf of my client. I simply call them and ask them how they would describe working with me. I let them speak and I take notes. I then email them a 2-3 sentence testimonial written based on our conversation and ask them if it correctly articulates what they said. This can be a time saver, because oftentimes folks with good intentions just don't get around to writing out their own testimonial.

For new agents, my suggestion is to get some testimonials that are generic and written to show sellers that you are trustworthy. If you don't have a lot of past clients, you can get some testimonials from your previous career. Here's an example of a testimonial from a previous co-worker: *"Ray is great to work with and has always been a team player. He is very honest and always put my interests above his own."* You can see how this type of testimonial can really come from anyone – and isn't specific to selling houses. Get at least 7 of these for your testimonials section.

☐ Special Report: Top 4 Reasons Homes Don't Sell.

Some years ago I put together a special report entitled *Top 4 Reasons Homes Don't Sell*. At the time I was working with lots and lots of Expired listings, and after listing hundreds of them I began to notice a pattern as to why these properties failed to sell. Obviously the top reason was price, but there were more subtle reasons like having bad photos or having an agent that other agents in town don't want to work with. Sometimes an inexperienced agent will not know how to hold a deal together, so a listing could fall out of contract and fail to sell. This document helps sellers see that you understand why homes don't sell and assures them that you will avoid those pitfalls.

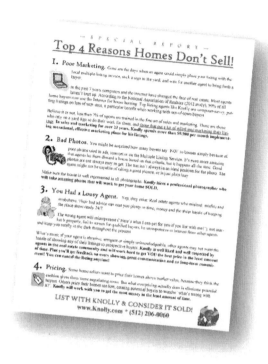

☐ Agent Interview Sheet.

Your Agent Interview Sheet is an ingenious document designed to completely crush your competition. It dispels the common consumer view that all agents are created equal and gives your clients the confidence to trust you with their most valuable asset. It also reinforces that they are making the right decision in hiring you. This sheet is particularly useful when a seller is considering interviewing more than one agent.

I recently talked with a seller who was looking to interview 14 agents! Yikes! Her property had failed to sell with her previous agent, so she wasn't going to make the mistake of hiring the wrong agent this time around. With this one sheet alone she was able to narrow her list down to just two agents that she wanted to interview – me and one other. 24 hours later she called to inform me that they were listing with me. This one document helped her eliminate 12 competitors.

Most sellers won't want to interview 14 agents. In fact, according to a recent NAR survey, nearly 70% of sellers interview just ONE agent prior to listing their house, so much of what I will teach you in this book will be geared toward getting you to be the one that gets in front of them first!

On the other hand, about 30% of sellers will want to interview more than one agent. This interview sheet will help you gain the advantage over your competitors.

I always want to know if a seller prospect is considering interviewing more than one agent. If they are, I will make sure that they use my interview sheet to conduct these interviews.

Here is the script that we use:

You: Cathy - are you going to be interviewing more than one agent for the job of selling your house?

Prospect: Well yes actually, I'm thinking about interviewing three.

You: That's great Cathy. Let me ask you – what specific criteria are you using to decide which agents you will allow into your house for a sit down interview?

Prospect: Uhhh – Well... I want to make sure they are good and I have to feel comfortable with them.

You: "That's great, Cathy! You know I've found that there are 10 specific questions you should ask any agent before you agree to list your house. Since I work with real estate agents every day, I know which questions you absolutely need to ask. In fact – I recommend that you ask these questions over the phone before you agree to meet with them. Think of this as a job interview process. You don't want to waste your time sitting down with anyone who doesn't meet the qualifications for the job. By the way Cathy – I've typed up those 10 questions and I can send you a copy. Would that be helpful to you?"

Prospect: Absolutely.

You: Wonderful, Cathy. I'll go ahead and email it over to you. It's a handy one page PDF with the top 10 questions and it already contains my answers to those questions. There's also space to write down the other agent's answer. You'll simply let the other agent know that you have a few questions to ask – and that you will get back with them if you would like to meet in person. It's a pretty simple process.

Prospect: Great! Thank You!

The beauty of the agent interview sheet is that you get to decide the questions you use! You should also include a portion where the seller can add up the score (how many questions were answered correctly). You can come up with whatever questions you feel are appropriate, and you don't have to use 10. Whenever you provide this information to a potential seller, they will feel indebted to you for providing them with a system they can use which makes their life easier. You also have a convenient excuse to call the seller back and gain their confidence. This form is definitely a game changer.

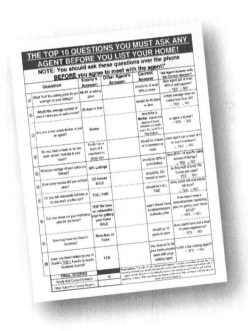

☐ Top 10 Reasons to Trust Me with the Sale of Your House!

People love Top 10 lists. Since securing the listing begins with securing the trust of the prospect, you want to give your prospects reasons why they should trust you with the sale of their most valuable asset. Your top 10 list also reinforces to the prospect that they are making the right decision by hiring you. Think of 10 reasons why someone should trust you with the sale of their house. Write down these 10 reasons and then expound on each one with a sentence or two.

☐ Seller Homework (Page 1): Why My Home is Special

My good friend and mentor Rand Smith taught me the importance of having Seller Homework in my pre-listing packet. It has been an invaluable addition!

This sheet helps you get the full scoop on the property so that you can write a glowing property description. On this fill-in-the blank sheet, your seller will list the features they really enjoyed most about their house, the type of person they think would love it, how they would best describe their house to a potential buyer and what features they liked most about the neighborhood/area.

Another trick is that whenever I write the *property description* for the listing, I use many of the adjectives and pick up on the features and benefits that the seller keyed in on. They love it! When they read my property description they always feel like I nailed it, and they often will say "Knolly, you described it perfectly!"

Filling out this sheet also helps your seller prepare to sell and to emotionally detach from the property.

Here is the information we request on this special form:

- Home features that we have really enjoyed: _____.

- The type of person I think would love this home most is: _____.

- ...because of these features: _____.

- How would you describe your home to a buyer?
  _____

- What are the features you like most about your neighborhood/area: _____.

☐ Seller Homework (Page 2): My Property Upgrades.

Knowing the specific upgrades that your client did to the property helps you to get your client top dollar. This sheet gives you negotiating leverage over the competition and also helps you write great ad copy for the listing.

This sheet allows the seller to list all of the upgrades that they made to the property including the interior, exterior, landscaping, and additional buildings.

Your seller will list the approximate amount they spent on each upgrade (or the approximate value of the upgrade if they did it themselves). Once you total up all the upgrades, you can use this total as negotiating leverage. I'll show you how in Chapter 16.

☐ Seller Homework: Property Information Sheet (Pages 3 and 4)

For my team, I designed a 2 page form which we call the Property Information Sheet. This sheet serves as a checklist of the most important property features and allows you, your seller or a team member to quickly check off the key features of the house. Although your MLS may also have such a document, it will generally be too exhaustive. Your sheet should focus on the listing features that are most important to potential buyers (based on the most popular online search criteria).

A few years after developing this document, I began experimenting with asking my sellers to fill it out. As a result, we now save at least 20 minutes on each listing appointment and the information is more accurate. Now we simply make this document part of the seller homework.

Here's the script to effectively use when requesting that the seller fill out this information:

You: You know Steve, we used to fill out this information ourselves, but you know what we found?

Seller: What's that?

You: In order to get you top dollar for your house, we found that it is best for the homeowner to fill out this form. We don't want to miss anything. Since you've lived in the house for more than nine years and I've only been at your house for a little over an hour - you are far more qualified to put down the most accurate information. Does that make sense?

Seller: You bet it does! I'll get it filled out right away.

You: Awesome Steve! It shouldn't take you more than 20 minutes, and you can email it to me!

☐ Top Tips on Preparing Your Home for Sale

This is a two-page checklist that you can use to guide your seller on the top things they can do to prepare their house for sale. This checklist allows the seller to walk through the house on their own and identify the things they should do to prepare their property for a successful sale and to get top dollar.

These tips give the seller no future excuse when negative showing feedback is received. It also allows you to sell their house faster and for more money.

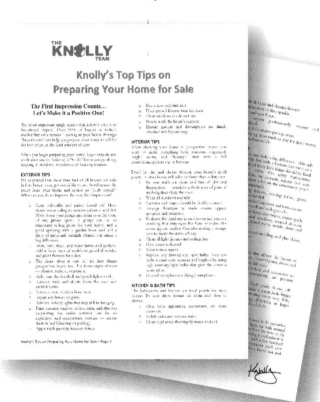

☐ Top Tips on Showing Your Home.

This one page document gives your seller a checklist of best practices when it comes to showing the house. It also gives them no future excuse when negative feedback is received as a result of their house not being show-ready.

You will want to encourage your sellers to give a copy of this checklist to everyone who is living in the house (and to tenants) so that they can also get in on the act. Don't expect your sellers to simply remember the things that you've told them regarding preparing their house for sale and handling showings. Using written checklists (that you can point the seller back to) is a much better system.

Tool #3. Virtual Listing Presentation (Your Promo Reel)

You should think of the Virtual Listing Presentation or pre-listing video as your *"promo reel"*. Every famous person has one.

This virtual listing presentation is a 3 to 10 minute video that highlights you and your team. This video will serve as a condensed and highly concentrated version of your listing presentation, designed to win the trust and confidence of your prospective seller before they meet with you.

In this video you will emphasize your marketing plan, how your team operates, pricing the house, how commission works and why the prospective seller should trust you with the sale of their house.

It is amazing to see the impact that your pre-listing video has on your prospects when it is coupled with your seller book and your pre-listing package. A few weeks ago I was at a listing appointment and the seller would not stop smiling the entire time we were together. Because the seller had already viewed my pre-listing presentation, read my book and reviewed the pre-listing package, there wasn't really much to discuss except price. We sat there reviewing the price while the seller kept smiling at me and saying *"Yes, Knolly – whatever you think is best is OK with me. I'm trusting your judgment on that."*

Once your sellers read your book and watch your "movie" they will feel like they already know you and trust you. In fact, when you effectively integrate these tools into your listing business, you can cut half of the time off your listing appointment.

Your Listing Tools Also Serve as Recruiting Tools

You should think of everyone in your database (and especially your past clients) as newly recruited soldiers in your army. When you arm your soldiers with the right tools, they can go out on the battlefield and recruit for you until the cows come home. Your tools help you create clients for life and raving fans.

Follow-up Call Script for folks you have given your book to:

You: Hey Kelly! Hope all is well. I just wanted to see how you are enjoying the book and see what your thoughts are?

Prospect: Thanks again! You know I'm still taking a look at your book but we haven't really decided what we are going to do yet.

You: That's great, Kelly. Take your time. You can always count on me for free advice so call or text me anytime you have a question. I'm the expert.

Prospect: Awesome! I sure will.

You: Great. By the way Kelly, who else do you know that's thinking about selling? I'd love to send them a copy of my book as well.

Prospect: You know, I can't think of anybody right now.

You: No worries, Kelly. Can you do me a favor?

Prospect: Sure.

You: Any time you run across someone who is even hinting about selling their house, ask them if it's OK for me to send them a free copy of my book. You already know I won't pressure them, I just want to help as many folks in our community as possible.

Prospect: You bet I will!

You: That's great, Kelly. Simply get their name and number and text it to me – or better yet, simply pick up the phone and

CALL ME. I'll make sure to get in touch with them so I can send them a free copy of my book on your behalf.

Prospect: Sure, will do!

You: Thanks Kelly! I'll check in with you in a few weeks. How's that?

Prospect: Great!

Now you can email the prospect this simple follow-up email:

Hi Kelly,

It was so great talking with you today. Thanks again for your time.

Like I mentioned, if you come across anyone who is thinking about selling (even if they are just tossing around the idea), I would love to send them my new book on your behalf.

I have found that many sellers want to weigh all their options without necessarily wanting to sit down with a real estate agent early on. My book helps guide them through the entire process, so they can make the best decision for their family.

I have found that it's best if you just get me their name and phone number so I can follow up and send them a copy. You can always email me their info or text me if it's more convenient.

Thanks again Kelly! I'll check back with you in a week or so.

With the above scripts, you are training your sphere of influence to develop the habit of sending you the contact information of potential sellers. If they simply give your contact information to these prospects, chances are those prospects will never call you. Many people have a difficult time reaching out to someone (cold calling) that they don't know, so you will lose lots of potential prospects unless you train your contacts to send potential seller's information directly to you.

Post-Closing Seller Script:

Here's one of my favorite closing table scripts. After you have closed escrow on the listing use the following script:

You: Thanks again guys for letting me represent you in the successful sale of your house. Are you satisfied with the job I did?

Seller: You bet we are! You got it sold!

You: Awesome! Well, right now what I need most is more inventory. Remember we still have lots of buyers looking for houses, not only in your area but all over town. I'm going to give you five copies of my book. Feel free to pass them out to anyone you run into who is thinking about selling their house.

[Hand them an envelope or small box containing copies of your book].

Seller: You bet we will!

You: And by the way, I'll be calling you from time to time, just to check on you and of course to see if you need any more copies, or

know someone looking to buy or sell. Would
that be OK?

This system is much more effective than giving your
client a stack of your business cards at closing. Guess what
will happen to those cards? Nobody knows. Your stack of
books however will be readily handy for your sellers to pass
out at a moment's notice. Besides, your clients love being
able to hand out an *item of value* to their friends and family.

A Note about Copyrights.

Make sure that the content you create for your book,
pre-listing package and video is unique. United States
Federal Copyright law prevents anyone from editing and
reusing existing copyrighted material without the express
permission of the copyright holder. The federal government
has placed a penalty of up to $150,000 for copyright
infringement. One way around this law is to obtain a license
from the copyright owner for a license fee.

Don't Reinvent the Wheel

When I wrote my seller book and put together my pre-
listing package, it took me roughly 300 hours total. It's a
good piece of work up front – but it now saves me more than
340 hours each and every year. Likewise you can choose to
write your own book and compile your own pre-listing
package from scratch or, if you don't want to reinvent the
wheel – *you can simply license my completely editable version!*
I created a generic version of my book that any agent can

begin using with little to no editing. You simply add your picture and name to the cover and the book becomes yours!

License Knolly's Complete System (Editable Book, Pre-Listing Package and More)

Having your own book, pre-listing package and pre-listing video will help you win far more listings, serve as powerful recruiting tools for your clients and radically shorten the amount of time you spend with seller prospects.

As a coach, I have repeatedly had my coaching clients ask me if I would be willing to let them purchase an editable copy of book, my pre-listing package, video script and various other listing business forms which I have created to run an efficient listing practice. While my focus was on teaching them how to write their own book from scratch and how to put together their own pre-listing package, I found that weeks and even months later they still would not have their book written or their pre-listing package compiled. My coaching clients were losing tens of thousands in potential commission income by not utilizing these important tools.

These tools took me hundreds of hours and years of testing to perfect. I realized that by allowing agents to utilize editable versions of my own time-tested tools – I was also able to allow them the opportunity to begin getting more listings right away by eliminating hundreds of hours of the time they would need to invest in creating these tools from scratch.

Therefore I have put together a full collection of customizable tools which will allow you to instantly have your own 80 page seller book, pre-listing package, pre-listing video script forms, and several other key tools that you can use in your listing business right away – all completely editable and completely paid for by your sponsors. You can order or get more information at SuccessWithListings.com.

These tools will allow you to get more listings now, maximize your Success with Listings, and shave about 3 hours off each listing you take, get more listing referrals and save money in the process. These tools allow you to look like a top agent overnight.

How Much is it?

When developing the pricing for the complete toolkit, I considered the cost of one on one coaching. Top Listings Specialists willingly pay $1,000 per month ($12,000 per year) for a one-on-one (1:1) coach, and they continue to do so because their coach holds them accountable and helps get them results. When pricing my complete system, I endeavored to make the cost affordable, so I priced it less than top agents pay for one month of coaching! You pay for it once, and it's yours to use for the next twenty years – or for the rest of your career. The lifetime license fee is regularly $995, however we have it on our website at the discounted price of only $595 (or 6 convenient payments of only $99).

A 24/7 Virtual Assistant

Imagine hiring a virtual assistant to be your promoter, doing nothing but going out and helping you generate listings. That's what you book and pre-listing package do. They work for you while you are sleeping!

Now imagine paying this person a one-time fee and having them work for you for the rest of your career! That's what you get when you snap my complete toolkit into your listing business.

Getting Your Complete Seller Book and Tools for *FREE*

To allow us to be able to license it to others at no charge, we incorporated a *Preferred Vendor Directory* right onto the back cover, so that the complete cost is paid for by your preferred vendors.

You can license my book and get your books printed at no cost to you! It's rather simple. Your customizable book comes with an editable back cover. On the back cover there are 6 ad slots for service trades and one banner position for a preferred vendor. You will earn at least $900 each and every

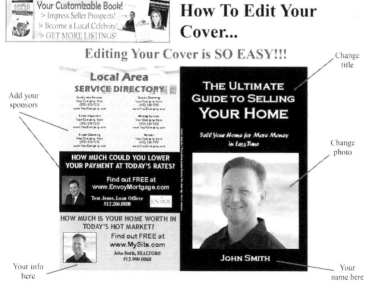

year that you are using this tool! This means your sponsors cover the entire cost of licensing your book plus you can print more than 300 copies a year at no cost to you.

On my website (www.SuccessWithListings.com) I give you a complete system for generating your book sponsors including call and email scripts and a back cover template that you can snap in.

Tools Included in My Complete System:

The tools including in my system are:

- ✓ Your Complete Seller Book (editable)
- ✓ Easy to Edit Book Cover
- ✓ Complete Vendor System to cover the entire cost and generate annual revenues to you (comes with vendor email and call scripts and vendor payment form)
- ✓ BONUS 1: My Editable Pre-Listing Package
- ✓ BONUS 2: My Virtual Listing Presentation (Pre-Listing Video) with editable video script
- ✓ BONUS 3: Job Descriptions for 14 Team Members (editable)
- ✓ BONUS 4: Listing Team Training Manual (editable)

Your Complete Seller Book

This is my editable book with copyright license. No need to pay a ghostwriter.

Your Editable Pre-Listing Package

Editable version of the pre-listing we use every day to list and sell properties. 14 pages of documents that you can edit and use in your business.

Your Virtual Listing Presentation (Pre-Listing Video)

You get a copy of the pre-listing video that my team uses to educate sellers along with an editable script so you can easily create your own video.

Job Descriptions for 14 Team Members

Comprehensive list of editable job descriptions for 14 different team positions.

Administrative Assistant | Buyer Specialist | CEO
Executive Assistant | Marketing Assistant | Office Manager
Listing Manager Showing Assistant| Team Runner
Short Sale Processor | Short Sale Listing Manager | Team Agent
Telemarketer | Transaction Coordinator

Your Listing Team Training Manual
24 pages and completely editable, this is the same manual I use to train my listing team members.

For more information or to get yours go to: www.SuccessWithListings.com.

Final Thoughts

Whether you decide to use the tools I have created or develop your own is up to you. Either way I admonish you to begin implementing these important tools in your business immediately so that you can reap the rewards of more listings, more income for your family and more time to enjoy life.

In the next section (chapters 6-10) let's take a close look at how to generate all the seller listing leads you will ever need.

Chapter 5 Homework

- ☐ Write/Compile your complete Seller Guide
- ☐ Write/Compile your complete Seller Pre-Listing Package and Seller Homework Packet
- ☐ Create you Seller Pre-Listing Video
- ☐ Take a look at SuccessWithListings.com to see how you can license all of my listing tools for FREE by partnering with preferred vendors so that you don't have to reinvent the wheel by creating these items from scratch.

Section

II

Finding the Listing

Chapter 6
Lead Generation for Listing Leads

What is the first and foremost important activity of a successful Listing Specialist? Of course you already know the answer: *lead generation*.

In ancient times, our forefathers were hunter-gatherers. Back then, people migrated with their food source and hunting for the next meal was not an *optional* exercise. No matter how scarce the surrounding food supply seemed, our ancestors would relentlessly chase their prey until they achieved success. For them, failure meant starvation and death. So when the food supply was abundant, they stockpiled and carefully preserved and stored the surplus. In good times and bad times they never took their eye off the ball.

If you want to be successful, you are not at liberty to treat lead generation like an optional exercise. Lead Generation is the ONE activity which allows all the other aspects of your career to become a reality. Prospecting is the cornerstone of your career.

When you take on a new listing, what is the ultimate goal you are hoping to achieve for your client? *A successful sale.* What is the ultimate goal you are hoping to achieve for yourself? *A paycheck and a client for life.*

In order to receive a paycheck, you have to have a closing. In order to have a closing, you have to have a contract. In order to have a contract, you have to have an offer. In order to have an offer, you have to have a listing. In order to have a listing, you have to have a client. In order to have a client, you have to prospect. In order to have a prospect, you have to lead generate. Lead Generation is the catalyst that burgeons into paychecks.

Time Block for Success

A successful Listing Specialist will conduct their lead generation activities in the morning hours, typically before noon.

In Chapter 1 we looked at *A Day in the Life of a Successful Listing Specialist.* There you saw that 9 AM to Noon is a pretty typical time block for lead generation. Generally speaking, 2 to 3 hours a day (or more), Monday through Friday is preferable. Handling your lead generation in the morning hours, when you are at your peak performance and maximum energy level is the way to go.

In order to achieve success with your lead generation activities, you will need to block out your daily lead gen time in your calendar. Set it there as a hard and fast daily appointment, and don't break the routine.

The 4 Stage Lead Lifecycle

In real estate all leads have what I call a four stage lead lifecycle. This is true not only for real estate, but for any area of sales.

Most agents speak about and focus on just one stage in this process, *lead generation*. In fact, this is only the *first* step in what is a four-step process. Generating leads without capturing, incubating and converting (lead follow-up) will not necessarily lead to clients. Those who focus merely on stage one will miss many a payday.

In order to be achieve Success with Listings you absolutely have to take most seller leads through the entire 4 Stage Lead Lifecycle. Stages 2 through 4 are the stages that determine if a lead will live (and reward you monetarily along with the possibility of repeat business) or die (and reward you with nothing).

>**Stage 1:** LEAD GENERATE
>
>**Stage 2:** LEAD CAPTURE
>
>**Stage 3:** LEAD INCUBATE
>
>**Stage 4:** LEAD CONVERT

Stage 1: Lead Generate

We call this *Lead Generation*. This is the step where the hook is baited and you are 'fishing' for leads. Lead Generation involves marketing and promotion, and a variety of other tactics required to generate a lead.

Stage 2: Lead Capture

We call this *Lead Capturing* or *Lead Receiving*. This is the stage where the lead actually falls into your hand and you catch (or capture) it. During this stage you have the lead captured, but it is uncertain whether or not this lead will actually turn into a *paycheck* for you. Hard work and diligence is required in order to take the lead all the way to the pay window.

Stage 3: Lead Incubate

This is what I call the 'nurturing' stage. As my mentor Rand Smith says, *"In order for someone to work with you, the possibility of trust has to exist."*

Think of this as the step where you are getting the lead to trust you. You are nursing the lead and trying to get them to see that working *with* you is a better choice than working *without* you. You are working to show them that you can be trusted.

Sometimes the lead incubation process is quite lengthy. Other times, (depending on the lead source, your skill level and contact frequency) it happens very naturally and quickly.

Step 4. Lead Convert.

Leads that are converted have graduated to become *clients*. In order to take a lead all the way to step 4, you absolutely have to *connect* with them. What I mean is, a connection between you and them has to have taken place.

It is unfortunate that many real estate agents completely drop the ball when it comes to stages 2 and 3. Many of the Type A personalities (High Ds on the DISC profile) that I train try to take a lead from Stage 1 directly to stage 4. They want to generate the lead and immediately convert them. If the lead doesn't convert right away, they move on to the next one. Don't make this mistake. Stages 2 and 3 are where the magic happens. If you want to build your listing business to the highest level it can possibly be, you will have to get good and consistent at capturing and incubating your seller leads. You can easily double your business just by making sure your leads are captured and incubated. These leads can often turn into clients, months down the road. If you do not focus on these critical stages, then many of your potential listings (and paychecks) will simply fall through the cracks.

You'll be happy to know that you can delegate steps 2-4 to your team members if they are highly trained and skilled at converting leads (yes, it truly is an art form). You can also make use of drip email campaigns and other systems to help you capture and incubate your leads.

Handling Objections

Oftentimes listing agents completely fumble the ball when a seller prospect throws out an objection. I have witnessed an agent's energy change and I have watched them go on the defensive when objections are raised. While the agent may attempt to mask their emotions, this subtle change from positive to neutral or negative energy is immediately picked up by the prospect, and defeat is imminent if the agent cannot recover quickly.

As you move toward mastery in the lead generation game, you will continue to encounter objections, yet the more skilled you become, the easier these objections will be to navigate through.

What Is An Objection?

Think of some words that you would consider being synonymous with the word *objection*. What comes to mind? Typically we think of objections as *obstacles*.

What I want you to realize is that *an objection is not rejection*. An objection is an *opportunity*.

Let's say for example that you are talking to a prospect about listing their property and they throw out an objection such as *"I like what you have to offer, but I haven't seen your signs in our neighborhood"* or *"Your fees seem higher than the other agents that I've talked to"* or *"What makes you think you can sell my house when my previous agent couldn't?"* With these questions, what is the prospect really saying? I believe they are saying *"Knolly, I think you can probably sell my house and I want to list with you. Can you please confirm for me that I am making the right decision?"*

Remember, an objection is not rejection. An objection is an opportunity. If the prospect did not want to explore the idea of listing with you they would not throw out an objection in the first place.

Think about the way you make big decisions. Before you swipe the card on that $400 purse, a flood of questions races through your mind. *"What's your return policy?"* *"When did you say the newer designs are coming in?"* *"What if I find it for less somewhere else?"* Why do you get this barrage of questions right before you make a big decision? The reason is that we are programmed to not want to make a big mistake. We throw up objections to protect ourselves. We want confirmation that we are making the right decision before we fully commit. We may also want to know where the escape hatch is (or whether or not there is one) before we jump on board. Once our objections are handled, we can feel safer about moving forward.

As a Listing Specialist, when you handle objections effectively you are reaffirming to the prospect that they are making the right decision by hiring you to list their house.

If the prospect did not want to list with you in the first place they wouldn't have any objections. Instead of asking questions they would simply tell you that they are not interested. Again think of when you were pitched a product to purchase. If you were not interested you would simply tell the salesperson "no, thank you" and move on. You wouldn't stand there and began asking questions about the product unless you were considering the idea of buying it.

In order to handle objections masterfully, you need to master the material in this book and learn your scripts backwards and forwards.

Why Agents Don't Prospect

There is a wide array of excuses that real estate agents provide for why they do not prospect regularly. No excuse is warranted or valid. Lead Generation is a daily activity.

Lead Generation is critical to your success. Next I would like to address some of the most common excuses that I've heard for not prospecting. Let's examine them together.

Excuse #1: *"I'm so busy! I just can't seem to find the time!"*

Imagine our forefathers waking up and thinking *"I've got a lot of things to do today, so I guess I won't go out hunting. Feeding my family can wait."*

In our businesses we can easily become distracted by that which is *urgent* and forget about that which is truly *important*. Everyone and everything may seem to be vying for your attention, but nothing deserves it more than your lead generation time.

No matter how busy your world gets or how much business you currently have in your pipeline, you should never take your foot off the lead generation pedal. Your time block for lead generation should be anchored to your schedule and honored daily.

Excuse #2: *"I've tried to time-block but I keep getting distracted."*

Allowing yourself to become distracted means that you are not correctly protecting your time block period. Be sure that everyone in your family and your office understands the importance of this activity. In ancient times, nothing was more important than hunting. This still holds true today. Imagine a family member discouraging the patriarch from going on the daily hunt, because of some other matter.

Purposely protect your lead generation space by hanging a note on the door that says "LEAD GENERATING. PLEASE DO NOT DISTURB." Close the door if you can. Also, take any snacks, coffee, water and other supplies with you into your lead generation bunker. Even the distraction of leaving your desk to fetch a drink of water or a coffee refill may prove fatal. If you are less than supremely disciplined when taking short breaks, then you should be anchored to your desk until you have achieved your goal for the day (lead generate for 3 hours, make 20 contacts, set 2 appointments, etc.).

Excuse #3: "I just can't get in the habit of time blocking."

You absolutely can get into the habit of time blocking because you already time block now. In fact, you have learned to time block since the day you were born.

Do you go to sleep every night? That's a time blocked activity. Do you brush your teeth, shower and get dressed every morning? Each of those is a time blocked activity. Do you eat meals every day? That's a time blocked activity. When you worked a 9-to-5 job, did you go to the movies during your work hours? Of course not, because you time blocked 8 hours for work and did personal activities during your off work hours! Even when you go to the movies you are time blocking 2-3 hours of undisturbed time.

You already know how to time block and you do it every day. If you are not time blocking for lead generation in your real estate practice, then you have not yet come to realize the correlation between prospecting and paychecks.

- Prospecting = Paychecks
- Not Prospecting = Poverty

Excuse #4: *"I don't know what to say."*

Knowing what to say is critical and oftentimes we fail to lead generate because we are afraid that we either don't know what to say or we will say the wrong thing.

Knowing what to say is a matter of training and learning your scripts. As you master the material and learn the scripts in this book, you will know exactly what to say to your prospects.

Excuse #5. *"I don't know what to do."*

You've time blocked your schedule and plopped yourself down at your desk promptly at 9 AM. Now what? Obviously, knowing what to do during your lead generation time is very important.

For a Listing Specialist, lead generation is the activity of generating new seller leads.

During your lead gen time, you should be:

1. Prospecting for new seller leads (lead generation).

2. Following up on your existing leads (lead incubation).

3. Implementing marketing plans.

Overcoming the Fear of Prospecting

Some agents are actually afraid to lead generate, because they fear rejection.

You can greatly reduce or eradicate this fear by coming to realize this one simple truth: *It's Not About You.* Yep – it sounds like a cliché, yet it is so true at so many levels.

Working with a seller is first and foremost about helping a person in need. You are helping someone else achieve success. Firstly you are adding value to them. Coincidentally you are receiving value in return.

For example, let's pretend you are a master roofer. You decide to go on a 2 week mission trip to a remote village to help the villagers restore their roofs, which are in terrible disrepair. You hop on a plane and take a grueling 13 hour flight. Then, after a 2 hour bumpy and dusty jeep ride through a remote and unnamed road, you arrive at your destination.

Now then, what do these villagers need? A new roof. Why are you there? To put as many new roofs on as you can over the next 2 weeks. Are you confident that you can do the job? Of course! You are a master roofer.

The only question that remains is – *will the villagers allow you to help them to get what they need?*

What if some of the villagers don't allow you to help them? Perhaps a foreigner has done them wrong in the past, or they just grew up with the notion of not trusting others. You show up with your sleeves rolled up and tools in tow. You knock on the door and your interpreter explains why you are there. The villager looks at you and smiles, but shakes his head *"NO."* The interpreter pleads with him, as it is clearly obvious that his roof is one of the worst in the village and it is leaking badly. Unfortunately the villager remains suspicious, rejects your act of kindness and ultimately shuts the door in your face.

You feel rejected.

But ask yourself, was this rejection about you or is it about them? Of course it's about them. It has nothing to do with you because you are eminently qualified to achieve success for them. If this villager had allowed you to, you could have placed a gorgeous new roof on their hut within four hours. You have no choice but to move on to the next house. Luckily for them, they are not so resistant. After a bit of conversation through the interpreter, they follow you around the outside of their hut as you point out what you are going to do for them. They invite you in with open arms. They even celebrate their new roof and thank you by preparing you a delicious local dish.

Your Prospects Have to Be Willing to Allow You to Help Them.

When you are rejected by a prospect it is usually not about you, it's about them. People come to us with a boatload of past experiences, trust issues, and the like. Our job is to help them overcome their fear, apprehension and trust issues so that we can help them get what they want. You will use your skills, your scripts, your tools, and your notoriety simply as leverage to help your prospects make the right decision to hire you for the job of selling their house. Once they hire you, you can confidently move forward to help them achieve success.

As Listing Specialists, we must let go of ego. We must become servants who are singularly focused on knowing what our clients want and need, so that we can serve it up to them.

On the other hand, if they choose not to hire you don't take it personally and don't be offended. It's okay. It wasn't meant to be. Place them in your incubation system and move on to the next one.

If someone does not allow you to help them to succeed it is not about you it's about them. Likewise, when someone does hire you, it is still not about *you* it is about them. Understanding and internalizing this simple truth will help you overcome your fear of rejection and your fear of prospecting. Shake it off and move on.

Of course you should have 100% confidence in yourself, knowing that you are the best person for the job. You should always be improving yourself, your skills, your tools, your systems and your tactics.

Where Will Your Leads Come From?

Becoming a top Listing Specialist requires a nonstop supply of listing leads. As it turns out – there are only three sources that all the leads you will ever need will come from. I call these the 3 Lead Generation Buckets.

I am convinced that the reason most agents do not realize their highest success potential is because 1) they are not primarily focused on listings, 2) they do not have the right leverage and 3) they are not consistency generating leads through the 3 lead generation buckets.

It may help to think about the three lead generation buckets as the three legs of a stool. Suppose you wanted to stand on a heavy duty 3-legged stool (you know, the tripod style). It will support and distribute your weight quite nicely. What would happen though if you took one of those legs off and tried to stand on it? The stool simply would not support you. What if you took two of the legs off? You would end up flat on your back. Sadly most real estate agents are trying to stand on a one legged stool – and that one leg that they do have is busted and in disrepair.

The 3 Lead Buckets (the 3 legs of your stool) are:

1. **SOI** (your sphere of influence).

2. **Farm** (your geographic farm).

3. **Niche** (your specialty).

From these 3 buckets you will generate all of the leads that you will ever need. During the rest of this section, (the next 4 chapters) I will show you how to tap into these 3 lead buckets and how to implement them into you daily lead gen schedule so that you will be able to generate, capture, incubate and convert more leads than you ever thought possible.

Chapter 6 Homework

☐ Develop your system for capturing, incubating and converting the leads you generate.

☐ Create your time-blocked lead generation schedule.

☐ Set up your lead generation bunker.

Chapter 7 - SOI
Your Sphere of Influence

The first lead generation bucket that we will be discussing is your *database*, also known as your sphere of influence (SOI). This will understandably be your largest and most important bucket.

Retaining a current client is more important than generating a new one. You have already invested a great deal of time and energy cultivating the relationship you have with these folks, and they already command your loyalty.

Unfortunately a great many real estate agents spend vast sums of money, time, attention and energy trying to generate new relationships while completely abandoning their current ones. If you orphan your clients your competitors are waiting in line to adopt them.

Keeping in touch with your SOI is critical! Your SOI is made up of past clients, people you know and people you've met.

According to a recent survey conducted by the National Association of REALTORS® (NAR), when selecting an agent to sell their house 7 out of 10 sellers chose their agent based on a referral by a friend, neighbor or relative, or they used their previous agent. That means 70% of your business will come from or originate from someone in your database. This is what we call repeat and referral business.

Another survey conducted by the NAR revealed that 84% of sellers say they are likely to use the same agent or recommend that agent to others. That means 84% of your past clients would refer you or reuse you! That's not bad. Yet how many people actually do reuse the same agent again or refer them to their SOI? Shockingly, the research points to just 9%-11% of them. This is a remarkable disconnect. Why is it that nearly 90% of the folks who say they would refer you or use you again never do? The answer is obvious. *You are not staying in touch with them.*

Based on the aforementioned statistics, 70% of your income should come from your SOI. Now let's convert this data into a little math exercise. Let's say that your goal is to net $100,000 this year. Let's further pretend that you were adequately marketing to your SOI on a consistent basis. According to the data, $70,000 of the $100,000 income you earn over the next twelve months will come from this one bucket alone. However, if you do not stay in touch with your SOI, this $70,000 bucket dwindles down to right around $9,000. Ouch.

Let me explain it another way. When it comes to eating out, many people base their decision to try out a new restaurant on the restaurant's star rating. If a restaurant has 4.5 out of 5 stars (based on numerous patron reviews), would you eat there? Absolutely. Would you eat at a restaurant that received 1 out of 5 stars (with numerous patron reviews)? Not likely. That establishment would likely be on their way *out of business*. The research shows that when you abandon your sphere of influence, your rating drops from 4.5 stars to a 0.5 star! That's a half a star rating! Ouch.

So the question is WHY AREN'T YOU STAYING IN TOUCH WITH YOUR SOI??? Think about the question. What is your excuse? Why are you willing to give up so much of your potential income?

Throughout my career as a trainer I've heard a variety of excuses as to why agents are willing to forgo the vast sums of wealth that should be continually springing forth from their database. If 70% of your business will come from your SOI wouldn't it make sense to spend most of your lead generation time, attention, effort and marketing budget on this group? Of course! Yet most agents seem obsessively and obstinately focused on following every new scheme, tactic, and strategy that comes along promising to deliver fresh new leads. In other words, they choose to spend the majority of their time focusing on and marketing to *complete strangers* while ignoring those who already know, like and trust them. Such thinking is foolish and should be abandoned immediately.

An Easy-to-Implement System

So how do you get your SOI to become your raving fans, keeping your name and face at the top of their mind, and sending you business left and right? It's simple, you have to stay in touch with them and you have to recruit them into action.

After coaching and training tens of thousands of agents, I have come to understand that the reason why the majority does not keep in touch with their SOI is because they get so wrapped up in their current production that they get tunnel vision and are singularly focused on the next deal. Soon the weeks fade into months, and the months fade into years. What they lack is an easy to implement "stay in touch" plan.

At the Knolly Team we developed an easy 18 touch SOI campaign. I teach the K-I-S-S method. *Keep it Simple Stupid. Keep it Simple Sweetheart.* Or my favorite – *Keep it Super Simple.*

Your Easy Stay-in-Touch Plan

The Knolly Method

1. **Monthly E-Newsletter** to your database (12x/yr).
2. **Quarterly mailing** to your database (4x/yr).
3. **Semi-annual call** to your database (2x/yr).

This super simple plan only requires a few hours a week to implement.

Your Monthly E-Newsletter

For our monthly Newsletter we use MoreSolds.com. MoreSolds is a CRM (Client Relationship Manager) that I created several years ago for my team. We wanted a system that was robust and feature rich, yet easy to use, so we created our own. We now make our CRM available for free to anyone who wants to use it. The newsletter module is called *RealtyRave* and is only $4.95/mo. It takes less than 5 minutes to set it up and then it's automated and works for you month after month, keeping you in touch with your sphere.

Too many agents get caught up in manually piecing together articles, and when the monthly chore of compiling a customized newsletter becomes too time-consuming, they abandon doing it altogether.

Your primary focus is on touching your clients each and every month. The articles should be made up of short and relevant content.

The beauty of MoreSolds is that our E-Newsletter editor researches what is trending that month and includes shortened versions of those articles. They handle all of the back end work so you don't have to. Plus it is automatically customized with your photo, logo, contact information, *Featured Listings* link, *Property Search* link and more, so it looks like YOU created it.

Research the various systems available and pick the one you love. Regardless of what program you use to send out your email newsletter, it should be *'set it and forget it'* simple. In other words, you want to use a system that you can set up once and your newsletter will automatically go out each and every month, like clockwork.

Quarterly Postcard Mailing

Each quarter, mail a jumbo sized (5 1/2" x 8 1/2" or similar size) postcard out to your database.

Rather than sending a new postcard each quarter, simply print up a batch and send the same one every three months.

For example, if your database is 250 people, you would simply print 1000 postcards and send that same postcard every three months.

If you try to change up the design of your postcard every three months, you will invariably discontinue the campaign because you simply won't get around to getting the job done.

Remember – your goal is simplicity. Yes, you could create a new postcard every quarter but that is completely unnecessary. Again, the point of the mailing is to tap your SOI on the shoulder and remind them that you are still in business and that you still *need* business. Make it easy on yourself by printing up one batch of postcards and using that same one throughout the year.

Your postcard should double as an *item of value* (IOV). My favorite for shelf life is a Preferred Vendor Directory. You could also consider including the following:

- Friends and family discount coupon (i.e. $500 off your next transaction);
- Referral Reward (i.e. $50 Visa gift card);
- Free House Valuation;
- Free copy of your book (a free printed copy of your seller book; see chapter 5).

Print & Assign

When it comes to delivering your postcards, simply have them printed and assign the job of mailing them to your Admin. If you don't yet have an Admin, you can entrust the job to your kiddos, a neighborhood student, or anyone else willing to help. When the mailing is due, simply drops off the box of cards, addresses labels and postage stamps, and have the person get your mail-out ready and sent. Delegating this helps you automate the process while you stay focused on the most dollar productive activities.

Semi-Annual Phone Call to Your Database

Twice a year you will want to pick up the phone and call your SOI. Again this is solely for the purpose of continuing to stay in touch with them.

You can easily spread those calls out evenly throughout the year. For example, let's say you have a database of 300 people. This means that you will make 50 phone calls each month, or 12 calls each week. It should take you no more than forty minutes to an hour to make those 12 calls. Considering that you should be time blocking for lead generation at least 2-3 hours each day (Chapter 6), these calls are both wonderful and profitable, and can easily be incorporated into your lead generation time.

Script!

You: Hi Penny its _____ - how are you?

SOI: Great! it's good to hear from you. We are doing well, how are you doing?

You: I'm doing awesome, Penny. Hey Penny, the reason I'm calling is just to touch base and see how things are going. The last time we talked your daughter Suzy had just gotten a new puppy and your son Charles was about to graduate from high school.

SOI: [talks about what's new while you take notes about what's new in their life and enter these notes into your CRM]

You: Penny - thanks again for taking the time to catch me up on what's going on with you guys! Right now my business is doing well but I still have a big problem that I was hoping you could help me with.

SOI: Sure... What's up?

You: Penny, my biggest problem right now is with our inventory. Our listings are selling fast and we need more! I'm looking to help 2 more families to buy or sell before the end of the month. Who do you know that's thinking about buying or selling?

SOI: hmmm... You know... no one comes to mind right now.

You: Thanks Penny. I really appreciate your help. As always Penny, if you happen to overhear anyone talking about selling - let them know that you'd love to have your agent give them a call with some free advice. Then just text me, email me or better yet, CALL ME with their contact info. Can you do that for me?

SOI: I sure will!

You: Thanks again Penny! By the way - I'm also going to be sending you a few copies of my new book... it's a complete Seller's Guide that you can pass along to anyone you run into that's thinking about selling.

SOI: Wow, that's great!

You: Thanks again Penny - you have a great day!

SOI: You too!

Follow Up Email:

Hi Penny,

It was so great talking with you today. Thanks again for your time.

I was delighted to hear about how Roxanne is going off to college and about your job promotion! Congrats to you and Steve on both accounts! [Here you are inserting a sentence or two about your phone conversation/highlights of what you discussed]

Like I mentioned, if you come across anyone who is thinking about selling or buying (even if they are just tossing around the idea), I would love to help!

I have found that it's best if you just get me their name and phone number so I can follow up with them. CALL ME with their information and I promised to give them the same level of service I provide to all my close friends and family. You can always email me their info or text me if that's more convenient.

I am looking forward to helping 2 more families buy or sell before the end of the month, and I look forward to your help!

Thanks again Penny!

Enter the Call Notes into Your CRM

It is important that you enter your notes about the call into each client's contact record on your CRM. You know how your doctor pulls out a clipboard at your annual physical and briefly discusses your medical history that you discussed with her the year before? Clients love it when you

can briefly restate what you discussed on the last call with them. When they see that you were paying attention to what is going on in their life, they will become all the more loyal and will want to strongly support you. You may also find it helpful to visit their Facebook and LinkedIn page, so you can catch up on what's going on with them before you make the call.

What if You Don't Already Have a Database?

Putting together your database from scratch is easy. Simply get out several sheets of paper and write down the names of everyone you know (your doctor, dentist, previous coworkers, church friends - everyone). Shoot for at least 200 names. Now all you have to do is track down their contact information and input them into your CRM. You can easily recruit your children or a neighborhood student to help you with the data entry. If you already have a list on an electronic spreadsheet, you can easily import the data into your CRM.

Do You Already Have a Database?

If you already have a database, awesome! Good for you. Your homework assignment will be to clean it up! Chances are it's outdated. You will need to go through your database with a fine-toothed comb and update all of your contacts while adding any new ones you have written down. This will require some research and phone calls to your existing database.

Here's a sample call script to folks you haven't talked to in a while:

You: Hi John! It's _____

SOI: Oh - Hi!

You: You know John, it's been a while since we've talked. Frankly, I apologize for not being in touch with you.

SOI: Oh, I understand.

You: Thanks John. You know from this day forward I've decided to commit myself to staying in touch. My goal is to call you about every six months, just to see how you, Jill and the family are doing. Would that be okay?

SOI: Sure!

You: Awesome! Well let me just make sure that I have all your current information. Is your home address still 301 N. Hickory Cove?

SOI: Yep

You: Awesome. And is this the best number for you?

SOI: Yep

You: Great. What's your current email address?

[Keep going along these lines until you have updated all of their contact information]

You: Thanks again John! As I mentioned, I'll be contacting you about every six months just to see how you guys are doing. Plus Penny – I have a pretty large database with folks in almost every profession you can think of, so let me know if you ever run across anyone looking for a job, or if you need a good handyman, painter, roofer, electrician, attorney or whatever!

SOI: Great! I sure will.

You: Awesome! Oh - one more thing John. My biggest problem right now is with our inventory. Our listings are selling fast and we need more! Who do you know that's thinking about selling?

SOI: hmmm... You know... no one comes to mind right now.

You: Thanks John. I really appreciate your help. As always John, if you happen to overhear anyone talking about selling - let them know that you'd love to have your agent give them a call with some free advice. Then just text me, email me or better yet,

CALL ME with their contact info. Can you do that for me?

SOI: I sure will!

You: Thanks John! By the way - I'm also going to be sending you a few copies of my new book... it's a complete Seller's Guide that you can pass along to anyone you run into that's thinking about selling.

SOI: Wow, that's great!

You: Thanks again John - you have a great day!

SOI: You too!

After your call be sure to send a follow-up email using your version of my previously discussed follow up email script.

Once your database is squeaky clean, it will stay that way by implementing your 18 touch plan.

Developing and maintaining your SOI is the best way to reach optimal success in the real estate business. Your database will consistently reward you with repeat and referral business when you consistently stay in touch.

Real Estate CRMs

Using a great real estate CRM will allow you to efficiently and effectively stay in touch with your SOI. There are a wide variety of CRM software products on the market. You should be using one that will allow you to stay in contact with your clients in a much more effortless manner. Give our free MoreSolds CRM a try, if you don't already have an easy to use cloud based system.

Developing Your Inner Circle

Now that we have thoroughly examined an easy program for consistently reaching your SOI, I want you to consider creating your own *inner circle*. An inner circle can make big things happen in your listing business.

Having an inner circle is another biblical principle. In his ministry, Jesus had thousands of disciples, yet he hand-picked just twelve to be part of his inner circle.

Your inner circle will be the cream of the crop, hand selected from your SOI.

Did you realize that you could effectively do 100 real estate transactions a year from an inner circle group of just 25 people? You could if those 25 individuals were highly connected people that would each commit to sending you just one referral each quarter.

Your inner circle will be individuals who you can count on for multiple referrals each year. You will want to stay in contact with this group more frequently, and perhaps have a periodic client appreciation parties/events just for them.

Anchoring Your Goals into a Higher Purpose

Personally, I am very big on the concept of paying it forward and giving back. I would love to see you anchor your real estate goals into a higher purpose.

I believe that our mission in life should be tied to a higher purpose. I'm convinced that my duty on earth is to serve God and others. That's what leadership is per Jesus' own example.

Imagine if you took a little from each commission check you earn to help a needy cause.

One example is helping to put wells into villages that don't have safe and potable water.

Another friend I know spent years raising money to build incredibly nice mini-houses (huts) for villagers who spent the majority if their lives living in cardboard boxes situated on a land fill. These little huts were some of the cutest you've ever seen and cost only about $5,000 each.

What my wife Josie and I personally do is we have the title company where we close our transactions wire 10% of our funds from every closing directly into a "ministry" account. It's a separate account and we call it *God's Account*. Although we realize that the biblical practice of tithing is no longer a mandate, we still love and follow the principle as it is always a good practice to pay it forward.

We use the money in God's account to fund missionaries, feed the poor, help those who fall on bad times, assist widows and orphans (for anything outside of ourselves). This is not something we have ever shared publicly because we don't do it for publicity. We are absolutely sure that we get more benefit from giving than those who are the recipients. We just personally feel compelled to pay if forward - and we have been allocating 10% of our income for more than 20 years. We do it from a spirit of gratitude and thankfulness. We started doing this in 1992 and we have never stopped. Back then we were both making less than $7 an hour and our monthly household income was less than $2,000 with both of us working full time jobs! It was tough to do, but the Lord has always blessed us with an abundance and taught us to fully trust in His provision.

Let's look at an example of how anchoring your purpose into a higher calling works.

Let's say for example, that Cynthia is a busy Listing Specialist. She is committed to reaching her goals and she is also committed to giving back. Cynthia does the research and finds out that for $3,000, she can fund a well for a village in a third world country. Just one well would provide clean and safe drinking water to more than 300 villagers, greatly reducing infection and disease in that area.

Now let's say Cynthia has a goal to list 40 houses this year. She decides to donate $300 from each closing to her "well" project.

This means that for every 10 houses that Cynthia closes, she can provide funding for one well. Therefore, once she reaches her closings goal for the year, she would have also reached her higher goal of providing fresh drinking water for four villages.

Cynthia's goal is now firmly anchored into a higher purpose. Instead of having a goal to sell 40 houses, her goal this year is to put in four wells.

As Cynthia is calling on her SOI to solicit listing referrals – instead of asking past clients to help her reach her goal of selling 40 houses this year, she can ask them to help her reach her goal of providing safe drinking water to 4 villages.

For every client that her inner circle refers her, they are actually helping make the world a better place. Meanwhile they are making Cynthia's world better too. It's a win-win.

Cynthia: Hi Jim, it's Cynthia over at the Baker Team. How are you?

Jim: Oh, Hi Cynthia – we are doing well, how about you?

Cynthia: Awesome Jim. Hey – I'm calling because we have a wonderful new project that I wanted to let you know about, so you can help me spread the word.

Jim: Great, what's up?

Cynthia: You know Jim – My team and I found out that people in Haiti are literally dying because they don't have access to fresh drinking water. We also found out that we could put a well into a village that would provide clean and safe drinking water for over 300 people, and save lives. Our team is going to cover all the costs; we just need your help getting the word out. Does that sound like something you could help with?

Jim: Sure! How can I help?

Cynthia: Well Jim, our goal is to put in 4 wells this year that will serve over 1200 people. Basically for every house we close this year we are donating a portion of the proceeds to this project. For every 10 properties we close we can fund a well.

Jim: Cool!

Cynthia: So Jim, all we need you to do is send us the contact information of anyone you run across that is thinking about buying or selling. Every referral you send us will go toward helping with our big goal of putting wells into these villages! Doesn't that sound great?

Jim: You bet!

Cynthia: Thanks Jim. I knew we could count on you. I'm going to be keeping track of our goal and keeping you updated periodically. By the way - how many referrals do you think you can send me over the next 12 months?

Jim: Well... I don't know - maybe five.

Cynthia: That's great Jim - I'll put you down for five. I'll also email you some more for information about this incredible project! Thanks again Jim!

Jim: You bet Cynthia!

Using the script above, all Cynthia would have to do is keep contacting her sphere of influence. If she contacted 20 inner circle contacts and each person made a commitment of 2-3 people, she can count on 40-60 referral leads this year from this target group!

In order for the program to be a success, Cynthia will have to hold those who made pledges accountable. She will do this by writing down each person's commitment and then tracking it on a spreadsheet. Each quarter she can send out a spreadsheet showing exactly where things stand. Her quarterly report can show the names of those who pledged referrals, the number of referrals that they pledged, the actual number of referrals that they have sent (year to date), and the referrals remaining to be sent. The report would also show how many wells have been put in and how many there are to go. She can follow up her quarterly report with a phone call thanking those who are making good on their pledges and encouraging the ones who have not.

Your clients love to get behind a project that is for the good of others. That's why anchoring your goals into a higher purpose can help you achieve what you want faster. Now then, if Cynthia were simply to call her sphere of influence without a higher purpose goal, her message would not have the same affect. Imagine Cynthia just calling her database and letting them know that her goal was to increase her wealth by selling 40 houses this year, or simply to help 40 families buy or sell. This doesn't have the same ring. Her sphere of influence can feel much more motivated to help her reach an altruistic goal of serving 4 villages.

There are literally hundreds of different things you could do to pay it forward both domestic and abroad. You could provide scholarships, help kids pay for summer camp, fund art classes or music lessons, provide wheelchairs for the elderly, home restorations for veterans, fund self-improvement classes, help rescue animals... the list goes on and on. Pick something that is near and dear to your heart, figure up the cost, factor how much you are willing to donate (percentage or fixed amount) from each closing and go to work getting your SOI on board with your higher purpose!

In doing so you will be a blessing to others, allow your SOI an opportunity to pay it forward, and provide for your family.

You should think about this as a "project" and run it as such, on an annual basis.

Here's an example of a project to provide wheelchairs for the elderly:

1. **Project Purpose**: Provide wheelchairs for the elderly.
2. **You closings goal**: 60.
3. **Cost per wheelchair:** $400.
4. **Amount you decide to donate from each closing**: $100.
5. **12 Month Project Goal:** Provide 15 wheelchairs for the elderly.

With this example, your unit goal is 60 closed units over the next 12 months. You find out that you can purchase rehabbed wheelchairs for around $400 each, and you decide to donate $100 of each closing toward the project. Once you reach your unit goal, you will have provided 15 wheelchairs for the elderly.

That's $100 per closing x 60 closings = $6,000 ÷ $400 (cost of each wheelchair) = 15 wheelchairs.

Let's say you need 100 referrals in order to project 60 closings. Your group of 20 people will need to commit to sending you an average of 5 referrals per person. If your inner circle is 40 people, you would only need 2.5 referrals a year from each person.

As you can see, anchoring your goals into a higher purpose is a wonderful way to achieve your goals while simultaneously making the world a better place.

Final Thoughts

Your sphere of influence (your database) is by far the most important of the three buckets you will focus on during your lead generation time. Spend the time it takes to get your pristine database together, and begin incorporating the tactics in this chapter into your daily time block. In doing so, you will reclaim the myriad of paychecks that you are currently letting fall by the wayside.

Chapter 7 Homework

- ☐ Sign up to an Online CRM service (you can use MoreSolds.com or any other service you like).
- ☐ Create or clean up your SOI database list.
- ☐ Launch your monthly E-Newsletter.
- ☐ Design your postcards and have them printed.
- ☐ Create a call schedule for calling your SOI 2x/year.
- ☐ Develop your Inner Circle.
- ☐ Create a *project* so that you can anchor your goals into a higher purpose.

Chapter 8
Geographic Farming

Farming is your second lead generation bucket. Although this bucket probably won't be as large as your sphere of influence, over time it can grow to create a substantial portion of your income.

A geographic farm is in area of town that you specifically target with the express purpose of becoming well known in that territory. Once you pick your area, you will build your business there through consistent marketing, exposure, branding, involvement and advertising.

Imagine that you were running for mayor of your city. What would that look like? What kind of marketing campaigns would you employ in order to get the vote? Visualize your mayoral campaign. Well, farming looks the same way; only you are running for mayor of a smaller territory – more like a precinct, subdivision or an area of town.

Success at geographic farming requires having an action plan, a budget, being creative, doing some hard work, and being realistic in your expectations.

Most top agents that are seasoned have a geographic farm they work with, and many have been working those areas for years.

Picking Your Farm

Let's look at some criteria to consider when putting your farm together.

500+ Houses

A good farm will be made up of at least 500 houses. Ultimately, the size of your farm will depend on your sales goals. I know some agents who have a farm of 10,000 or more houses. My suggestion is to start with around 500 houses and increase the size of your farm over time.

Area Should Have Steady Turnover/Sales (7% Minimum)

The area you choose to farm should have a minimum sales turnover of 7%.

For example, suppose you pick a farm area with 500 houses. Using the 7% turnover rule, at least 35 houses per year should sell within your farm each 12 months (500 x 7%).

You should be able to use your local tax record data to determine the actual number of houses in an area or subdivision. Then, to determine how many houses are actually selling in your target area, you can do an MLS "Sold" report to see how many houses actually sold there in the past 365 days.

If you are having trouble coming up with these reports, your team leader, coach or broker should be able to help you.

The Average Sale Price Should Be Enough to Support Your Goals

One of the most obvious ways to increase your income is to increase your average sale price. Farming is one of the easiest ways that I know of to increase your average sale price, because you get to *choose* which neighborhoods and areas you want to work in.

Keep in mind that it costs the same to market to high-end neighborhoods as it does to low income areas.

At any rate, you will want to make sure that the areas you target are at least within your acceptable average sale price goals.

Your Farm Should Be Nearby

Dominating an area that is near where you work or live helps put the fun and excitement into farming. Your clients can drop by your office or you can pop by their house at a moment's notice. Plus you get the added benefit of getting to see your marketing efforts at work on a constant basis, as you drive through these nearby areas.

If you choose a farm area that is too far away from your home or office, you will find yourself regretting making that long drive. I recommend that you keep your farm area within 5 to 10 minutes of where you work or live, if at all possible.

Of course you can take listings in a very large area, if it's part of your MLS and if you are familiar with the area, but I do not recommend that you farm in those faraway areas.

Personally I used to take listings in five counties. I don't mind driving an hour to a listing appointment, but I don't farm in those areas. Your farm should be close to your home base.

"What if the Area I Want is Already Dominated by a Competitor?"

I suggest you begin with an area that doesn't appear to be heavily farmed or heavily dominated currently. Drive around and check out the signs that are out. You can also run MLS reports to see who dominates the listings in that area.

If you feel that you absolutely must break into a particular area, go ahead and begin farming there. If that area is already heavily farmed by another agent, just realize that it can take longer to make headway. It can be done, but the fruits of your labor may come further down the road.

Farming on Foot

Get out and walk the neighborhood at least once a month. You can hit as many as 100 homes in a three hour time block.

Have an Item of Value.

Hand the homeowner something of value. If they aren't home, you can leave it at the door. This can be a newsletter with valuable coupons, a calendar of events, a sports schedule or a vendor trade directory.

Brand Yourself

Remember, your goal is to become famous in the areas that you serve. To be well known you will have to brand yourself. This means including your photo and name (or team name) in all of your items of value. In fact, it is recommended that your name, photo and logo make up approximately 30 percent of the marketing piece.

Get Involved.

It is important that you get involved in your local community as much as possible. City Council meetings, HOA meetings, PTA, church, local committees and neighborhood watch are all examples of ways you can get involved and serve the local area. Remember, you are running for the office of *"Real Estate Major"* of your farm!

Area YouTube Channel.

You can easily start a YouTube channel for the various neighborhoods that you serve. Interview local business owners and local restaurants and feature them and their businesses on your channel. You can also talk about new businesses and municipal services that are coming into the area.

Here Are Some Of The Folks You Can Interview For Your YouTube Channel:

- Restaurant owners/managers;
- Local Banks and Credit Unions;
- Government officials;
- Hospital/emergency clinic directors;
- Large employers;
- Service providers.

Interview Examples:

- Interview a local landscaper in the spring with questions like: *"When is the best time to fertilize your lawn?"* and *"When is the best time to begin planting spring Annuals?"*

- Interview a local gym owner about the best exercises for folks who work in an office environment or just ask questions about their facility and what they have to offer the community.

- Interview a local health organization to find out what services are available to the local community.

- Interview a new restaurant or your favorite area boutique shops.

Open House a Lot!

Whether you like doing open houses or not, the fact remains that open houses can serve a major purpose when your goal is to dominate your farm area through branding. Having 20 to 30 signs on the street corners around your farm area every weekend is a strong way to create a credible and sustained presence in your farm. Once you have a listing in your farm area, do as many open houses as you can.

Personally invite the neighbors to your open house event. This is hard work but it is a proven method. Some of the visitors to your open house could be future sellers and at your open house event they will get to see your stellar marketing in practice.

Every Door Direct Mail (EDDM)

EDDM is an incredible gift introduced by the United States Postal Service. With EDDM, you can send a jumbo postcard to every home in your farm area for less than twenty cents each. You don't even have to affix the postage stamps or address labels. You simply pick the area you want your postcards *delivered* to, fill out a form, and deliver the postcards to the Post Office.

Farming for FREE

To enjoy ultimate Success with Listings, I believe that you should strive to employ LOW or NO COST strategies. Farming does not have to be expensive; in fact it can be *free*. Say what!? Yes, it's true.

Using EDDM currently costs less 20¢ per house to send your mailing piece.

Now let's suppose your farm was 500 houses. Mailing to your farm would cost just under $100 in postage. All you need to do is invite four service providers to participate in your mailer. Each trade will receive a small ad on the back of your postcard and they each invest just $25. Now how much will it cost to you to mail your marketing piece? *Nothing.*

If you charged each one $40, you would cover the postage and the cost of printing your postcards as well.

Local trade vendors make good candidates. For forty bucks they can piggyback on your mailer and reach 500 houses. At just eight cents per house, that's a phenomenal deal. If your farm were 1000 houses you would charge $80 per trade, and so on. You can also include more than 4 trades and bring the price down further for each participant.

"Who are the Best Trades to Partner With?"

Below is an alphabetical list of some of the best local trades you can consider partnering with.

- ☐ Air Conditioning;
- ☐ Appliance Repair;
- ☐ Attorneys;
- ☐ Auto Repairing & Service;
- ☐ Burglar Alarm Systems;
- ☐ Carpet and Rug Cleaners;

- ☐ Cleaning Services;
- ☐ Computer Service & Repair;
- ☐ Concrete Contractors;
- ☐ Contractors – General;
- ☐ Deck Builders;
- ☐ Doors – Garage Doors;
- ☐ Dry Wall Contractors;
- ☐ Electrical;
- ☐ Fence;
- ☐ Flooring;
- ☐ Florists;
- ☐ Foundation Repair;
- ☐ Furniture Dealers;
- ☐ Glass – Auto, Plate, Window, etc;
- ☐ Handyman Service;
- ☐ Hardware Retail;
- ☐ Home Inspection;
- ☐ Home Remodeling;
- ☐ Home Warranty;
- ☐ Insurance Agent;
- ☐ Lawn Maintenance/Landscaping;
- ☐ Locksmith;
- ☐ Mason Contractors;
- ☐ Mortgage Lender;

- ☐ Moving Services;
- ☐ Painters;
- ☐ Pest Control;
- ☐ Plumbing Services;
- ☐ Roofing Companies;
- ☐ Septic Installation;
- ☐ Siding Contractors;
- ☐ Storage – Household & Commercial;
- ☐ Title Companies;
- ☐ Tree Service;
- ☐ Windows.

"How Long Will it Take to Begin Seeing Results?"

Farming takes time. Just like creating success in other areas of life, it boils down to time on the task over time. If you are effectively marketing to your farm utilizing all of the strategies in this chapter, it can take several months to begin seeing steady results.

Achieving success with farming is a commitment. Success has a lot to do with the activities you are doing, and sticking with the program. If you are not seeing the results you want, then more than likely you are not doing everything I've discussed in this chapter, you are not giving the program long enough to succeed or you have unrealistic expectations.

An Ideal Farming Plan:

Here is an ideal plan for working your farm:

- ☐ Bi-weekly farming on foot (3 hours/wk with an item of value);

- ☐ Bi-weekly interview and YouTube post (popular local restaurant, business or person of interest);

- ☐ weekly open house (3 hours/wk; can be assigned to your Buyer Specialist);

- ☐ Monthly postcard mailing via EDDM (can be assigned to your Admin);

- ☐ Attendance of a community event (once a month).

Setting Realistic Expectations

Oftentimes agents give up on farming when they don't see the results that they expect very quickly. Again, Success with Listings is about time on the task over time. It's also about having realistic expectations.

You should aim for a goal of having a 20% listing market share in your farm area. I've seen agents grow to a 50%+ market share in their target area, but 20% is a realistic, doable and worthy goal.

What that means is that if there are a total of 40 property sales a year in your farm area, your goal will be to eventually grow your market share in that area to the point where you are listing 20% of the houses that sell there annually. In this case success would mean that at least 8 of those 40 sales are your listings.

For some this number may seem low but eight sold listings is nothing to sneeze at. For example if your gross commission were $7,500 from each of those listings, then your GCI from this bucket will be $60,000. That's a great return on investment considering that you don't have to spend much more than a few hours a day a few days a week sowing in that field. If your goal is to sell 20 houses, then all you would have to do is increase the number of houses that you market to by broadening the territory of your farm.

Door Knocking in Your Farm (Circle Prospecting)

Tom Atwood, CEO of The Five Doors Network at Keller Williams Realty recommends that you Circle Prospect around your open houses, new listings, pending listings and just-solds. Circle Prospecting is the process of knocking on 100 doors around the "subject property." You can even circle prospect around a property you've sold in the past, or one that your office sold or currently has listed.

"The door knocking script around circle prospecting is real simple," says Atwood. *"The best way to build rapport with a stranger is to get them to talk about their favorite subject: themselves."* With this script, you will do just that. You will get prospects engaged and then you will earn the right to ask for their business.

JUST LISTED Door Knock:

You: Hi, Mr. & Mrs. Neighbor, my name is _____ with _____ Realty. I'm hoping you can help me! I just listed your neighbor's house at 123 Main St and I was hoping you could share with me 2 or 3 reasons why you love living here?

You: .....oh awesome! That will really help me in delivering you a new neighbor! By the way, now is your time to have a hand in selecting your new neighbor. Who do you know in your network that's thinking about making a move? I know this is a tough neighborhood to get into and inventory is really scarce....

....thank you so much for putting me in touch with those people....

[If no names come to mind ask the neighbor to call you directly when they do, better yet ask them for their contact info so you can follow up]

You: Lastly, because this house is going to move so quickly, my next challenge will be how to help all of our clients find the next house that will be coming available in the neighborhood. We already are talking to dozens of potential buyers. That's what makes us different than other REALTORS®, we actually prospect for buyers for our sellers! So, do you know anyone that's also thinking about making a move?

This is only the first knock! Once the house goes Under Contract you go back to let the neighbors know!

CONTRACT PENDING Door Knock:

 You: Well actually that great house at 123 Main went under contract in only 4 days.... Here's my stack of offers of other buyers who wanted to buy in the neighborhood but got outbid.... It's evident that prices are on the rise. Do you know of anyone since our last chat that's thinking about making a move?

JUST SOLD Door Knock:

Now then, once the house closes escrow you go back to let the neighbors know!

 You: Hi Mr. and Mrs. Neighbor, we wanted to hand off the latest sales report in the neighborhood and let you know that Mr. and Mrs. New Neighbor just moved in down the street and they are awesome people so please welcome them to the block when you get a chance. I'd love to send you my monthly newsletter so would it be ok to get a personal email address so we can keep you better informed with the trends of the local market?

A Final Word on Farming

Geographic farming is an incredibly important bucket in your listing business. If you are not currently farming, you are foregoing a large chunk of potential income, and you are not effectively serving the areas where you live. You should grow where you are planted.

Begin putting together your farming strategy today, and make it a part of your overall marketing plan for the rest of your listing career.

Chapter 8 Homework

☐ Pick your Farm (select an area based on the criteria I've outlined in this chapter).

☐ Create your farming piece (item of value that you will provide when farming on foot).

☐ Create your YouTube channel and decide what content you will be adding to it.

Chapter 9

Your Niche

Now we come to your third and final lead generation bucket – your Niche. According to Webster, a niche is aptly defined as *"a specialized but profitable corner of the market."*

Let me ask you a few important questions. As a real estate agent, what sets you apart? Well for starters you are a Listing Specialist. The fact that you are singularly focused on sellers most certainly sets you apart.

So what do you offer that most other agents in your office or area do not? Why should a client use you versus the agent in the office next to you? Having a niche handily answers both of those questions.

Having a niche (or multiple niches) sets you apart from the pack.

What is Your Specialty?

Why Have a Specialty?

Let's take a lesson from the medical industry.

A few years ago a substantial and comprehensive nationwide study was conducted by the Centers for Disease Control and Prevention (CDC) division of the U.S.

Department of Health and Human Services. The purpose of the study was to compare the work schedules and salaries of physicians in various specialties.

In the study's key findings, the following information was revealed.

- ✓ Annual visits per general physician are 30% higher than visits per specialty physician.
- ✓ Twice as many general physicians (40%) worked evening and weekend hours, than did specialty physicians (19%).

Another comprehensive study found that the average annual salary for a specialist MD in the United States is around $339,738; while the annual salary for a general practitioner is around $186,044.

Based on the study's findings, in the medical field a specialist earns an average of $153,694 more than a general practitioner.

The bottom line is that, on average, general physicians will have 30% more annual visits, they are twice as likely to work nights and weekends and they will earn 45% less than a specialist.

So why is it that specialists work far less and earn far more? *Because they are sought out, in demand, and relevant.*

Don't Box Me In

On the face of it, having a niche may seem counterintuitive. When asked *"What do you specialize in?,"* the urge to say *"I do it all"* is very strong, because we don't want to turn away any potential business. Specializing can actually feel limiting.

You may already be apprehensive about the idea of marketing yourself as a "Listing Specialist," and now I am asking you to specialize in a niche! You may be wondering *"Knolly... won't that alienate me from the buyer side of the business? Won't that limit my opportunities?"*

The answer to these questions is yes and no. While it is true that specializing will definitely shrink your pool of potential clients, it is equally true that you can grow your business by exponential proportions through niche marketing.

Let me give you one case in point. Cardiologists (medical doctors who specialize in heart disease) are sought out, in high demand and very relevant. Heart Disease is the leading cause of death in the United States, accounting for approximately 1 in 4 deaths annually. Each year, more than 700,000 Americans have a heart attack. Coronary heart disease alone costs the United States about $108.9 billion each year. Heart disease is the number one killer of women and is more deadly than all forms of cancer combined. While 1 in 31 American women die from breast cancer each year, 1 in 3 will die of heart disease.

Just glancing at the statistics, it's no wonder that cardiologist are among the highest paid medical doctors in the industry. Yet the truth is, when an MD chooses to specialize, they inevitably, by default, must cut out a large percentage of potential business. The truth, general practitioners have far more potential business than a cardiologist ever will. That's because only about 6% of the population currently suffers from heart disease. By specializing in this one narrow field, cardiologists are, in effect, cutting out 94% of the American population. Put another way, cardiologists are completely irrelevant to 9.4 of every 10 Americans. Nevertheless, for the 6% of Americans who need them, they are highly sought out, highly in demand and highly relevant. They can charge a lot more than an average MD and still have a long waiting list.

Having a niche makes you the cardiologist of the real estate world.

I once saw an agent's business card that read "Specializing in commercial, residential and land." Indeed the tendency to be a "jack of all trades" is very strong in our business.

The truth is, you can become very big by becoming very small.

A Division of Your Business

You should thing of your niche is a division of your business or a department of your company.

Your niche does not have to define you but it does set you apart. I say this because many agents don't want to be "pigeonholed" or boxed-in by becoming too well known for a specific niche.

In my own case, for many years I specialized in short sales. As a result, I was able to help hundreds of families avoid foreclosure while earning a substantial income for my family and my team members. I became known as the "short sale king" of Austin, TX and many agents still refer their short sales to my team. I also became a national trainer and taught thousands of agents how to effectively stay in the business during the economic downturn while helping their clients avoid foreclosure. When the distressed market began to dwindle, some of the agents in my office were concerned about my future business, because they had misperceived that short sales were all that I knew how to do. In reality, what actually happened was that, after the economic collapse of 2008, this particular bucket became much larger than my other two buckets. Once the economy improved and this bucket began to shrink back to a more appropriate size, my other two buckets grew proportionately. Don't be afraid of dominating a specialty – just be sure that you have your other two buckets (your SOI and your Farm) working at the same time.

What Will You Specialize In?

The options are almost limitless. Here are a few ideas:

- For Sale By Owners (FSBO)
- Expired Listings
- Homes with Pools
- REO/Bank Owned
- Luxury
- Homes on one or more acres
- Short Sales

- New Construction
- Golf Course communities
- First time home sellers
- Seniors
- Farm and Ranch
- One story homes
- Waterfront
- Condos
- Homes with outbuildings
- Divorce
- Probate
- Investment properties
- Land tracts

As a Listing Specialist, you may want to begin with just one listing niche. Once you have maximized that one, you can add another.

It is easily possible to have multiple niches and have different agents on your team as administrators over each niche. This would be akin to having a medical practice with a resident cardiologist, an orthopedic surgeon and a radiologist on staff.

Remember, you can get quite creative when it comes to selecting a listing niche. My buddy and fellow trainer Stuart Sutton has multiple niches, one of which is properties on one acre or more (www.1acreplus.com). The idea here is simple. *If you have a home on 1 acre or more, why would you hire a real estate agent who specializes in cookie-cutter neighborhoods when your home is obviously unique? If your home is on 1 acre or more you should hire Stuart to sell it!*

My friend Diadra Ackols actually specializes in listing and selling *churches* in the Atlanta Georgia area.

Yes – churches.

She and her business partner Cheryl Gosa call themselves the "Church Ladies". If you need to buy or sell a church in the Atlanta area they are the ones to call! Churches aren't cheap either. As a minister of the gospel myself, I once looked into what it would cost to purchase a church building (and then I quickly looked out of it)! Working in this niche gives The Church Ladies the unique ability to run their business as a ministry. There are many churches that they represent which are not even listed on their website, because, for obvious reasons, many pastors and/or congregations don't necessarily want to publicly advertise that they are selling! Therefore, they actually have their own *secret list* of churches for sale. The specialty not only brings them a large number of sellers, but also brings them a continual supply of buyers (ministers and investors) looking to purchase church properties.

Your job will be to do the research and decide which niche you will want to get involved in. Then launch! Depending on which niche you decide on, your path to learning that niche (or at least learning where to go for the specific training) is probably just a series of Google searches away.

Marketing Your Niche

Your niche marketing will be unique and separate from the marketing that you do to your SOI and Farm. This is because you are targeting a completely different audience with your message.

Your Core Set Of Secret Weapons Will Be the Following:

- business card
- jumbo postcard
- flyer
- niche website
- YouTube channel

Business Card.

The back of your business card is a prime marketing canvas. In addition to the business card that you use in your listing business, you should also print a specialty business card specifically for your niche. Don't overlook this inexpensive but effective advertising medium.

Business cards are so cheap that it doesn't make sense to not have a different one for each niche you specialize in. For example, if you decided to specialize in working the divorce niche, you would have a separate business card that bulleted your qualifications as a *Divorce Sale Expert*. When meeting with prospects facing divorce, and divorce attorneys, having this specialized business card will go a long way toward gaining their trust and confidence. One look at your business card will assure them that you are the right person for the job, since you obviously specialize in divorce sales.

Jumbo Postcard.

A standard postcard is 4" x 6." A jumbo postcard is generally 5" x 7" or 5 1/2" x 8 1/2." Jumbo postcards serve as a professional looking mini-flyer. You could also choose to use a brochure, but I find that a jumbo postcard generally stands out better, and is more portable, not to mention the fact that it is snail-mail ready without having to use an envelope.

Flyer.

In addition to your jumbo postcard, I recommend that you also have an 8 1/2" x 11" flyer that contains the same messaging as your jumbo postcard. A full page *sales sheet* is the good old-fashioned go-to marketing piece. Even if you don't actually print them up, you want to have this flyer available as a downloadable PDF on your website.

Niche Website.

I strongly believe that you should have a separate website (with a unique domain name) dedicated to each niche listing business you have. At the very least, you should have a page of your website completely dedicated to each niche you serve with a unique domain name that points to that particular page.

The ROI on a niche website is so ridiculous, that only ignorance (which would no longer apply) or laziness could be cited as a reason for you not to have one. If you do it yourself, a niche website can cost $10 a year or less.

There are online software services that will allow you to build a website for free. Your only true cost would be the annual registration of your domain name.

For an example, check out one of my niche sites at www.ShortSaleWebsite.com.

If you don't want to go that route, you can easily hire someone to build your site or choose from a number of *template websites* (sites which are online sites that allow you to build your own website).

YouTube Channel.

Once you get more involved in video, you want to launch your own YouTube channel specifically for your niche. The cool thing is, YouTube will allow you to create separate channels under one account.

You will want to increasingly migrate your business to video. With over 1 billion users, YouTube is the clear winner when it comes to free video hosting.

You can use your channel to describe what you do and how you do it, and even to interview some key allied resources in your niche business or to post testimonials (case studies) from satisfied clients.

Your Niche Creates a Persona and a Perception

Being a specialist creates a unique persona in the minds of your prospects. It also creates a deep and positive perception. The fact that you specialize in what they need makes hiring you a near no-brainer. Having a niche also gives you amazing TOMA (top of mind awareness).

Take for example Stuart who sells homes on 1 acre or more. He receives referrals even from fellow real estate agents, because everyone knows he specializes in that niche. Likewise, any of the past clients he has helped in this specialty will naturally refer any of their friends who need to sell their 1 acre plus properties. In the same way, Cheryl and Diadra receive many referrals from real estate agents who have clients that are looking for churches. And any time someone that they know runs across anyone hinting about moving to a larger church, the *Church Ladies* immediately come to mind and receive the referral.

When you have a unique specialty, it singles you out as the person to call. Even an individual who personally knows several real estate agents will call you to sell their home if they believe that your specialty requires that they hire you for the job.

Final Thoughts

So there you have it. All you have to do is pick your niche and begin going for it. I'll be rooting for you all the way! Having a niche will set you apart from the competition and help shore up your listing business. This is your third lead bucket and the third leg on your stool.

In the next chapter, we will look at how to combine these 3 lead generation buckets into one powerful and rockin' listing business!

Chapter 9 Homework

- ☐ Decide on your Niche Market
- ☐ Create marketing materials unique to your niche
- ☐ Develop a niche web page or website

Chapter 10
Putting it All Together

In Chapter 6 you learned how important daily lead generation is and we looked at a very specific system for creating time in your schedule to lead generate.

In chapters 7 - 9 we discussed the 3 lead generation buckets where virtually all the leads that you will ever need for your listing business will come from. The old proverbial excuses of not having enough time or money to generate leads are no longer valid for you or your listing business. You already have all the time you need (3 hours a day), and all of your lead generation activities can be done with low to no cost. Likewise the excuse of not knowing how to generate listing leads no longer exists for you.

All 3 Buckets

In chapter 6 I talked about how your 3 lead buckets are like the legs on a sturdy stool. If you have all 3 in place and in great shape, the stool will support your weight. To adequately support the weight of a thriving listing business, you should have all 3 lead gen buckets in place.

Using the 3 Lead Generation Buckets to Reach Your Goals

Now that you have decided to focus on the 3 lead generation buckets of a top Listing Specialist, let's take a look at how you can use these buckets to help you reach your goals.

Based on your numeric goals exercise (Chapter 4), how many listings appointments per year do you need to achieve your annual net income goal? Once you've figured up that number, we will spread it across your 3 buckets.

Let's say that your annual net income goal is $100,000. In order to net $100,000, based on the data you input in the *Goals Calculator*, you would need to go on 34 listing appointments over the next 12 months.

Your Economic Goals:		
Your Net Income Goal (GCI):	$ 100,000	1
% Paid to You from Team/Broker:	70%	2
Your Average Commission %:	2.80%	3
Your Average Sale Price:	$ 237,440	4
Your Average Gross Commission is:	$ 6,648	
Your Average Net Commission is:	$ 4,653.82	
Your Production Goals:		
Your Annual Listings Taken Goal:	26.5	
Your Monthly Listings Taken Goal:	2.2	
Your Annual Listings Closed Goal:	21	
Your Monthly Listings Closed Goal:	1.8	
Conversion Rate on **Appointments**:	78%	5
Conversion Rate on **Closings**:	81%	6
Annual Appointments Required:	34	
Monthly Appointments Required:	2.8	

Now all you have to do is spread that goal across the three buckets.

Example:

Total Appointments Goal: 34

- SOI: 17 appointments (50%);
- Farm: 8.5 appointments (25%);
- Niche: 8.5 appointments (25%)

With this exercise you can begin to see that your listing appointment goal is not so overwhelming after all! Go ahead and work up the numbers yourself, based on your goals from chapter 4. I recommend you stick with a formula of 50% of the leads coming from your SOI and the rest of your leads split between your Farm and Your Niche.

Reread chapter 4 if you haven't already developed your numeric goals and entered them into my Goals Calculator.

Many Listing Specialists make the unfortunate mistake of thinking that all of the listings they take have to come from just one source. By spreading your leads across the 3 lead buckets, you can see that your goal is very achievable. If you focus on these buckets you will have three separate and simultaneous streams of listings leads and be able to build your listing inventory to the highest it can possibly be.

Since you are time blocking each morning for lead generation (Chapter 6), you will want to break up your daily time block to account for the 3 buckets.

Sample Lead Generation Time Block Schedule

3 hours/day 9am - Noon

- Monday: SOI
- Tuesday: Niche
- Wednesday: Farm
- Thursday: SOI
- Friday: Farm.

As we discussed in Chapter 6, during your lead gen time, you should be:

1. Prospecting for new seller leads (from one of the 3 lead buckets).
2. Following up on your existing leads.
3. Implementing your marketing plans.

The Sample Lead Generation Time Block Schedule above is an example of what your lead generation schedule might look like with respect to your lead bucket focus. Every morning will be dedicated to lead generation, lead follow-up and implementing marketing plans.

Chapter 10 Homework

☐ Make sure that your SOI, Farm and Niche lead generation systems are in place.

☐ Put together your own Lead Generation time block schedule spread across the 3 lead generation buckets. Use Chapter 6 to help guide you.

☐ Spread your listing appointments goal across the 3 lead buckets to determine how many listings appointments you are going to need to do from each bucket.

What's Next...

Next let's move on to actually working with sellers! In the next 2 Sections (chapters 11-18) I will outline my 46 step listing system in great detail so you can move on to building your successful listing career.

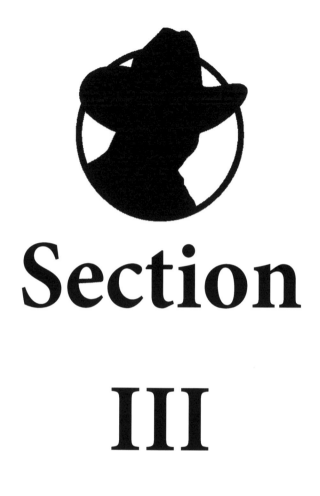

Section

III

Securing the Listing

Chapter 11
Pre-Listing Questionnaire and Research

Welcome to Section 3! Congratulations! You have officially made it to the meat and potatoes of the material! I will now dedicate Chapters 11-18 to documenting for you my 46-step listing system in detail. You will want to use these chapters as a companion guide to walk you through each new listing you take, as you move forward toward mastery.

Step 1: Generate Seller Prospect

Success with Listings begins with *Lead Generation*. In Chapters 6-10 (Section 2) you learned how to time block for lead generation and how to generate your seller prospects using the 3 listing lead generation buckets. Be sure to execute and implement what you learned in this section so that you can build a solid and ongoing pipeline of listing leads and seller prospects.

Step 2. Initial Phone Consultation with Seller Questionnaire

When a potential seller calls have your Admin handle the call and ask the seller prospect several key questions. The tone of the conversation should be friendly, conversational and not too lengthy. Your Admin basically needs to ascertain several key pieces of information and stress to the caller that they made the right decision to call you!

Here is the basic information that should be gathered during this initial call:

1. Seller's Name.

2. Property Address.

3. Seller's best phone number.

4. Seller's best email address.

5. How the Seller heard about you.

6. Approximately how much is currently owed on the house.

Prospect: Hi this is Bob - is Knolly in?

Admin: Hi Bob - Knolly is on an appointment right now but I'd love to have him call you back as soon as possible. Are you thinking about selling your house?

Prospect: Uhh - yes. We are just thinking about it right now but we have a few questions for Knolly.

Admin: That's awesome Bob. Knolly is the best. He'll get you top dollar. Let me just get a little bit of information from you so I can have him call you back.

Prospect: Sure.

Admin: Bob, what's the property address?

Admin: Great - What's the best number for Knolly to call you back at?

Admin: Oh - and what's the best email address for you?

Admin: By the way Bob, how did you hear about Knolly?

Admin: Thanks so much Bob. By the way - what's your best guess of how much you owe on the house?

Admin: Thanks again Bob. I'll get all of this information over to Knolly and he will be giving you a call back shortly.

After asking these questions, have your Admin forward you the questionnaire along with a copy of the tax record (and a CMA if they are trained to do them) for you to use when you call back the prospect. Your Admin will also send your prospect a follow up email (step 3).

You should always endeavor to call the prospect back as quickly as possible (within 1- 4 hours), *but do your research first.*

One point that I want to make at this juncture is that much of the material I am teaching you in this course is written for your *Administrative Assistant* (Admin). This is because I am making the *calculated assumption* that you currently have (or will soon have) an Administrative Assistant. Therefore, I have written this training guide so that it doubles as a training system for your Admin, so that you don't have to reinvent the wheel by needing to create your own training document for them. You can easily highlight the portions of the material that your Admin will handle. Better yet, just give your Admin a copy of this training guide so that he or she will be fully on board with your listing system from A-Z.

Obviously if you do not currently have an Admin person, you will perform the functions I have outlined for them. As one person put it, *"if you don't have an assistant, you are one."*

In my own case, I was only in the business for about 60 days before I recruited my wife to assist me. By the time I was in the business eight months I hired my first full-time Admin, Barbara Riordan, who still works with me today. Most real estate agents that I coach absolutely *should* have an Admin person. In this course, you are learning how to have a successful high-volume listing business and an Admin will be critical and integral to your ultimate success and will be your first and most critical hire. In Chapter 20 I will show you when and how to hire an Admin. I'll even show you how to get a virtual assistant (VA) at a very affordable rate.

Step 3: Send Seller Prospect a Follow-up Email

Within 10 minutes of hanging up on the call, your Admin should be able to fire out a follow-up email to the seller prospect. Doing this helps to build further rapport and impress your future client. They quickly begin to see how professionally your business is handled, and the fact that you have a well-oiled machine.

Here's the email template we use:

Hi there Jim,

Thanks so much for taking the time to discuss your home with me. We are very excited that you are considering the possibility of listing with The Knolly Team. I have forwarded your information to Knolly and he will be in contact with you shortly. He is eager to discuss more about your property and how we can get to SOLD.

Knolly has lived and worked in the Austin area since 1988 and we have helped more than 1000 families achieve their real estate goals. We hope that we can add you to our family of satisfied clients.

Thanks again!

Step 4. Input the Prospect into Your Database

Make sure that your Admin adds the prospect's information to your database immediately. At the Knolly Team, our Admin adds the prospect to our database as a *"lead"* so that they show up on the *Leads* section of our MoreSolds CRM. The added advantage here is that the lead can also be assigned to any team member, so that it will prominently show up on their dashboard when they login.

Step 5: Do *Comparative Market Analysis* (CMA) and Research

It is so awesome to receive a new seller lead! After all, seller leads are what you have worked diligently for during your lead generation time, and you've got one! It's very tempting to contact the seller right away to strike up a conversation and set an appointment, however you should *do your research first.*

You should review the tax record information and the CMA on the property before calling back the prospect.

When reviewing the tax record you are looking for things like what year the house was built, how long the seller has lived there, names of all owners, the original mortgage balance (and type of loan), any foreclosure postings, home features, previous MLS activity, lot size, etc. The tax record tells a story so read through it thoroughly and see what story it is telling you.

Once you have reviewed the tax record data, you can then pull up the house using Google's *Street View* feature to see exactly how it is positioned in the neighborhood or area. Perhaps it's on a busy street that backs up to a highway or maybe it's nestled on a quiet cul-de-sac. If necessary, you can even go one step further and do a Google search of the neighborhood to find out even more information about the area.

Doing this kind of review only takes about 10 minutes and it helps you to come across more confidently and gain more rapport on your call with your prospect. This doesn't mean that you will discuss all of the details you uncover during your initial call, it simply means that you will be able to have a much more intelligent conversation and psychologically you will feel much more prepared to discuss the property and the seller's needs.

For example, doing prior research allows you to say things like *"You know Bob, it looks like your house is pretty close to the railroad tracks. Now for some agents that would be a challenge, but I've got some specific strategies that I use to overcome that objection and get you top dollar. Besides, the train only runs twice a day"* Or you could say something like *"You know Susan, I did a good bit of research on your property. Isn't your house the one with a second-story balcony situated on that large cul-de-sac?"*

Likewise you will want to review the CMA to see how quickly houses are selling and at what price. I generally recommend that you be fairly tightlipped about your ideas on pricing until you meet with the homeowner face-to-face. However, you still want to be educated on pricing *before* you have your initial phone conversation with the seller. On the call you will want to find out their ideas on price while not disclosing your own thoughts. I'll show you how to do that in the next step.

It is very important to be well educated prior to conducting your consultation call. As I've said before (and will continue to repeat), in today's environment you've got to win the listing before you ever have your face-to-face meeting with the client. Not doing your homework before having the initial phone consultation will undoubtedly result in a less than optimal first impression for them, and less confidence (lower energy) for you.

How Price is Determined

Price is determined by what a buyer is willing to pay for a house. Ultimately, at the end of the day, market price is set by the buyer. Therefore it is imperative for you to dig and discover exactly what buyers are currently paying for a house as similar to your seller's as possible.

Let's say a buyer is willing to pay $415,000 for a house in a certain area. The buyer and seller agree on the price, the transaction moves forward and ultimately the house closes. Once the sales price is published, the SOLD price is then used as a comparable factor for all future home sales of similar houses in the area. Let's suppose the market takes a downturn and buyers are no longer willing to pay $415,000 but $390,000 for the same house. As the market begins to shift downward, the sold data will begin reflecting lower sold prices which will then reset the current market value. The same happens when the market shifts upward. Higher sales prices replace the lower home sales data.

What is a Comparative Market Analysis (CMA)?

The CMA is a side-by-side comparison report of houses currently for sale and houses that have SOLD in the same neighborhood or area as your seller's house. A CMA is an extremely helpful tool that you will use to determine what the market is saying. The CMA will typically include *Active* listings (listings currently for sale), *Pending* listings (listing currently under contract), *Closed* sales (listings that have recently sold) and *Expired* listings (listings that failed to sell).

CMAs can vary widely depending on the knowledge, skill level and experience of the agent inputting the search parameters, as well as the data fields that are chosen. This is a delicate and critical job that will help you achieve maximum success for your client. Since price is the most important factor involved in the sale of your client's house, you absolutely have to thoroughly learn and understand how to do an accurate and competent CMA using your MLS's software. Once you learn how to do CMAs, you will see that the ones you produce will become increasingly accurate in their reflection of what the market is currently saying.

Doing the CMA

Putting together CMAs is actually a very fun exercise. It's a great time to explore the market virtually, and each CMA you do helps to build your experience and give you insights on what the market is currently doing.

My Top Tips for Putting Together a Great CMA

Since there are a variety of different MLS software systems out there, I won't be able to provide you with step-by-step instructions here. However I would like to share with you some of my top tips for doing a great CMA.

1. Get trained! If you haven't done a lot of CMAs using your MLS's current system, I highly recommend you take a class at your local board to become thoroughly competent at using the vast array of features that your MLS software offers. You might even be able to take the courses online or go through some online tutorials. Also, ask your broker or the technology expert at your office to tutor you on how to do a CMA using your MLS system.

2. Under *Property Type*, many MLS systems will default to *House*. If your listing is not a freestanding house, be sure to select the correct property type (*house, condo, manufactured, mobile, townhome, etc*).

3. When you do a CMA be sure to check multiple *Status* types (*Active, Pending, Sold, Expired*) so that you can get a good mix of comparables.

4. Use a *Date Range* of 90 days or less if houses are selling relatively quickly. You can go 120, 150 or 180 days or less if the current market is turning slowly.

5. The tighter you can hone in on the *Area* around the subject property, the more accurate your CMA will be. For example, in Texas, we have a lot of

subdivisions, so I generally will try to pull comparables from the same subdivision. If the subject property is not in a subdivision, you might want to do your CMA using the "map search" feature of your MLS. This feature will allow you to manually select the area (even specific streets) around the subject property, by drawing the perimeters of your search on a map.

6. Under *Square Feet*, use a range that is within a few hundred square feet (up or down) of the subject property. For example if the subject property is 1825 square feet you would search for comparable properties from 1600 – 2000 square feet. If the subject property is 3486 square feet, try a search parameter of 3300 to 3600 square feet.

7. Under *Year Built*, put in a date range that is within a few years of the subject property. For example if the year built is 2004 you would search for properties built between 2002 and 2006.

8. Try using comparibles that have the same number of stories as your seller's property. This can be important because price per square-foot can vary widely depending on whether the subject property is a one-story or two-story. Generally speaking you do not want to include comparables that are two-story if the subject property is one story, or vice versa.

9. If possible, you want to have at least 3 to 5 comparables for each of the following categories: *Active, Pending and Sold.* You can also include

Expired listings if there are any. If you are getting more comparables than you need, you can simply tighten up your search parameters *(year built, square footage, date range, etc)*, or select only the comparables that are the closest match.

10. Do a *Simple CMA*. A Simple CMA (sometimes called a *Summary CMA*) is the kind that shows all of the data on one page. I highly recommend this type of CMA when doing the listing presentation as it is much easier to follow.

11. Also do a *Full CMA* report. A full CMA report (also known as a *Complete CMA*) is one

with multiple pages, lots of additional information and photos. These CMAs can be 20 or more pages and they do look impressive. They can be a little harder to follow though, during a listing presentation, but they definitely have their place. You will want to do full CMA in addition to your summary CMA. I'll show you how to use the full CMA in addition to the summary CMA in Chapter 13.

12. A great way to practice putting together a CMA is to select a sample subject property and have your team leader, broker or a top Listing Specialist you trust do a CMA on the property, while you do one of your own. Compare the two CMAs that were created, yours and theirs and see if they are identical or what the differences are. Do this multiple times until you feel confident about doing CMAs. Have the person walk you through how they did the CMA.

"What if my prospect calls me and wants to discuss the details of selling their house before I have time to do my research? Or what if I don't have an Admin to handle the initial call?"

In situations like this you can simply tell the prospect that you will get back with them within 20 or 30 minutes. You don't need to tell the seller that you are going to do some research and then call them back. You simply need to get the pertinent information we discussed in step 2, and set up a time to call them back. I have an easy script for you.

You: Hi this is _____ with The Prosperity Team.

Prospect: Hi there, this is Karen Smithers - I'm calling about my house.

You: Awesome Karen! Are you thinking about selling?

Prospect: Well, kind of. We are considering the idea of selling.

You: Karen I'm so glad you called. I actually can't talk right now but I saw your call pop up and I didn't want to miss it! Can I call you back in about 30 minutes?

Prospect: Sure - no problem

You: Karen - what's the property address?

> You: Awesome! What's the best number to call you back at?
>
> You: Oh, and Karen let me jot down your email address.
>
> You: Perfect! Oh, by the way Karen, how'd you hear about me?
>
> You: Cool. About how much do you think you owe on your house?
>
> You: Awesome Karen! Hey - I'll call you back in about 30 minutes!

This quick script will allow you to have a window of time to quickly do your research and then be able to call your seller prospect back.

Obviously there will be some circumstances where you will want to speak with the prospect right away. For example, if you are contacted by an *expired listing* owner you will want to set an appointment right away because you realize that there are other agents in your market vying for that same listing.

Know Where the Lead Came From

Pay close attention to the source of the lead. I always emphasize to my team that the most important question to ask a seller prospect is how they heard about us. Why is it important to know the source of your lead? Most agents believe this information is important because it shows them what marketing activities are working so that they can correctly allocate their marketing budget accordingly. Knowing what marketing activities are working and which are not is certainly important, but it is *not* the primary reason why you want to know the answer to how the lead heard about you. *Knowing the lead source will completely direct the tone of your conversation and determine the time you will need to take.*

Knowing where the lead came from will help you determine if you need to shorten or lengthen your initial phone consultation (step 6) and your listing appointment (step 11).

For example, a prospect that heard about you through an internet ad or a billboard will be handled very differently from one who was referred by her sister.

Remember that 70% of sellers chose their agent based on referral or previous experience. People do business with people they know, like and trust.

A referral is a *transfer of trust*. Generally speaking, a prospect that has been referred to you will trust you to the degree that they trust the person who referred them. For that reason, I usually will endeavor to find out how well they know the person who referred them. For example just last week an agent referred me a seller who is outside of her service area. When I called the prospect back I asked *"I see you were referred by Linda Jones. She's awesome! How well do you know Linda?"* The prospect then proceeded to tell me that Linda had sold her best friend's (of more than 20 years) house and came highly recommended. This information allowed me to shave my listing presentation time in half.

Well – now that you've done your research it's time to call your listing prospect! Let's move on to the next chapter where I will show you exactly how to conduct the phone consultation and set up the listing appointment.

Chapter 11 Homework

- ☐ Role Play the Scripts in this chapter.
- ☐ Review several Tax Record documents to see what story they are telling you.
- ☐ Learn how to do both a Simple CMA and a Full CMA.

Chapter 12

Conducting the Phone Consultation and Setting the Listing Appointment

Whew! Your hard work is paying off and you are moving closer to securing the listing! In this chapter you will learn steps 6-8 of the 46 step process. During these next few steps you will be working to build a rapport with your seller prospect by getting to know them and understanding their specific needs. You will be setting the listing appointment and setting up the stage for a slam-dunk listing presentation.

Step 6. Phone Consultation with Seller Prospect and Set the Listing Appointment

The purpose of the phone consultation with your seller prospect is to ascertain the answers to just a handful of very important questions so that you can better assist and advise the seller. You want to get further insight on the seller's motivation and state of mind, build a bond, generate rapport and *connect* with the seller.

By the time that the seller prospect contacts you, you can rest assured that they are pretty serious about selling their house. Perhaps the only question that remains for some of them is whether they will hire you or go with someone else. They want to be confident that you are the right person for the job. Of course many of the prospects that contact you will already be sold on listing with you, because you have followed the lead generation system that you learned in Chapters 6 through 10 and you are implementing your tools (Chapter 5).

When the seller ultimately contacts you they have probably thought about the idea of selling for *many* months or perhaps even years. The call to you is a culmination of many hours of thought, prayer and likely lots of research.

Generally speaking, the idea of sitting down with a real estate agent to discuss the sale of their property is not something that most people relish. It's important for you to understand that you represent for them the end of the line in their decision making process. They have already discussed the matter with their family, friends, boss, coworkers – and they have done lots and lots of online research, talked with their neighbors, reviewed your website, browsed through Zillow and much more.

Think about when you go to purchase a vehicle, a computer or any big ticket item. The last individual you want to talk to is a salesperson. When you step onto the car lot or into the computer store you are prepared. You have Googled into the wee hours of the morning. You have checked the online reviews. You already know everything there is to know about the item you intend to buy. In fact, many shoppers are bypassing the whole brick and mortar experience, and opting to shop online instead. Those who shop online do so because they feel that it is more convenient and that it saves them time and money. Additionally, they get to bypass the pesky salesperson.

In Chapter 2 I shared with you 10 reasons why you should focus on listings. Let me give you another one. I have found that, in general, *sellers are much more committed to the process than buyers*. Once the seller signs the listing agreement, they have made a very solid psychological and legal commitment to move forward with the process. Most of them will tell you that they want to have the whole process wrapped up within the next 90 days.

When a buyer signs a Buyer Representation agreement with you, they are also committing to you. However, unless they are on a short timetable, buyers can stretch out the time it takes to find the perfect home, or put their plans on hold at a moment's notice. Looking at homes is fun for many buyers, so it's not a big deal to go out tire-kicking just to see what's out there. Maybe that perfect house will magically appear, or maybe not. In contrast, selling a house isn't nearly as much fun as buying one, so sellers are typically much more committed to the process.

Once a motivated seller signs a listing agreement, it is very rare that they will decide to take their house off the market. They are typically intent on seeing it through.

Here are the questions you should be sure to ask when conducting your initial phone consultation:

1. How did you hear about me?
2. What's motivating you to sell?
3. Was your house previously on the market?
   a. If yes, what kind of activity did you get?
   b. What was it priced at?
4. What will you do after you sell?
5. Is the property occupied?
6. How soon do you need to sell?
7. How much are you looking to sell for?
8. What will you do if your house doesn't sell?

Let's analyze each of these important questions so that you can better understand the purpose and principles behind each one.

Question 1: *"How did you hear about me?"*

Toward the end of Chapter 11, I shared with you my thoughts on why knowing where the lead came from is so important. Again, knowing where the lead came from will help you determine if you need to shorten or lengthen your phone consultation and your listing appointment. If you already have the answer to this question (based on the initial call from your Admin in step 2), simply restate the answer to stimulate a discussion.

If the prospect heard about you through your SOI, you could say something like:

You: Hey Sheila, it looks like you were referred to me by Karla Johnson. I sold her and Rick's house last year and they were very pleased with my results. How well do you know Karla?

Since a referral is a *transfer of trust*, you want to use this information to reassure the seller that they are making the right choice by hiring you.

If the prospect heard about you through your farming efforts, you could say something like:

You: Sheila - it looks like you received one of my postcards in the mail. That's awesome. I am the neighborhood expert for Legend Oaks, and I'm very familiar with the houses in your area.

If the prospect heard about you through your niche marketing, you could say something like:

You: Sheila - it looks like you received one of my postcards in the mail. I am an expert at selling homes on one acre or more and I have a steady list of buyers looking for properties like yours.

With the dialogue around this first question, you are establishing to the prospect that they made the right decision by calling to discuss their needs with you.

Question 2: *"What's motivating you to sell?"*

Defining the seller's motivation is critical because it is their *reason* for selling. It is the anchor that you will keep coming back to. They could be moving across town or out of state for a job transfer, or relocating for other reasons. They may be looking for a better school district for their children. Understanding their motivation helps you get on board with their objectives, so that you can serve them fully.

According to Inman News, the 3 most common reasons for selling are 1) family-related, 2) work-related and 3) housing related.

If a homeowner receives a job transfer, gets a new job or simply finds the daily commute unbearable, she/he will often make the decision to sell and purchase a property closer to his or her workplace. Other common reasons for relocating include 1) being closer to church or family, 2) the desire to live in a different city or a better part of town, 3) better home amenities, 4) a growing (or shrinking) family, 5) personal hardship or 6) simply the desire to upsize or downsize.

For those facing a hardship, the most common hardships include:

1. Loss of income
2. Increased expenses
3. Medical problems
4. Divorce/Absolved relationship
5. Death in the family

TOP 10 REASONS PEOPLE MOVE:

1. New or better home
2. Moving out on their own
3. Cheaper housing
4. New job or employee relocation
5. Moving closer to work
6. Lower crime rate
7. Wanted to buy a home (for those renting)
8. Loss of employment
9. Better weather
10. Due to natural disaster

(Source: Bekin Moving)

Question 3. *"Was your house previously on the market?"*

Regardless of whether you think you know the answer to this question or not, ask it anyway. Even if there is no prior evidence of the house being on the MLS, you may learn a lot with this question. The prospect may say something like "*We were thinking about selling it back in 2012 but found out we were upside down and couldn't sell without doing a short sale.*" Or they may say "*well – we tried to sell it on our own but didn't get any serious offers.*" If I find out that their property was previously on the market I will ask the follow-up questions of "*how much activity did you get?*" and "*what was it priced at?*"

Question 4. *"What will you do after you sell?"*

This question will oftentimes reveal just how motivated a seller is to sell.

Most people tend to plan their future in advance, especially when it comes to relocating. If the seller sounds unclear about their future plans it may indicate that this could be a "*distress sale.*" A distress sale occurs with someone is *forced* to sell as a result of a hardship, such as financial, health, death in the family, divorce, job transfer, etc.

Question 5. "Is the property occupied?"

If the property is not currently occupied you will want to know how long it has been vacant. I went on a listing appointment last week where the house had been vacant for three years – and it was in a nice subdivision! Needless to say the house was in disrepair – so we had to price it accordingly. This question might also reveal whether or not the house has been rented out. Tenant rights are very strong in most states and you will want to see a copy of the lease since it will likely convey with the sale and could limit the potential pool of buyers.

Question 6. *"How soon do you need to sell?"*

It's always helpful to determine how quickly the seller is looking to get their house under contract. Knowing the seller's time frame also helps dictate your pricing strategy. Some sellers want to get the entire process over with quickly while others want to drag it out a bit.

You will also use the information you gain from this question during your listing presentation (while presenting the CMA) to help calibrate the seller's time expectations (based on actual sales data) if they are unrealistic.

After listing and selling over 1000 houses I have learned that the *"restless point"* for many sellers is right at 60 days on the market. For some reason – once the house hits 60 days on the market the sellers get pretty antsy. For that reason I aim to price their house so they will sell within 45 days or less. In a really hot market sellers can begin getting anxious at around 30 days and in a very slow market 90 days may be the anxiety point. At the end of the day, the actual days on market will be determined by the price of the house, the property condition and current market conditions in the area where the house resides.

Question 7: *"How much are you looking to sell for?"*

It is extremely important to understand where the seller's mindset is with regards to what their house is worth. I absolutely want to know this information before I have a sit-down meeting with the seller. Again – if you don't already have a very strong rapport with the seller I do not recommend that you discuss your thoughts on pricing or market data with the seller during your initial phone consultation. In other words – I want the seller to reveal to me what their thoughts are on the price without me revealing to them what my thoughts at this point.

Keep in mind that your phone consultation is primarily a fact-finding mission. Your objective is to understand exactly what the seller hopes to accomplish and what their current perception of reality is with regard to the current market. You will then use this information during your listing appointment to help educate the sellers in the areas where their perspective may be skewed, and to help them reach their goals.

Sometimes sellers do not want to reveal what they are thinking regarding price. This is usually because they have a feeling that the price they have in mind is a bit high. They may think that you might scoff if they told you. Sometimes they won't want to tell you their price for fear that you will attempt to talk them down. Some sellers will want you to show your hand first, which I don't recommend you do. In some cases you will have to ask the question three or four different ways in order to get the seller to open up with their thoughts about price.

 Here's the script I developed for getting your prospects to divulge their ideas on pricing.

You: So John, how much are you looking to sell for?

Prospect: Well - I don't know - you're the expert! That why I called you. What do you think it's worth?

You: You know John - you're absolutely right. I am the expert. I'm really good at getting my clients the most money possible in the least amount of time. That's why your cousin Jane referred you to me! John - I'm going to be doing lots of research on your house to see what the market is saying. But you know John - I've found that a lot of my clients these days are really in tune with what is going on in their neighborhood. Are you pretty in touch with what's going on in your area?

John: I think I am.

You: That's great. What have you seen houses like yours going for?

219

John: Well my neighbor down the street got $245,000 for his.

You: That's awesome, John! Is that what you were hoping to get?

Prospect: Well, I was hoping to get a little more than that. I'm hoping we can get at least $250.000.

You: Terrific! So what's the number that you absolutely would not go below?

Prospect: I don't think we would go any lower than $245,000.

You: That's great John - let me run the numbers and see what the market is saying. We can review that information when we get together.

It is important that you do not reveal your feelings on price at this juncture. When the prospect reveals their ideas on price you should react with zero judgment. Say something like "that's great, John" or "awesome" and move on. You can discuss the market data at the listing appointment.

Q: *"What if the prospect still won't tell me their thoughts on pricing?"*

Let's say that at this point your prospect is still having a hard time giving you a value. I find the following script usually will do the trick.

You: You know John - I can see that you really would like to rely on me to share with you what the market is saying about price - so I'm

> going to be getting the research done right
> away so I can present the data to you when
> we sit down together. I'm eager to get you
> the most money possible.
>
> Now John - there's an exercise that I do with
> my seller clients that they find very helpful.
> If you don't mind playing along would you
> mind closing your eyes for just a moment?
> John - when it comes to selling your house for
> top dollar - based on your home's present
> condition - I want you to close your eyes and
> think of a price. I want you to think of a
> number that would put a smile on your face.
> Now reach up and grab that number and pull
> it down. John - what number did you pull
> down?

This last-resort script seems a bit radical but almost always does the trick!

Q. *"What if the prospect is way high on their idea of price?"*

During the call, if you find that your seller prospect is way off in their idea of the price – avoid the temptation to react negatively. Let's say you are talking to a prospect whose house is worth around $300,000. If they tell you they believe their house is worth $350,000, react simply with *"I see"* or *"interesting."* You should wait until you have a sit-down meeting with the seller to dig deeper and show them the data.

Q: "What if the seller's idea of value is pretty low?"

Again – I always recommend that you not escalate into a deep discussion about pricing over the phone. If the prospect is spot-on with their pricing avoid the temptation to react with excitement. For example, let's say the prospect tells you that they think their house is worth $240,000 and your research points to a price of around $250,000. It would be quite natural to respond enthusiastically with something like *"Awesome John! We can certainly sell it at that price! Let's get it sold!"*; however, I don't want you to tip your hand at this point. An overenthusiastic response from you could indicate to the prospect that you are looking for a quick and easy sale. You can calmly respond with something like: *"You know John – my intention is to get you the highest price possible. Let me take a close look at what the market is saying right now so we can put the most money in your pocket."*

Q: "Why is it so important to NOT discuss pricing on my initial phone call?"

People do business with people that they know, like and trust. Unless you have already built an incredible rapport with the seller prospect, I firmly believe that you should not discuss pricing in great detail on your initial call.

For most sellers, the price of their property is a *very sensitive* topic. If you vocally disagree with the seller's thoughts on pricing at this early juncture you can quickly find yourself ostracized. It becomes you against them. The truth is – most sellers are slightly unrealistic in their expectations of what their house is worth. Sellers take it very personally when you don't agree with them or have a difference of opinion. The pricing conversation can quickly erode their confidence and trust in you. Yes, my friend – the truth hurts – and pushing the truth on your sellers in the wrong way, or at the wrong time could hurt *you*.

On the initial call with the seller prospect, you want to build as much rapport as possible. You want to win their trust and gain their confidence. You want them to leave the call with a smile on their face. Few things can reverse rapport more quickly than discussing the most sensitive topic of their property: *price*.

There are a few exceptions where you might break this rule. One obvious exception is if you already know that you will be hired. For example if a past client or friend is calling you to list their house and you know you already have the job – why not do the entire listing presentation over the phone? I've done many listing appointments over the phone and over Join.me or Skype. Obviously nothing replaces a face-to-face conversation, however there will be many instances where you must discuss the entire transaction remotely (for example, if the seller lives out of state or if you are out of town).

"Help! The seller is completely unrealistic about their ideas of pricing and I don't want to waste my time or theirs."

Another exception you can make with regard to revealing the market pricing over the phone is with sellers who are *completely* unrealistic in their pricing thoughts. Even in cases like this I would not recommend that you discuss price on the first call. This way your initial call can conclude with lots of joy and cheer and your follow-up call can be more of a "wake up" call.

You: Hi Theresa, it's Connie - how's it going?

Prospect: Great!

You: You know Theresa – the reason I'm calling you back is because I was able to do a good bit of research... and I looked at what the market is doing in your neighborhood... and based on the data I had a few questions for you. You mentioned that you would like to get $350,000 and the data shows that most of your neighbors have been selling for around $280,000 - $300,000. My job is to get you the most money possible – so my biggest concern is with the appraisal...

You would have a conversation like this to avoid wasting your time with a seller who is completely unrealistic or who probably needs to wait to sell (depending on their motivation for selling).

In Chapter 13 I'll give you 10 scripts to use when you are up against a seller who wants to price their house above the current market value.

Question 8. "What will you do if your house doesn't sell?"

This question is designed to flesh out the options that your seller has in the event that the house doesn't sell. Of course almost any house that is priced correctly *can* sell, but you do want to know what their backup plans are. Knowing the seller's contingency plan helps you to gauge their motivation level as well.

If the seller says something like, *"Oh – if we can't sell it we will just stay here. We just want to test the market for now,"* then they might not be 100% committed to seeing the process through, or they may not *really* need or have to sell.

Of course if they say something like *"we don't have an option to not sell. My job transfer takes place in 90 days and we don't want to lease out the house and become landlords,"* then you know they have a high level of motivation.

Set the Appointment

Once the client has answered all of your questions, SET THE APPOINTMENT.

You: Thanks Michael for taking the time to talk with me about your house.

I can pull together the market data this afternoon and meet with you tonight at 4 or would tomorrow afternoon at 2 be better?

Prospect: uh.... Let's do tomorrow at 2

You: Great! I'll see you then. By the way Michael, did you have any other questions for me before we meet?

Prospect: No... I don't think so.

You: Excellent! Oh - and I'll be dropping off my new book and info packet at your house later today. If no one is home we will just leave it at the front door. Be sure to review the packet before we meet, as it contains

> valuable information which will allow you to
> get top market price for your home.

Give your seller a few time options and endeavored to meet with them during your daily listing appointment hours of 1-5pm.

Think about it this way, your clients don't meet with their dentist or their doctor during nights and weekends. They take time off of work to meet with these practitioners during their posted hours. In the same way, clients should be able to meet with you during your preferred hours. After all, the sale of their most valuable asset is at least as important as having their teeth cleaned!

Obviously there will be times (especially when you are establishing your reputation) when you will have to meet with sellers on a weekend or evening and that's okay for now. The more well-known and in-demand you become, the more willing your prospects will be to meet you during your scheduled hours.

Keep the Dialogue Conversational

Although your main goal on the call is to build rapport and get your questions answered, you want to keep the dialogue conversational. Don't make it sound like you are conducting a questionnaire. In truth, you are really simply *having a conversation*, and as you are talking with them you are bringing up questions. Also keep in mind that you are getting to know them, so it is completely appropriate to have a normal conversation intertwined amongst these 8 questions, asking them about themselves and their family and getting as much detail on what they do for a living, what they like, their interests, etc.

How Much Time Should the Phone Consultation Take?

Conducting a phone consultation will take about 10 to 15 minutes. You can begin the conversation with something like: *"Thanks again John for calling me... by the way how much time do you have to talk right now?"* It could be that the prospect is on their lunch break or just doesn't have much time to talk.

Sometimes consultations can take much longer. As long as rapport is being built, that's OK. Just don't give away a lot of precious information and data. Save that for the face-to-face. If you reveal all of your thoughts about the house over the phone, the client may not feel it is necessary to meet with you.

Step 7: Send Seller Prospect a Follow-Up Email

Now it's time to cement the conversation with a follow-up email. Sending a quick follow-up email helps to further build rapport and displays your professionalism. I simply use a template email from my CRM and tweak just a few things in it.

Follow-up Email Template:

Hi Michael,

Thanks so much for taking the time to talk with me.

It was really good speaking with you! Please visit my home seller website at: http://www.MyListingSite.com

As I mentioned, I recently finished a book that better outlines the home selling process.

I also put together a video with much more information about what we offer. You can access both on my site. My team and I would be honored to work with you to get your home SOLD. I have already reviewed the information on your property and I am confident we can get it sold for you.

I look forward to meeting with you tomorrow at 2.

To Your Success,

Step 8: Drop Off Your Pre-Listing Package

Drop off your pre-listing package along with your seller book (Chapter 5) as soon as you can. As soon as your phone call with the prospect is concluded, you want to try to get your pre-listing package in route to their house. This can be done by you, your spouse, your runner or your Admin person.

If no one is home, simply leave the package at the front door. If the homeowner is home, have the person dropping off the package greet the homeowner and hand them the package with your compliments. You may also choose to drop it off at their job – which could create a great impression and additional dialogue with their coworkers. Keep mind, however, that the sellers may want to be discreet about the fact that they are considering selling.

When dropping off the pre-listing package:

Your Admin: Hi Mr. Smith. Knolly asked me to drop off this package with you. He's looking forward to meeting with you tomorrow at 2.

Step 9: Draw Up the Listing Docs

Once your call is concluded, and you have set an appointment, it's time to have your Admin type up the listing docs, using your preferred forms software.

To save time, have your Admin create a template set of listing documents which will already have all of your standard information filled in.

Step 10: Confirm the Listing Appointment and Request that the Seller Homework Be Filled Out Ahead of Time

In your pre-listing package you dropped off with the seller, you included the *Seller Homework*. We discuss this in detail in Chapter 6. You should always endeavor to have the seller fill this 4 page homework packet out before you meet with them.

You: Hi Michael - it's _____.

Prospect: Hi there!

You: I'm looking forward to meeting with you tomorrow at 2. As I mentioned – our meeting shouldn't take more than 40 minutes – unless you guys have additional questions.

Prospect: Sounds good.

You: Now Michael, before I come out I need you to do me a big favor.

Prospect: OK.

You: Well, you know how professional doctors or dentists will ask you to fill out a few forms before you arrive to their office? We have a similar practice. In my packet you'll notice that there are four yellow sheets labeled *Seller Homework*.

Prospect: Oh - okay.

You: Michael - these forms allow me to get you the maximum market price possible. I need you to fill out these forms ahead of time.

Prospect: No problem.

You: Awesome! Oh, and one other thing. In addition to the homework, I just need you to have two house keys ready for me when we meet. Can you do that for me?

Prospect: Sure.

> You: Great, Michael! So I'll see you tomorrow
> at 2, give or take 10 minutes for traffic.

Always ask your seller to complete their homework and have two keys ready for your appointment. Filling out your homework forms helps the prospect to psychologically commit to listing with you. These forms also help the prospect to emotionally detach from the property and mentally begin the selling process.

Additionally, the Seller Homework can help to greatly reduce the time spent at the listing appointment! Just imagine that you arrive at the house and the seller has their homework filled out and two shiny keys sitting on the kitchen table. What does that tell you? It's a clear signal to you that you've already secured the listing! There is no need to roll out your full dog-and-pony show. You can move straight to the pricing conversation and get the listing docs signed.

For the aforementioned reasons it is important to make sure that the Seller Homework is filled out before you arrive. You can ensure that it is by mentioning it in your appointment confirmation call, as demonstrated in the above script. I recommend that you make your confirmation calls about 3 to 4 hours in advance of the appointment. Alternatively you can make all of your confirmation calls for the following day the evening before.

You will notice in the script above that the tone of your call uses the assumptive clause *"I'm looking forward to meeting with you tomorrow at 2pm"* versus asking *"Are we still on for tomorrow at 2?."* With this assumptive script you are taking the position that the sale of perhaps their most valuable asset is a very important and meaningful event for the sellers and that there is no possible way they would want to cancel or reschedule. Of course if they absolutely cannot meet with you for some reason that has arisen (illness, they are double-booked at that time, etc) they will let you know, so there's no need to ask the direct question of whether or not they can still meet with you. Asking this as a question instead of posing it as a statement (as per my script) only gives them an easy out.

Offering a FREE CMA Service

Q: "On my website, I offer sellers a free market analysis. Since I send the prospect a CMA before I talk with them how can I avoid the pricing discussion before meeting with them!?"

Great question! In today's fast-paced environment, more and more seller prospects want access to quick data. They want to quickly find out what their house is worth. To accommodate this desire, there are many national home-valuation websites that have popped up over the years. Indeed – one of the best ways to generate seller prospects is to offer a free CMA.

Even though I strongly believe that the pricing conversation between you and the client should happen after you have built a good amount of rapport, I am completely in favor of you offering prospects a free CMA as a service. I'm okay with this approach because your prospects won't attach any negative feelings to you when they receive the market report. It is simply hard data on a report they requested.

If you provide a free CMA service (and you should) the trick to converting these leads to clients is in how you conduct the follow-up.

I recommend that you compile the CMA and then do a quick follow up visit to the house to view the property and build rapport. You simply need to contact the prospect so that you can drop off your pre-listing package, your book and "finalize your CMA."

Set Up a Quick Property Walk Through

 Here's the script for requesting a quick visit:

You: Hi Terry this is Knolly over at the Knolly Team. Listen, Terry - I'm finalizing your Free Home Valuation report and I just need to do a quick walk-through of your house so that we can get you the most accurate data. It won't take me more than 3 to 5 minutes tops. I can swing by tonight around 6 and do the quick walk through and I'll be out of your way quickly.

It's important that the prospect knows that you aren't going there to make a sales pitch or *sell them*. The prospect may respond with something like:

Seller: Well - we aren't really ready to sell right now. I'm not sure tonight would be a good time.

You: You know Terry, I completely understand. Providing a free home evaluation to the residents of Legend Oaks is my specialty. I want to make sure that I am getting the highest value possible for you - and quickly seeing your house is essential. I promise I won't be discussing anything about *selling* your house. I just want to walk through your house quickly and I'll be on my way. It won't take me more than 3 to 5 minutes. I can swing by around 6.

Walk Through the House

Once you get to the house, be true to your word. Quickly walk through the house and look around. Take the pre-listing packet containing your book, pre-listing package and video and hand it to the prospect.

You: Hey, Terry - it's so nice to meet you! I promise it won't take me more than 3 to 5 minutes to walk through your house. Thanks again for your time. Oh by the way - I brought you the book that I wrote for folks who are thinking about selling. It contains lots of great information that you and your husband can review together.

Walk through the house with a clipboard or your smart phone for taking notes. Look around with keen interest in a few areas while taking notes. This shows the seller you are accurate and thorough. Before you leave try to set a solid listing appointment.

Close for an Appointment

You: Terry - I have to say you have a wonderful home here. I would love to interview for the job of getting your house sold. I'm confident I could get you the top market price. Are you available to meet this Thursday at 3 or would Friday at 2 be better?

If the seller isn't open to setting an appointment (perhaps they aren't ready to sell just yet) thank them for their time and let them know you will be sending their completed market analysis via email. Then email the CMA to the seller as soon as possible, using your template email script:

Email Script:

Good Morning Terry,

Thanks so much for requesting your FREE Home Valuation. It was great meeting you and Gary.

I have attached the comprehensive valuation I put together for you as promised. Please review the data and let me know if there are any questions.

Please also refer back to my home seller website at: http://www.YourSiteHere.com. I recently finished a book that better outlines the home selling process. I also put together a video with much more information about what we offer. You can access both on the site.

If you are considering selling, my team and I would be honored to work with you to get your home SOLD. I have already reviewed the information on your property and I am confident we can get it sold for you.

Let's set up a time to meet as soon as you are available if you are considering the idea of getting your house sold.

Thanks again, Terry!

Once you've sent the CMA via email, follow-up with a phone call and attempt to set up a face-to-face appointment with the homeowner. Even if the seller says they aren't interested in selling right now, a sit down appointment with the seller *now* can help you secure the future listing – even if it is a year down the road.

Next Steps

Well, then… now that you've set the appointment, let's spend the next chapter together taking a detailed look at how to conduct the listing appointment to assure maximum success!

Chapter 12 Homework

☐ Review the 8 Seller Questions and Role Play/Practice the scripts around these important questions

☐ Role Play the Scripts in this chapter.

☐ Make sure your book and pre-listing package is finalized (Chapter 5)

☐ Create your own Free CMA Service for clients in your SOI, Farm and Niche.

Chapter 13
The Listing Appointment

Now we have come to the listing consultation! You finally made it – you are meeting with your sellers and the excitement is flowing!

At this point I want to commend you for all the hard work and effort you have put in to make it to what I call "center stage."

Step 11: Conduct the Listing Appointment and Secure the Listing

Have you ever witnessed a performer that you previously had never heard of really shine in a performance? Sometimes they go on to become an *"overnight"* sensation. Make no mistake about it; their rise to fame didn't happen overnight. You and I did not get to see all the years of hard work or all that occurred to help get them to that one performance where they just stole the show.

In Chapters 3 and 4 you pondered deep questions and you developed goals that are unique to you and your career. In Chapter 5 you launched your book (your complete Seller Guide) and you put together an incredible *press kit* (your pre-listing package) and pre-listing video. In Chapter 6 you developed a disciplined daily regimen and a precise lead generation system, and you overcame your fear of prospecting. In Chapters 7-10 you implemented your precise strategy for generating a non-stop supply of SOI, Farm and Niche seller listing leads. In Chapters 11-12 you conducted all of the necessary pre-listing preparation. Finally, it's show time.

Tragically, a good many real estate agents drop the ball when it comes to properly prepping for this big moment. They just want to get leads and go out on appointments, without having a solid foundation, and without having the specific systems in place that will lead to immediate and sustained success. These agents are flying by the seat of their pants. By contrast, you are calm, cool, collected and confident, because you have taken the time to build the firm foundation that will support your listing empire.

You are now about to sit down with the sellers and walk away with the listing. This is your audition. This is your job interview. This is your time to shine.

Again – in today's competitive environment you must seek to win the listing before you ever sit down face-to-face with a seller prospect. Your well-crafted pre-listing tools and systems will greatly tip the scales in your favor and can cut down or eliminate the time that you need to spend convincing the prospect that you are the right agent for the job.

Deciding who they will trust with the sale of their most valuable asset is a little war that rages in the mind of every seller prospect. By putting a much better foot forward, you can win the battle and annihilate the competition in one fell swoop. You have set the stage and your client's mind is at ease. Yes, my friend – becoming a top Listing Specialist is akin to warfare. Winning a battle takes strategy, skill, timing and the right weaponry. The same is true in the listings game. In time you will be able to make it look *effortless*.

In this chapter I will share with you my *award winning* listing presentation. Although I (and my team) have used this same presentation on more listings than we can count, I strongly encourage you to get your hands on as many successful listing presentation scripts as you can. There is more than one script that can lead to success, and in time you will likely amalgamate the perfect presentation script that works for you.

Prepping for the Appointment

In general every successful listing presentation will follow the following format:

- **Step 1:** Meet and greet the seller; place your bag/folder down where you will be meeting with the sellers.

- **Step 2:** Walk through the house taking notes and building rapport with the sellers.

- **Step 3:** Sit down with the sellers and discuss the sale of their home (listing presentation) including what you have to offer, your plan for getting it sold and pricing.
- **Step 4:** Close (seller signs the listing paperwork).

Make Sure that All Decision Makers Will Be Present

You will want to make sure that all decision makers will be present. This will prevent you from having to make multiple presentations and it will help all parties involved in the decision making process to fully understand what you have to offer without them having to hear it second hand.

Always Arrive on Time

In order for someone to do business with you, the *possibility* of trust has to exist. When someone is just getting to know you, they are constantly scanning for the signals that you are subconsciously sending. For this reason, you have to keep your word and exceed their expectations. Little things like not calling when you say you will or arriving late can send up little red flags and work to undermine trust. The good news is that once people know and trust you, they relax their guard. Even so – you should always seek to exceed your client's expectations.

Getting to your appointment on time is essential to setting a good first impression. I recommend that you arrive about 3 to 5 minutes early. Sit in your car and relax, meditate or pray for a few minutes and arrive to the door at the scheduled time.

If traffic in your area is unpredictable and you need to build in a few minutes of leeway add this script into your confirmation call:

 You: Sam, I'm looking forward to our meeting at 4 PM tomorrow. I'll be leaving from another appointment and should get there right around 4 - give or take 10 minutes for traffic. Is that OK?

Again – at this point meeting or exceeding the seller's expectations is critical, so if you think traffic may hold you up some you can simply build in that expectation and get the seller's permission.

Park on the street in front of the house or across the street. Avoid parking in the driveway if possible.

Turn Your Fear into Excitement

It's completely normal to have that slightly queasy feeling just before you sit down for a listing appointment. You drive up to the house, park your vehicle and look straight at the home – and then you start to get that little feeling. It's Showtime! The butterflies are fluttering!

Think back to when you did your first public speaking – yikes! For performers, it is natural to have a touch of fear before you are about to give a live performance to an audience. In this case – you are about to do a presentation and the audience will be just one or two people. You get a bit of an adrenaline rush and perhaps a nauseous feeling in your gut.

If you previously met the owners when you dropped off your pre-listing package you will feel much more comfortable when it's show time. Eventually, as you build confidence and experience, this awkwardness will dissipate substantially.

Another tip I've learned is to *turn your fear into the excitement.* In the human body, fear and excitement manifest themselves in almost the same way. An accelerated heart rate, stammered speech, sweaty palms and slightly shaky hands can be symptoms of a person who is either scared to death or one who has just won the lottery.

It is very important to channel your fear into excitement. To do this the first thing you have to remember to do is *smile.* Whenever you sense that feeling of fear creep up on you I want you to tell yourself this affirmation: *"That's not fear - that's excitement!"* Repeat the affirmation a few times while smiling. This is how you can channel or convert your fear into excitement.

Being able to shine at the listing appointment takes preparation and *great energy.* You have put together your seller book and an awesome pre-listing package. You have mastered your scripts and dialogues. You have researched the market and arrived with a flawless CMA. You are confident. Now all you have to do is turn your fear into excitement and let your positive energy radiate throughout the entire presentation.

Look Like You Came to Get Hired

You are going on an important job interview and it is critical to look the part. The first time you sit down in front of your prospects you should look absolutely amazing. No, this is not a black-tie affair – but it's pretty close.

You are there to ask a prospect to trust you with their life savings and award you with a nice chunk of their equity. For example, when you go on a listing appointment for a $350,000 listing, you are asking the seller for a $21,000 check. Do you realize that 40% of American workers earn less than $20,000 a year?

Regardless of how your clients choose to dress, you should be stunning. I don't think you should break this rule even for good friends or family.

Remember that most people are overly critical and judgmental when they are first getting to know you. Looking your best gives the prospect one less thing to critique – and puts a positive checkmark in your column.

This brings us to the subject of breath. You will be sitting in close proximity to people and your breath should be fresh. An agent with bad breath could be perceived by a seller prospect as one having poor hygiene or neglect. A seller could ask themselves *"If this guy can't even take care of his breath, what kind of job will he do with our house?"* It may sound silly but prospects will spot every little red flag they can – because they are very afraid of putting their trust in the wrong person. To eliminate bad breath, have your teeth cleaned every three months, floss daily, brush your teeth after meals and scrape your tongue. Carry an extra toothbrush, toothpaste and mouth rinse with you, so that you can implement good oral hygiene while on the go. If you suffer from chronic halitosis, you may want to download Dr. Harold Katz' free ebook entitled *"The Bad Breath Bible."* You may also need consult a dentist to insure that your condition isn't a result of tooth decay or gum disease. Breath mints will only mask the odor for a few minutes – and you should absolutely never chew gum while on a listing appointment!

In addition to fresh breath, you should also be well groomed: fingernails clipped and clean, good hygiene, neat facial hair, etc. Flawless. You are there to sell yourself above all else. YOU are the commodity the seller is buying.

A spritz of perfume or a dash of cologne is okay, but please don't overdo it! Your seller may have allergies and your strong (although fragrant) odor may be a distraction throughout the entire presentation.

You can have great wisdom, the best strategies, outstanding counsel, a fantastic marketing plan and a spot on pricing strategy, but if you arrive disheveled, smelly or uncouth, doubts will be created in the mind of the seller.

After mastering the art of listing houses – you will be able to look at just about every listing appointment you go on as a guaranteed paycheck. Envision yourself as a top Listing Specialist in your market. Your appointment conversion rate is above 90%, you work only with motivated sellers, and your listings are all priced correctly. Your business is highly leveraged, so you are spending only about three hours of your personal time on the lifecycle of each listing. And most of all, as a consultant, you are placing the interests of your clients first. You are achieving perpetual win-wins for both you and your clients. You are achieving success for your sellers and, as a byproduct of their success you are achieving success for yourself. When your client reaches their goals, you will in turn reach yours.

Greet the Seller and Set the Time Expectation Up Front

When you first arrive you should greet and thank the seller.

Script! Hi John and Mary - thanks so much for agreeing to meet with me today. Our time together won't take more than 40 minutes - unless you have additional questions.

Here you are simply setting the time expectation. Be realistic. Early in your listing career it will typically take a lot more time to get through a listing appointment – perhaps an hour or more. However, if your prospect has already received your seller book and pre-listing package 30 to 45 minutes should suffice.

Next you should ask the seller if you can place your things on the kitchen table (or wherever you are going to be meeting with them).

Ask for the Seller Homework

Look around and see if you can spot the seller homework packet and 2 keys you requested. If you see them – hooray! Thank the seller for getting the homework completed. If you don't see it anywhere – simply ask *"Were you able to complete the homework forms?"* Pay close attention to their answer as it may indicate how much work you will have to do while you are there on the appointment. Their answer may also reveal their motivation or their willingness to follow your direction.

If the sellers have completed the homework then you are one step closer to getting the listing. Thank the sellers for filling out the homework and reemphasize that you are going to use the information in these documents to get them the highest price in the least amount of time. Don't casually grab the documents and put them away. Review them with keen interest for about 30 - 60 seconds or so. Look excited! Your affirmation of a job well done is their immediate reward for completing their homework assignment. You will also use this time as an opportunity to win the listing!

You: Wow, guys, this is great information! This is really well done. I love it. I can't wait to start marketing your property. I love how you wrote this sentence here. I already can see how we can use this information to get you the highest price.

Here Are Some Possible Excuses For Not Completing The Seller Homework And Probable Indications:

Seller: *"Oh – we were going to do that but we got busy."*

Such an answer could indicate that your seller is not very motivated or that you did not stress the importance of having the homework completed. You should always let the seller know that having the homework completed allows you to get the maximum price possible in the least amount of time. If you did clearly let them know this, then how could they let it slip? Are they really serious about selling?

Seller: *"We decided to wait and fill out the homework until after we interviewed you."*

This answer indicates that the seller is not completely sold on you *yet*. You will have to win their trust and confidence during the listing appointment.

Seller: *"What homework?"*

You obviously did not do an adequate job of explaining the importance of the seller homework. You should be reminding your seller about the homework on both the pre-listing call and on the appointment confirmation call (review Chapter 12).

Walk Through the House

Now go ahead and walk through the house with or without the seller. There are pros and cons to both approaches which I will discuss here.

Walking Through the House *with* the Seller

Truthfully speaking, for a top Listing Specialist most houses don't need to be *seen* to be *sold*. I have personally seen very few of the past 1000 houses that I've sold. After you've seen a few hundred houses (with rare exception) the grand excitement of seeing yet another house just isn't there. Regardless – you will need to turn on that excitement! The seller will be looking closely at your facial expressions and your body language. They are showing you their baby – the place they have called home for the past nine years. You need to be jazzed about it!

Having the seller take you for a tour of their house can be a great exercise for building rapport. You are asking questions, sharing a few laughs and breaking the ice. You are getting to know them better while they show you their most prized possession. The drawback here is that this approach is time consuming. Some sellers will want to show you every nook and cranny.

As you walk through the house – you can point out several key elements and how you will market them. You should also be taking notes.

Avoid giving the client too much home preparation advice during the walk through. At this point you are building rapport. I recommend you share with them all of your thoughts on prepping the home for sale *after* they list the house with you. Giving a seller a bunch of to-dos and negative feedback early on can undermine your rapport building efforts. Once the seller has signed with you, they have indicated that they are ready for you to take the lead and they are ready to listen to your advice. Also, some sellers want to sell their home *as-is* and price it accordingly, so for them it would be inappropriate to discuss home prep. Once you understand their objectives you can render the best advice. In my opinion, the appropriate time to render advice and counsel regarding preparing their house for sale is *after you have been hired*. I will discuss home preparation thoroughly in the next chapter.

Walking Through the House *without* the Seller

This is the fastest approach but it does not build much rapport. Therefore you will probably want to reserve this approach for sellers you already have a good rapport with – or for those who have already indicated that they will be listing with you.

You: Sally - let me take a quick walk-through of your house. I'm going to walk through it by myself because I want to see your house through the eyes of a prospective buyer. I'll be back in about 3 minutes.

Be Very Familiar with Your Listing Docs

Make sure that you are completely familiar with the listing agreement. Carry a blank copy of your standard listing agreement around with you and read it several times a day, until you are completely familiar with the verbiage.

At the listing appointment you will typically be reading the document upside down, so you should practice reading it that way as well. Also – clients do not want you to read the document to them word for word. You should be able to summarize what each paragraph states in a sentence or two and then move on, unless they have specific questions.

I also tend to refrain from calling this document a *contract* or an *agreement*. I simply call it paperwork. At the listing appointment, when it's time to review the document I'll say something like *"let's go ahead and review the paperwork."* I'll discuss this in greater detail shortly.

Always Take the Listing Docs with You on Your Listing Appointment

Even if the prospect tells you that they are not going to list right now or that they simply want to meet with you – you still want to have the listing documentation prepared and with you on the listing appointment.

I've only broken this rule a few times – and one of them was very painful. On this occasion, the listing prospect made it very clear with me that he did not want to sign anything but that he just wanted to sit down and have a consultation about selling his house. He would not be signing any paperwork. He repeated that several times during the call. I decided to just go on the appointment without the paperwork and, as it turns out, the appointment went very well. His wife was ready to sign so he asked me if we could go ahead and sign the paperwork. Nice! I had two other listing appointments that same day so I told him I would get back with him later and swing by with the paperwork. In the meantime, he had another listing appointment lined up with another very high profile competitor in my market. That agent was from my same office, and showed up after me with paperwork! My prospect did not tell me he was meeting with anyone else and I didn't ask, due to my overconfidence at how the appointment had gone. At that point, the seller was so warmed up about the idea of selling that he went ahead and signed with the other agent. I already had the listing in the bag, but because I failed to bring the paperwork with me I lost it. It would have been a $450,000 guaranteed sale, which is nothing to sneeze at in my market. I learned a powerful lesson and I have never repeated that mistake again.

Sitting Down With the Seller

Once you have finished walking through the house, sit down with the seller at the kitchen table. If you are meeting with more than one person avoid sitting in the middle as this will cause you to have to look back and forth throughout the entire conversation. Sit to one side of the sellers so that you can easily see them both. I like to sit on the left side of the sellers. Personally I have found that if you are still trying to build rapport it is best to avoid sitting directly across the table from the sellers. I feel like it breaks up the energy flow to have them on the other side of the table. However, there are many Listing Specialists I know who prefer sitting across from the seller. Go with what is most comfortable to you.

You should have a copy of your pre-listing packet, your seller book, a copy of the tax record, your CMA and the listing documents with you.

I recommend you have all of the documents in a customized presentation folder that you can leave behind. Your paperwork should be very neatly organized and not haphazard. Situate the paperwork in the order that you will be presenting. You do not want to be shuffling back and forth through the docs in the presence of your prospect. *Place the listing docs at the bottom of your presentation stack so that they are not visible to the prospect when you open the folder.*

As I discussed earlier, you should make it a point to go on every single listing appointment armed with a copy of the listing docs ready for signatures. Even if the seller tells you that they are simply *interviewing* agents and don't want to sign anything – you should be prepared to take the listing on the spot. However – you should avoid showing the paperwork until the time is right. If the seller sees the listing docs prematurely it may cause them to clam up or put them on the defensive.

Marketing and Price Script

On my listing presentations I begin by letting the seller know that *"there are two things that sell houses – marketing and price."*

You: John and Karen - I'd like to talk about two major things that sell houses - marketing and price. Marketing is what I have control over and price is what I'm going to give you control over - within reason. First, let's review our extensive marketing plan for your house.

I believe there are four things that sell houses: *location, price, condition* and *marketing*. The most important of these is *price*. However sellers almost always believe that *marketing* is the most important factor to getting their property sold. Whenever their house fails to sell, the seller will usually blame the agent – citing that the agent did not do enough to market their house. Rather than trying to dispel this misnomer (a futile task) you should go out of your way to provide and implement an incredible marketing plan for you listings. Doing so will both appease the seller and attract more business to you (both buyers and sellers). If the listing isn't selling the blame can then be cast on the correct culprit – price.

After letting your prospect know that marketing and price is what sells houses you can review with them your comprehensive marketing plan.

Your Seller Marketing Plan

Here is the script we use to present our marketing plan to our prospects. Remember though, since the seller has already received your pre-listing package, you may not need to go into as much detail on what you have to offer.

You: The first key element to selling your house is marketing. I believe that marketing is about *creating awareness* in the minds of as many potential buyers as possible. Simply put, *if buyers don't know about your house, it doesn't exist*. Because I have spent a lot of time marketing houses, I understand what it takes to get your house SOLD. Every week I come across sellers who have tried listing their house with another agent only to find bitter disappointment. Let's examine why.

In the past 7 years, computers and the internet have changed the face of real estate. Most agents haven't kept up. According to the National Association of REALTORS® (NAR) recent study, 92% of all home buyers now use the internet for house hunting. While most agents are struggling to keep up, my company has been immersed in the latest technology!

Besides not staying up to date with technology, less than 9% of agents are trained in the fine art of sales and marketing. That's because sales and marketing are nowhere in the training that agents receive in order to become *licensed*. The truth is most agents are good people; they just don't know how to do good marketing. Doing the kind of marketing that leads to a successful sale takes time, money and a great marketing plan.

The average agent in town uses a 3 point marketing plan. We call it the 3 P's of the average agent's marketing.

1. Put a sign in the yard

2. Put it on MLS

3. Pray that it will sell!

In my real estate practice, I employ the most comprehensive marketing plan you will find anywhere. I have a proven plan that will get your home SOLD faster and for more money; I focus my marketing efforts on five major categories 1) Outdoor Advertising, 2) Internet Advertising, 3) Print Advertising, 4) Premium Marketing and 5) Industry Marketing.

Sample Listing Marketing Plan

Now go ahead and review your comprehensive marketing plan with the seller. Here's the marketing plan I use. Go ahead and pick and choose the items you will employ, and feel free to add some more of your own!

1) Outdoor Advertising

- ☐ **Colorful Signage** - My signs are full color and printed front and back so they get noticed!

- ☐ **Direct Dial Number** - Buyers can call and get instant information from a live person!

- ☐ **24 Hour Info Hotline!** Prospects can call 24 hours a day and get information on your home. When a buyer calls I receive a text notification that someone has called about your property. The text notification has their phone number so I can call them back right away and schedule a showing!

- ☐ **Full Color Virtual Flyers** - Your listing will be assigned its own QR code, so buyers can pull up the up-to-date home information right from their smart phone or mobile tablet. On my virtual flyers I also include my buyer hotline, where buyers can call and get info 24/7.

2) Internet Advertising

☐ **Brokerage Websites** - My technology allows us to showcase your property on every major brokerage website. This means that your house will be featured on sites like Keller Williams, RE/MAX, Coldwell Banker, and all of the local mom and pop real estate outfits as well. So, even though you list with me, your house will be featured on just about every other brokerage site in town and throughout the nation.

☐ **National Channel Partners** - Through my unique relationship with my national channel partners, your house will be featured on popular websites like Zillow, Trulia, HGTV, Yahoo Homes, AOL Real Estate, Oodle and many more.

☐ **Affiliate Channel Partners** - Popular websites like those sponsored by Fannie Mae, Freddie Mac and many others will also feature your house.

☐ **Regional Channel Partners** - I market on hundreds of popular regional websites.

☐ **Craigslist** - I list and update your property on Craigslist regularly. My well-constructed ads generate a steady stream of buyer inquiries every day.

☐ **Search Engine Optimization (SEO)** - Of course you are familiar with search engines like Google, Bing and Yahoo etc. Your listing will be keyword optimized by my industry professional so that your house achieves high ranking status on the internet's most popular search engines.

☐ **Social Media** - I use Facebook, YouTube and many other popular social media platforms to market your property. I have lots of friends on my Facebook profile where your listing will be prominently featured along with my YouTube channel and several other key social platforms.

3) Print Advertising

☐ **Just Listed Cards** - I mail color postcards to your closest neighbors. Let your community help spread the word!

☐ **Real Estate Magazines** - I prominently feature your house in Real Estate Magazines carried at local restaurants and grocery stores!

☐ **Monthly Mailings** - I periodically send direct mail to local residents and my database, marketing my website that prominently displays your house as a premier featured listing.

4) Premium Marketing

- ☐ **Your Private Login Portal** - I provide you with access to your private portal where you can log in and see the status of your marketing campaign and track your transaction once it's under contract!

- ☐ **'Featured Listing' Exposure** - Your house featured prominently on my website in my Featured Properties section.

- ☐ **Professional Photographs** - When buyers are browsing the internet to search for properties, photographs do more to help sell your property than anything else. That's why I hire a professional photographer to take high-quality photos of your property.

- ☐ **Virtual Tour** - On my larger listings, I pay for a professional 360° panoramic virtual tour featuring several key areas of your house.

- ☐ **My Monthly e-Newsletter** - My e-newsletter is sent to my database of past clients and my sphere of influence each month, promoting the site where your house is prominently featured.

- ☐ **Electronic Feedback System** - Whenever your house is shown, I send an electronic survey to the showing agent. I encourage the agents to provide feedback on the showing so that you know exactly what buyers are thinking and saying about your house.

5) Industry Marketing

☐ My company's agents are working for you. It's true. That means I can tap into all of the agents at my brokerage, who are ready, willing and able to show and sell your house the minute any of their buyer prospects show an interest.

☐ Our entire MLS member agents are working for you. I mobilize all of these agents with my targeted marketing campaigns designed to provide them the exact information they need to get their potential buyers excited about seeing your house.

(after reviewing your marketing plan with the seller)

You: Susan, as you can see we employ the most comprehensive marketing plan you will find anywhere. Tell me Susan - is there anything else you think we should be doing that is not already included in our marketing plan?

Prospect: No... this looks good to me!

Getting it Priced Right

Once you get the seller's admission that your marketing plan is comprehensive and exhaustive enough to do the job, you can move on to the pricing discussion.

You: That's awesome, Susan! I'm so glad you agree that we have a comprehensive and

> effective marketing plan. As you can see –
> we've spared no expense to get your house
> sold in the least amount of time and at the
> highest price. Speaking of price - let's talk
> about our pricing strategy. Let's take a look
> at what the market in your neighborhood is
> saying.

Now you can reach into your presentation folder and pull out your CMA. When reviewing a CMA with a client use a one or two page summary format that shows *Actives*, *Pendings* and *Solds* on one page, as we discussed in Chapter 12. Try to get 3 or 4 comparables per category. You can also have a full comprehensive CMA with photos and greater detail to use as a reference, but you will primarily use a *Summary CMA* in your presentation because it is a quick and easy *at-a-glance* view of the market. A Summary CMA makes it much easier for a seller to quickly review and digest the information being presented. While it lacks the razzmatazz and impressiveness of a full-blown CMA, a Summary CMA gets the job done much more efficiently.

You: Susan - this market analysis shows what the market is doing in your area right now. At the top here you can see current properties that are for sale. We call these Actives. This is your competition. Now these here in the middle are currently under contract. We don't know what they sold for yet because they haven't closed - but we can see what they were asking. This last group shows houses that have already SOLD. Here we can clearly see what sellers are *getting* for a house similar to yours.

> Now the pending and actives we call this fantasyland - this is what sellers hope to get. Now as for the SOLDS - we call this *reality*. This is what sellers are *actually* getting.

Explain to the seller how to read the data in the columns (year built, square footage, price per square foot, days on market etc.)

Next, have the seller tell you their conclusions on pricing. Once you've educated the seller on how to read and review the market analysis you will want to have them draw their own conclusions. Armed with the right information your sellers can set the price they feel comfortable with (within reason). This way they can take ownership in the pricing of their property.

You: Susan - As we mentioned before the two things that sell houses are marketing and price. Marketing is what I have control over. I give my sellers control over the pricing. Based on what the market is saying - what price do you believe would create *value* in the mind of the buyer?

Once you have asked this question stop talking. The seller will often look down at the data again - as if to try and catch a glimpse of some hidden detail that simply isn't there. Let the market do the talking. Avoid the compulsion to tell the sellers what you think about the price. The truth is – you don't have any thoughts on the matter. The market speaks for itself – and it speaks very loudly.

Q: "What if the seller wants to price the house higher than it's worth?"

Most sellers have unrealistic expectations about what they can get for their house. They almost always want a little more than it is worth. Let's say your seller wants to price their house at $450,000 and you know that the market points to a price of $400,000 tops. Here are 10 of my most successful pricing scripts for sellers who want to overprice.

Script 1:

You: Susan... getting your house sold is all about creating value in the mind of the buyer. Do you believe that $450,000 will create value in the mind of the buyer?

Script 2:

You: Susan - what's the lowest price you are willing to go?

Script 3:

Hand the prospect a calculator and let them do the math.

You: So, Susan - what is the average price per square-foot that houses in your subdivision are selling for?

Prospect: $158 per square foot.

You: I see. Go ahead and punch in 158... and what is your square footage?

Prospect: My house is 2527 square feet.

You: Go ahead and times the 158 by 2527. What are you coming up with?

Script 4:

Susan - It looks like you want to get top dollar for your house! That's great. I also want to get you the most money possible because I'm on commission - and the more *you* make the more *I* make. We're in this together. Let's get you the top market price for your house. Based on the data what is the most a person has gotten for a house like yours?

Script 5:

You: You know, Susan - in order to get you the most money possible I'm going to have to sell the *value* of your house to a prospective buyer - and I'll have to use this market data to do it. Based on the data - how can we show a buyer that your house is worth $50,000 more than the market?

Script 6:

For this script you will have to pull out your comprehensive multi-page CMA which shows photos of the comparable properties and more details. You can also use your laptop, tablet or smartphone to pull up the houses that are most comparable and review the photos of these houses with the seller.

You: Susan – let's take a closer look at the comparables so we can get you top market price. I brought with me a more comprehensive market analysis which has photos and more details. Let's take a look at this one.

Now go through the details of each comparable, asking the seller specific questions like "how many bedrooms does this one have? How many bathrooms? How

many living spaces? What's the square footage? Great. Now let's take a look at the photos..."

You: Susan – based on the data that we've reviewed on this comparable house, would you say it is *nicer, not as nice* or *about the same* as yours?

Prospect: It's about the same I think.

You: I see. And how much did it sell for? I see.

Now you can follow this script by letting the seller do the math (from Script 3).

Script 7:

You: Susan – it is important to understand that most buyers will be using some form of financing when they purchase your house. This means that the buyer's lender will order an appraisal on your property. If your house does not appraise for at least the amount of the sale price, the buyer's loan will be rejected. This is often true even if the buyer is putting a large amount of cash down on the property. This is one of the major reasons why you will want to set the *right price* now.

Script 8:

For this script you want to show the seller the pricing pyramid graph.

You: Susan, are you familiar with how pricing affects showings? Research has proven that price drives traffic through a listing and that pricing a property correctly at the *beginning* of the listing process will attract the *most* potential buyers to your property. Fewer viewings results in fewer opportunities to receive a contract.

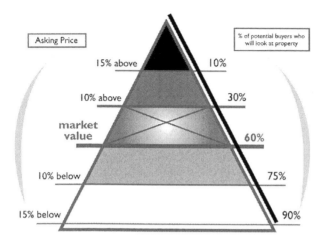

Script 9:

If the sellers are still being extremely stubborn about pricing their house correctly, then it's time to interject. For this exercise you need to draw a horizontal line. In the middle of the line you will write down what you believe is a fair market price. On the left side of the line you will put a price that is below market (low) and on the right side of the line you will write in a price that is above market (high).

You: Susan - the market seems to be pointing to a price of $158 per square foot. Are you aware of the message that our price sends to a potential buyer? For example on the left side here we have $375,000. This says to a buyer *'I need it sold yesterday!'* Such a message could make you appear desperate and we don't want that. Now let's look at this number on the right side - $450,000. Do you know when message this sends to potential buyers? This price says *'look - I don't care if*

I ever sell it!' Susan - we want to send the right message *now* by setting the right price.

Script 10:

This script is reserved for those who just won't crack. If you absolutely have to take an overpriced listing do it for a trial period.

You: Susan - Let's go ahead and *try* <u>your</u> price for 14 days. If we don't get it under contract in that time we'll adjust the price to what the market is saying.

In the listing agreement you will have the seller initial off on the 14 day price adjustment.

An Overpriced Home...

✓ Minimizes offers

✓ Lowers agent response

✓ Limits qualified buyers

✓ Lowers showings

✓ Lowers prospects

✓ Limits financing

✓ Wastes advertising dollars

✓ Nets less for the seller

When Looking At Market Price Show a Range

It is important that you show clients that the market price will fall within a range rather than pointing to a specific number. The range can be broad or quite narrow depending on the specific market area. For example if similar houses are selling for $98-$109 per square foot and the seller's house is 2500 square feet - the market price range could be $245,000 to $272,500. To hone in on a tighter price range you will need to compare the amenities and condition of the comparables with the seller's property. For example, after a thorough review, you might be able to see that the true comparables are selling for $102 to $106 per foot, which would give your seller's 2500 square foot property a price range of $255,000 to $265,000.

Get Price Adjustments Up Front

It is very important to get price adjustments signed off on *at the time you take the listing*. Oftentimes sellers are resistant to making price adjustments a month or two into the listing term. It is much easier to get them to commit to a price adjustment at the time you *take* the listing. This strategy alone will insure that a higher percentage of the listings you take actually close - providing success for both you and your sellers.

Build in two or three price adjustments spread a few weeks apart. You can add this into your listing agreement (if there is room for it under the *special provisions* paragraph) or create a separate addendum form that the seller signs off on:

Here's a Pricing Strategy example:

Pricing Strategy for 201 Main St:

Seller gives listing agent the authority to adjust the listing price as follows:

➤ Initial List Price will be: $425,000

➤ After 14 days on MLS, the list price of shall adjust to: $400,000

➤ After 30 days on MLS, the list price of shall adjust to: $390,000

➤ After 45 days on MLS, the list price of shall adjust to: $375,000

Ultimately, your goal is to launch the listing right out of the gate with the right price. If you are not able to do this for whatever reason you will want to get the listing priced correctly within the first 14 days. Ideally you will never have to make the 30 or 45 day price adjustments as your listing will be under contract by then.

Sellers may be a bit resistant to agreeing to price adjustments upfront, but it will still be much easier for them to agree to a pricing strategy now than trying to get them to agree to an adjustment later. You are already neck-deep in the pricing conversation so *now* is the time to get the seller's commitment on a solid pricing strategy.

Script!

[Script to use after you've used the pricing objection handlers and your client has a firm starting price]

You: So, Susan - It looks like you are leaning toward a price of $425,000. That's a bit higher than what the market is saying right now and we still have to contend with the appraisal issue. Are you absolutely sure you want to *start* at this price?

Prospect: Yes - let's try it at this price and see what happens.

You: OK, Susan. Let's give it a shot. Let's go ahead and start it at *your* price. If we don't get any offers within the first two weeks it means that the market is *rejecting* your price and we will need to adjust it to what the market is saying. Based on your starting price - here's the pricing strategy that I recommend.

At this point pull out the pricing strategy addendum and fill-in the blanks for 14, 30 and 45 days. Go ahead and have the seller sign off on the document. This way you will have your agreed price adjustments up front and there will be no need to waste your time getting the seller's written permission to lower the price each time you need to.

How Pricing Affects Showings

Research has proven that price drives traffic through a listing and that pricing a property correctly at the beginning of the listing process will attract the most potential buyers to your listing. Fewer showings means fewer opportunities to receive a contract.

Pricing Unique and Luxury Properties

For homes that are very rare and unique, I will often recommend that the seller also order an appraisal by a licensed appraiser. While we use similar criteria, software and systems as most appraisers, the appraiser will be seen by the buyer and the buyer's lender as a very credible source, when it is very difficult to clearly see the value of your client's property. We employ this strategy on our properties that are on 1+ Acres, luxury inventory (houses priced at $1 Million+) and other unique homes.

As-Is Pricing Strategy

The "As Is" pricing strategy is for sellers who lack the funds, ability or desire to properly prepare their property for sale.

After having your home inspected by a licensed home inspector, you can review the report and get any bids on the work needed. You can then properly price the house based on accurate knowledge of its condition.

"Hot Property" Pricing Strategy

This pricing strategy is particularly effective in all types of markets.

Generally, your seller will get a pre-sale property inspection report, correct all the items that are affordable, and then put the property on the market at or near the lowest price they are willing to accept for the property. In the right market, multiple offers may be possible using this strategy.

Getting Your Full Commission

Getting a client to agree to pay the full commission you charge is really a matter of creating a great *value proposition*. When clients can clearly see the value they are getting, they instinctively are in alignment with the fact that you are worth what you are charging. One of the key ways that you create value in the mind of the seller early on is with your Listing Tools (Chapter 5).

Present Multiple Commission Options

Another great strategy I learned from my mentor Rand Smith is to present the seller prospect with multiple commission options. This strategy helps show the seller that they are getting a great value from you. It also has the added benefit of assisting you in getting your full commission.

When I meet with sellers I let them know that I charge 8%, 7% or 6% depending on the marketing involved and the price range of the house. If I do agree to list their house for 6% then I let them know that I will charge them my *lowest* rate. I have found that it's best to have the various listing percentages permanently fixed into your listing agreement template. On the listing agreement you will circle the commission amount that you agree on and have the client initial the change. This is a very psychological exercise that assures the client they are getting a fair deal and prevents them from attempting to cut your commission. When you present your various commission options and circle one and initial the change, the seller instinctively understands you are cutting them a break and they typically lose their desire to fight with you on your commission.

 You: Susan - as you can see I implement a comprehensive marketing plan to get your house SOLD in the least amount of time and for the most money. I charge either an 8%, 7% or a 6% commission, depending on the property and the marketing plan we will need to employ. For standard properties (in a typical subdivision), and for past clients, friends and family I am willing to charge my lowest rate of 6%.

Explain How Commission Works

It is very helpful to explain to the seller how your commission is split. This exercise also helps to dispel the notion that you are making off like a fat cat with a big chunk of their equity.

Ask the seller if they are familiar with how the commission is split. Some will say they are somewhat familiar with it. In any case, proceed to quickly explain it to them. You can do the exercise with six crisp one dollar bills (or six business cards). Lay the six dollar bills out on the table and proceed to explain how the commission is divided.

 You: Susan - let me quickly show you how I will be dividing the commission I earn. The first thing I will do with my commission is pay the buyer's agent half of it. You see, Susan, I want to encourage as many buyers as possible to come see your house and I do this by paying the buyer agent half of my earnings **[grab 3 of the dollars and set them aside].**

As you can see, that leaves me with 3%.

I have chosen to align myself with a top brokerage in town which further helps to provide maximum exposure for your property. This dollar here goes to my brokerage. That leaves me with 2%. **[grab another dollar and put it on the stack with the other 3].**

Susan - Remember the comprehensive marketing plan that we will be implementing on your house? This 1% goes toward marketing and servicing your listing. **[grab another dollar and put it on the stack with the other 4]**

As you can see Susan – that leaves me with just one percent - which is what I live on. This is my paycheck. And from this I still have to pay taxes. **[now, hold up the last dollar left and fold a third of the dollar bill so that just 2/3 shows]**

When presented masterfully, this exercise will completely reshape the way your seller thinks about the amount you are getting paid.

Seller's Estimated Net Sheet

When making the decision to sell, sellers typically have 4 primary questions:

1. How much can I sell it for?
2. What will it cost to sell?

3. How long will it take?

4. How much will I walk away with?

At this point you have answered the first three questions for them and now it's time to answer the fourth. The Seller's Estimated Net Sheet allows the seller to see approximately how much they will walk away with after all expenses are paid.

You can arrive at the listing appointment with the estimated net sheet calculated based on the market value or you can quickly prep one at the listing appointment (using your laptop, tablet or smartphone). Either way, I don't recommend that you present this document until you have already agreed on a price and discussed your fees.

Endeavor to have this document as accurate as possible. Make sure the seller knows that the numbers can change (up or down) if their payoff balance, sales price or taxes are different than anticipated.

It is also a good idea to draft a revised Estimated Net Sheet with any offer you receive on the property and to present it with the offer. In Chapter 16 we will discuss the process of receiving and presenting offers in great detail.

Review the Listing Docs with the Seller

You should be very familiar with every clause in the listing agreement. This familiarity will allow you to quickly present the document (while reading it upside down) giving a brief overview of what each section states.

Sign the Paperwork

After reviewing the document ask the seller if they have any questions. If they don't – you're done! Go ahead and do your final close. Get the listing docs signed!

You: Susan, do you have any questions?

Prospect: No, not really. I think I understand everything.

You: Great! Let's go ahead and sign the paperwork so we can get your house sold!

Conducting the Listing Presentation at Your Office

Some agents have made a shift to conducting the listing appointments in their office. This strategy can be a tremendous time saver for you and create more efficiency for your seller. You can use many of the techniques outlined in this chapter when doing an in-office consultation. Make sure that you have a distraction-free conference area where you can hold your meetings. If you are considering this model, Find agents who are doing this successfully and interview them.

Always Give Honest Counsel

Always place the interests of the prospect above your own. For your seller this is a major life decision so you definitely want to know the driving motivation behind the person's decision to sell. Perhaps the seller just needs a little more space and a small room addition would do the trick for a lower cost than selling. Maybe the seller should consider converting their property into a rental investment. Listen intently and give your clients good and wise counsel on the various options that are available to accomplish their objective, regardless of how the decision affects you.

Last month a former client called me to list his house. He used to be a neighbor, and I had sold his house and assisted him and his wife on the purchase of their current home about six years ago. They have extensively remodeled the home they had purchased for $320,000, even going so far as adding nearly 1000 square feet to it. It is situated in a very desirable area of Austin. Their home has more than doubled in value and is now worth about $740,000. Their goal was to sell their house and make a move to another subdivision a few miles away where houses are priced between $750,000 and $900,000. Again, this was not a move up or a move down, but was more of a lateral move. Both the sale and purchase would be fairly easy transactions for me because both areas are red hot, with houses selling in an average of 14 days or less. Collectively, these two transactions would be roughly $1.5 million to $1.65 million in sales volume and the commission I would earn would be roughly $45,000 to $50,000.

As is my custom, I dug deeper so that I could thoroughly understand the seller's motivation. I always seek to know *why* the move is important to them, so that I can get on board and help them achieve their objectives.

During our conversation I learned that the seller owed about $320,000 on their current house so they had more than $400,000 in equity. They told me that their motivation for selling was to lower their overall debt and their monthly debt payments. They had about $60,000 of debt that they wanted to pay off through the sale of their house, primarily because the monthly payments on the debt was making meeting their monthly living expenses challenging. They were going to put about $200,000 down on the new house and pay off their existing debt. They were already pre-qualified and ready to go! The clear problem that I saw, however, was that they would now be stuck with a $550,000 mortgage. So while their unsecured debt would go down by $60,000, their secured debt (mortgage balance) would go up an additional $200,000. It just didn't make sense. Their primary motivation was clearly debt consolidation and reduction however the move would result in an even higher total debt on their portfolio. After a very frank conversation with them, they were able to come to the conclusion that selling their house was not the best option to accomplish their objective. By following Dave Ramsey's *debt snowball* plan, they could clearly see that they would be able to pay off their debt within the next four years or less. Of course they would have to live pretty lean in the meantime. We mutually concluded that it was not in *their* best interest to sell. That decision cost me two large commission checks, and I was very happy about it.

Every situation is different, and we must clearly advise our clients based on their objectives. As a consultant, we must place the interests of our clients above everything else, because their interests are all that matters.

Don't get me wrong here. I am not teaching you that your clients should make the decision that makes the most sense to you. I have had clients sell their property for a multitude of different reasons. Some just want a new or better home, others are forced to sell out of a hardship, some want to move away to better weather, some want to move closer to work, some want to downsize or upsize, some want to get their kids into a better school district, and on and on. Truthfully, most people sell and buy for *emotional reasons*. It is not my job to place judgment on their motivation, nor do I seek to challenge their reasons for wanting to sell. My job is simply to gain a deep and thorough understanding of why they are selling so that I can advise them correctly. Sometimes my advice will expose them to other options that do not involve selling, but it's up to them to make the decision on how they want to proceed. I don't try to talk them into a decision or out of a decision. I simply present all of the facts and let them make the decision that is best for their family.

In the aforementioned case, if my clients had simply told me that they wanted to make the move because they like the area in the other neighborhood better, then that's fine. Let's get it done! They could have even told me that they like the other area because the restaurants there are nicer. That would've been all right with me as well. In any case, I will always seek to expose my clients to all available options, and oftentimes, selling is the clear winner among them, but sometimes it is not. Either way is OK.

Q: "Knolly, should I discount my commission?"

Great question, but what do you mean by *"discount"*? In real estate sales, there is no "standard" commission and the commission that you charge is determined by you. Therefore, the term *discount* is subjective in and of itself. For example, if you generally charge a commission of 7%, then for you 6% could be a discounted commission. If you normally charge a flat fee, then anything under that flat fee could be considered a discount.

First of all, I definitely believe that you should have a *fee schedule* that clearly shows the rates that you charge. I also believe that you should charge your client a rate that you feel is commensurate with the services you are providing. I also believe that these fees should be in writing.

When clients see your rates in writing, it helps them understand that you are equitable. I'm certainly not advocating that you publish your fees on your website, but you should have them available for your clients to see during your listing presentation. I have a special document that actually explains my fees, and answers a few other common homeowner questions.

Imagine going to a restaurant where the prices are not on the menu. What about hiring someone to build your website that doesn't show you their rate sheet? How do you know that you're getting a fair deal? Just by seeing a person's rates in writing, people instinctively feel that they are getting a fair deal even if they believe the rates are high, because having your rates in writing conveys the idea that everyone is being charged the same or similar rates.

Whenever I have a contractor come to my house to give me a bid on work I need done, I instinctively make sure that my Mercedes is pulled into the garage with the door closed. I do this because I feel that their rates will automatically go up when they see the kind of car I drive. However, when a contractor pulls out a standard rate sheet that's typed up, I instinctively *feel* a sense of fairness. I feel like they are not basing my rate on the kind of car I drive, the house I live in or my income bracket.

When you discount your fees on a regular basis, word gets out. For example, when one neighbor finds out that you charged another neighbor a different rate, conflict can arise. *And they will find out.* One way to get around this is to have *purposeful* discounts. For example, you could decide to offer past clients a $500 or $1000 discount/rebate, etc. That too should be in writing.

Now that you have established what your rates are, deciding to discount that rate for a particular client will be both a *personal* decision and a *business* decision. Discounting your commission in a particular case is neither a right nor wrong thing in and of itself, rather it can be an either right or wrong thing for *you*.

Trust me, I've done my share of pro bono work, and it felt good to do because I felt it was the right thing to do under the circumstances. However, if you find yourself discounting your commission just so you can get the listing – you really need to take a much closer look at your value proposition. If clients are suggesting that you discount your commission then you are not doing a strong enough job convincing them that all agents are not equal and that they should hire you at all costs. On the other hand, some agents offer a discount commission even before the client asks for one, essentially robbing themselves if their hard earned income. Top Listing Specialists will tell you that less than 5% of the sellers they meet with will ask for a discounted commission, after they hear all that the agent has to offer. You must present your value proposition in an irrefutable way. Using the listing presentation outlined in this chapter and using your listing tools (Chapter 5) will help you do that. You must also present yourself with passion, conviction and *contagious confidence*.

Q: "What if the seller asks me to discount my commission?"

There are actually 4 things you have done that should prevent this from happening.

1. You have created a killer pre-listing package which clearly articulates your value proposition.

2. You have presented your seller with your exhaustive marketing plan for getting their house sold.

3. You have presented your seller with 3 different commission options and offered them your lowest option.

4. You have explained to the seller how commission works.

From these four things your seller can clearly see that you are worth your salt and that you will *earn* your fee. They will also see that they are getting a fair deal and that there is nowhere for you to "cut" commission.

Still, some people you encounter are born negotiators, so they will try to see if they can make you crack. If you are not okay with offering a discount, then you can use one of (or a combination of) the following scripts:

Script 1:

> **Use this script when the seller says that a competing broker will list for a lower commission. Pull out the 3 dollar bills (or 3 business cards) you used during the commission explanation exercise.**

> Prospect: The other agent says they will do it for 5%
>
> You: You know, John, I can appreciate that, but as I showed you earlier, this dollar goes to the brokerage, this dollar goes to the marketing and servicing of your listing and this dollar is your real estate agent's paycheck. Tell me, John, which dollar do you think they will be cutting out, their paycheck or the marketing and servicing of your listing?
>
> John, I won't skimp out on doing everything that is necessary to sell your house. I'm going to do a great job for you and I'm going to get it sold.

Script 2:

You: John, if you needed an important surgery, would you go with a surgeon who could get the job done with the *best chance of success*, or would you go with the one who charged the *lowest rates*? Unfortunately some homeowners don't use the same amount of discretion when selecting an agent. When you pick the wrong agent, you net less money in your pocket, have a less than stellar experience and it will take longer than necessary to sell. Although the other agent says they will charge you 1%, you can see that with my compressive marketing plan I could easily net you 3-5% *more* for your house, which will put more money in your pocket. You can trust me with the sale of your house, John. Let's go ahead and move forward and get it sold.

Script 3:

You: You know, John, I can appreciate that another agent has offered you a discount on the commission. As many sellers have experienced the hard way, not all real estate agents are created equal.

Think about it this way: If you had to undergo an important surgery, you would certainly search for the *right* surgeon. More likely, you would look for an experienced specialist; one that had perhaps performed hundreds or even thousands of successful procedures. In the same way, selling your house is a serious matter. You don't want to trust anyone but the right agent with your biggest asset. John, I'm the right agent for the job. You should hire me and let me go to work for you.

Script 4:

You: In the real estate world, the overwhelming majority of agents specialize in working with buyers. I am a Listing Specialist, and I specialize in working with Sellers. This unique specialization has enabled me to focus on and employ the best techniques for getting your house SOLD. When choosing the right agent to sell your house, you want to select a Listing Specialist. Hire me, and let me put my expertise to work for you.

Script 5:

This script is for sellers in a hot area where houses are moving fast.

You: So John, the other agent says they will sell your house for 1% less?"

Prospect: Yes,

You: So John, based on a $300,000 sale price, that's basically $3,000, correct?

Prospect: Yep,

You: "OK, John. I'll go ahead and add that $3,000 onto our list price. So we will start it at $303,000. Let's go ahead and complete the paperwork.

Script 6:

Use this script when competing with a "discount" broker.

You: Martha, my experience shows that discount agents provide the least amount of support in the areas you need them the most. Ask yourself this question: *Why would a heart doctor discount his services?* Generally speaking, it would be because they are either *inexperienced* (and need some patients to practice on), *undesired* or *not 'good enough'* to compete with doctors who charge regular or premium rates. That's the guy you probably don't want operating on you.

Script 7:

This is a variation of the script to use when competing with a "discount" broker.

You: John – I can understand why you are considering hiring a discount agent. Clients hire me because I have a proven track record for success.

You: John, have you ever been to a garage sale?

Prospect: Of course.

You: John... it's unfortunate that discount agents are seen as the *garage sale* of the real estate industry. When agents are out showing prospective buyers homes and they see a discount agent's sign in the yard, they will instinctively want to offer a 'discount price' for that property.

John, let's examine why this is the case.

[Now take off your watch and show it to your client].

You: Take a look at this watch. Now John, what do you think this watch would go for at a fine jewelry store?

Prospect: [Let the seller guess a price].

You: Absolutely, John! This watch would be priced at top dollar, and buyers will gladly pay the price it's offered for, because of the product presentation, the skills of the knowledgeable salesperson, and the perceived quality. Now, let's take that same watch out of the fine jewelry case and put it at a garage sale. Do you think it will sell for the same price it could command from the fine jewelry showcase?

Prospect: Probably not.

You: Right, John... at a garage sale, not only will buyers expect to pay far less for the same watch in the same condition, they will instinctively believe that the watch is *worth* even less than almost *any* price marked on it. That's because the watch is at a *garage sale*. The same effect happens when your home is placed on the market by a discount agent. We call it the *garage sale of the real estate industry*. When you list with me, you will place your property in the fine jewelry showcase where it belongs, and you'll net more than you would save by going with a discount agent. Let's go ahead and move forward, so we can get your house sold!

Q: "What if the seller wants to sell their House FSBO (For Sale by Owner)?"

You: For a variety of reasons, some sellers choose to try and sell their house themselves. It's certainly an option. Unfortunately, the statistical facts prove that homeowners will net *a lot less money, and take a lot longer to sell* when trying to sell their house themselves instead of hiring me to get it SOLD.

286

According to NAR's For Sale By Owner (FSBO) Statistics, 9% of U.S. homes sell FSBO. Knowing what goes into a top-dollar sale, it's not surprising that the data reveals the typical FSBO home sold for 18.65% less than similar properties that were properly marketed and exposed by a licensed REALTOR®.

Let's examine why this is the case. When a person decides to represent themselves in a court of law, the opposing attorney will immediately see an "opportunity." In the same way, prospective buyers will see an opportunity with someone trying to sell their own house.

The #1 reason most sellers try to sell on their own is to get out of paying the agent commission. Because I statistically net 4-5% more for my clients, they would actually lose a great deal of money (and time) trying to sell themselves. Let's take a quick look.

Suppose you decided to sell your house and the agent commission was 6%. Most FSBOs believe they are saving that 6% by selling themselves, but let's look at the facts.

In most cases, the FSBO will agree to pay a 3% (or so) commission to the buyer agent who finds a buyer for the house. This means the 'perceived' savings is now only 3%. However, when you take into account the fact that houses properly marketed statistically generate an 8% or higher sales price, it becomes apparent that selling yourself can actually net you a lot less than hiring me to do everything for you!

Working With a Prospect Who Is Looking to Interview More than One Agent

In Chapter 5 we discussed that, statistically, about 30% of sellers will want to interview more than one agent for the job of selling their house. If you are working with expired sellers, that percentage will be much higher. Whenever you hear that your prospect is considering interviewing more than one agent, you want to make sure they get your Agent Interview Sheet (Chapter 5) in your pre-listing package – preferably before they sit down with the other agents!

Prospect: I'm currently interviewing agents and I'd like to interview your team

You: That's great, Cathy. Let me ask you – what specific criteria are you using to decide which agents you will allow into your house for a sit down interview?

Prospect: uhhh – Well... (pause) I want to make sure they are good and I have to feel comfortable with them.

You: That's great, Cathy! I can appreciate that you want to interview more than one agent because you want to hire the right agent. You know I've found that there are 10 specific questions you should ask any agent before you agree to list your house. In fact – I recommend that you have these questions *over the phone* before you agree to meet with them. Think of this as a job interview process. You don't want to waste your time sitting down with anyone who doesn't meet the qualifications for the job. By the way, Cathy - I've typed up those 10 questions and I can send you a copy. Would that be helpful to you?

Prospect: Absolutely!

You: Great, Kathy. I'll go ahead and email it over to you. It's a handy one page PDF with the top 10 questions and it already contains my answers to those questions. There's also space to write down the other agent's answer. You'll simply let the other agent know that you have a few questions to ask - and that you will get back with them if you would like to meet in person. It's a pretty simple process.

Use the Texas Close

The *Texas Close* is simply to *extend your hand* out for a handshake at the time you are *closing* the seller for signatures.

You: Now, John, did you have any other questions?

John: No I don't think so.

You: Let's go ahead and put me to work John! [Extend your hand for a handshake]

You can use the Texas Close at any point that you feel it is appropriate to close the prospect and move forward with the paperwork. It's powerful!

Wrap Up

Congratulations! Always thank and congratulate your client when they list with you. Let them know that they've made the right decision to hire you, and that you and your team will be taking good care of them.

Now that you've gotten the signatures, let's move on to getting it SOLD! In the next section (Chapters 14-18) we will take a thorough look at what it takes to achieve a successful sale and we will cover Listing Setup, Listing Servicing and Contract to Close.

Chapter 13 Homework

☐ Become extremely familiar with your office's standard Listing Agreement

☐ Role Play the Scripts in this chapter.

☐ Practice and role play the entire listing presentation step by step, until you feel comfortable and confident with it.

☐ Practice doing some Estimated Seller Net Sheets

Section

IV

Selling the Listing

Chapter 14
Preparing Your Listing for Success

You have secured the listing. Yes! Great work. Now you can focus on having the seller get the house ready for the market. Shoot for having the house ready to go on MLS within two weeks or less if possible. In the meantime you can place your sign in the front yard with a *'Coming Soon'* sign rider.

Step 12:
Collect Property Survey

It's a good idea to obtain a copy of the property survey if one is available. The property survey is a diagram or sketch of a property showing the boundary lines (metes and bounds) of the property. The survey also shows the house, fence lines, buildings, pools and other property features. The seller should have a copy of the survey from when they purchased the home. If the seller can't find the survey they can typically try and secure a copy from the archives of the

Title Company or attorney where they closed on the purchase, if it has been less than 10 years or so.

The survey may be required or may need to be reviewed by any potential buyers. However, if any significant improvements have been made to the property (property additions, new fencing, pool, deck, outbuildings), the buyer or seller may need to obtain a new or revised survey.

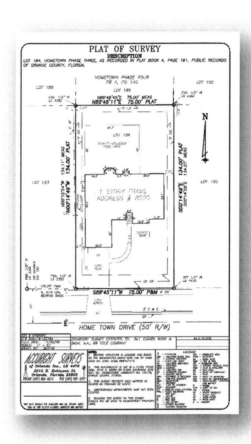

Step 13:
Prepare the House for Sale

Getting the property ready for the market begins with a truthful and honest assessment of the property's current condition. If your clients will be occupying the house during the selling process, you will need to endeavor to strike that delicate balance between the seller's comfort and stellar showcasing.

Houses that are marketed correctly, priced properly and prepped for sale will sell faster than all the others. Proper preparation allows your sellers to sell the house in the least amount of time and for the most money. This winning strategy also results in the least amount of inconvenience to your seller, because their house will only be 'on the market' for a short time (often less than 30 days) before it goes under contract. I never advocate spending a lot of money during this process. Unless the house is in grave disrepair, the time and money your sellers spend to get their house ready for market will typically be nominal.

In my opinion the single most important thing a seller can do in the preparation process is to *de-clutter* the house. Once their house is de-cluttered, the next items are *cleaning* and *painting*. These three items will not cost very much or take much time, but they make a huge difference and help sellers to get top dollar and sell in less time.

Knolly's TOP 3 Tips
to Prep Your Listing
De-clutter • Clean • Paint

 # 1: De-clutter. When you think about the idea of de-cluttering, think of floor space and counter space. Generally, you will want to display the maximum amount of floor space and the maximum amount of countertop space. Ask your seller to look around at the floors and counter spaces (including tabletops, desks, etc) of their house and identify things that don't belong and make these areas as clear as possible. If they have large pieces of furniture that are taking up a big chunk of floor space and can be eliminated, ask them to consider putting those items in storage or storing them in the garage. The more uncluttered and unencumbered floor space the buyer can see, the larger and more inviting the house will feel.

 # 2: Clean. A good deep clean is an absolute necessity after the seller has removed the clutter. This involves cleaning the house both inside and out. The floors, walls, baseboards, doors and all surfaces in the house should be thoroughly cleaned. If possible, the outside of the house and the driveways and walkways should be power washed. When it comes to cleaning, I recommend that my sellers either form a cleaning crew (them and 3 or more friends) or better yet, simply hire a cleaning service. A good deep clean should cost around $150 - $300 or so, depending on the size and condition of your house. If power washing is needed I recommend they hire a reputable contractor.

#3: Paint. Once the house is de-cluttered and clean, it's time to slap on some paint! Ask the seller to take a good look at all of the walls, baseboards, doors, window sills and ceilings around the house. In some cases they will just need to be touched up here and there; other areas will need to be entirely repainted. The seller should be objective and make a list. Then they can decide whether or not they will do the work themselves or hire someone. At $20 or less per gallon, paint is probably the least expensive way to make a dramatic improvement.

Property Repairs

I strongly encourage sellers to complete any minor and cosmetic home repairs that they can afford to. These include things like broken light fixtures, replacing light bulbs, torn screens, cracked caulking, broken tiles, leaking faucets, cracked windows, loose doorknobs, etc.

While most sellers may have been perfectly content to live with these minor items, they are a red flag to prospective homebuyers. Home buyers generally suspect that houses with small items in disrepair will likely have bigger items that have not been addressed. It's fairly easy for the seller to compile a list of things that need to be done and then pay a handyman to complete this list of minor repairs in less than a day. You should compile a list of reputable trades that you can recommend to your sellers. *What if the seller can't afford to do repairs?* No worries. You can simply use my *"As-Is"* pricing strategy from Chapter 13.

Digging Deeper
(Getting a Pre-Inspection)

For sellers who want to go one step further, a pre-sale home inspection can be ordered.

In my real estate practice, I have observed that more houses fall out of contract due to the results of the home inspection than for any other reason. For houses that are older than 10 years, getting a pre-sale home inspection is a good idea. The cost will generally be around $300 to $400. The inspection report will uncover any minor or major issues with the house and your seller should consider this a small investment to pay to protect themselves from the potential of a large future disappointment. Even if your sellers do not plan to fix the items uncovered in a home inspection report, just knowing and disclosing what the issues are will gain them a leg up in the negotiating process.

Staging

While de-cluttering, cleaning, painting and minor repairs will *prepare* the house for sale, staging is the process of *showcasing* the house for sale. According to a study conducted by the Real Estate Staging Association (RESA) homes that previously failed to sell, sold in 73% less time after they were professionally staged. The study was conducted with 174 vacant and occupied houses. Those homes averaged 156 days on the market without a contract before the homeowners decided to have them professionally staged. After staging, those same homes sold in an average of 42 days.

Another study by RESA of 410 professionally staged homes concluded that these homes sold 79% faster than similar houses that were not staged.

7 Seller Benefits to Staging Your Home

1. Professionally staged homes present and show better than competing houses for sale, including new construction homes and higher-priced houses.

2. Staged properties will sell faster when compared with houses that have not been staged. From the date of listing until the day of closing, home staging shortens this time frame, even in a slow real estate market.

3. Staged properties can increase the number of offers and selling price in hot markets.

4. Buyers view professionally staged listings as "well-maintained".

5. Buyers' agents recognize that professionally staged listings are "move-in" ready and are inclined to show staged properties.

6. Photos of professionally staged listings look better on the MLS, as well as in print.

7. Professionally staged listings "STAND-OUT" in prospective buyers' minds.

(Source: Real Estate Staging Association)

**You Can Use the Following
Top Tips Checklist for Your Sellers...**

Top Tips on Selling Your Home
(A Complete Checklist for Sellers)

The First Impression Counts... Make it a Positive One!

When you begin preparing your home, begin outside and work your way in. Make up a "to do" list as you go along keeping in mind the importance of first impressions.

EXTERIOR TIPS

It's estimated that more than half of all houses are SOLD before buyers even get out of their cars. Stand across the street from your home and review its "curb appeal". What can you do to improve the very first impression?

☐ Keep sidewalks and patios hosed off. Hose down house siding to remove cobwebs and dirt. Hose down your garage and clean your driveway of any grease spots. A garage can be an important selling point for your home, and a good spraying with a garden hose and just a drop of industrial strength cleaner can make a big difference.

☐ Mow, trim, weed, and water lawns and gardens. Add a fresh layer of mulch or gravel if needed and plant flowers for color.

☐ The front door is one of the first things prospective buyers see. If it shows signs of wear — clean it, stain, it, or paint it.

☐ Make sure the doorbell and porch lights work.

☐ Remove trash and debris from the yard and around house.

- [ ] Remove extra vehicles from view.
- [ ] Repair any fences or gates.
- [ ] Remove holiday lights that may still be hanging.
- [ ] Paint exterior window sashes, trim, and shutters (repainting the entire exterior can be an expensive and unnecessary venture — unless there is bad blistering or peeling.).
- [ ] Apply fresh paint or stain to wooden fences.
- [ ] Buy a new welcome mat.
- [ ] Place potted flowers near the door.
- [ ] Clean windows inside and out.
- [ ] Power wash the home's exterior.
- [ ] Ensure gutters and downspouts are firmly attached and functioning.

INTERIOR TIPS

When showing your house to prospective buyers you want to make everything look spacious, organized, bright, warm, and "homey." Start with a full housecleaning from top to bottom. Don't let dirt and clutter obscure your home's good points. A clean home will sell a lot faster than a dirty one.

- [ ] Be sure walls are clean and free of dirt and fingerprints — consider a fresh coat of paint if washing doesn't do the trick.
- [ ] Wash all windows and sills.
- [ ] Curtains and drapes should be freshly cleaned.
- [ ] Arrange furniture to make rooms appear spacious and attractive.
- [ ] Evaluate the furniture in each room and remove anything that interrupts the flow or makes the room

appear smaller. Consider renting a storage unit to move the items off-site.

☐ Clean all light fixtures and ceiling fans.

☐ Have carpets cleaned.

☐ Make minor repairs.

☐ Replace any burned-out light bulbs. You can make rooms seem warmer and brighter by using high intensity light bulbs that give the house a warm glow.

☐ Discard or replace any dying houseplants.

KITCHEN & BATH TIPS

The bathrooms and kitchen are focal points for most buyers. Be sure those rooms are clean and clear of clutter.

☐ Clear extra appliances, accessories, etc. from counters.

☐ Polish sinks and remove stains.

☐ Clean appliances thoroughly inside and out.

☐ Straighten and remove excess papers from kitchen memo area.

☐ Clean out your cabinets and drawers and add shelf paper and utensil trays to make them look as organized as possible.

☐ Buy a new shower curtain.

UNCLUTTERING TIPS

Eliminating clutter will give your house a more spacious look. By removing or storing things you don't need, you create a roomy, comfortable feeling that will be inviting to prospective buyers. If a house is too cluttered, buyers have trouble imagining themselves and their belongings in it. Remember, when in doubt—move it out!

☐ Clean out closets to display their roominess. Prospective buyers love to inspect for storage space, so it's important to make whatever closets you have look as spacious as possible. Another trick is to clear the floor space in closets. This simple strategy will make the closet 'appear' as large as possible.

☐ Be sure clothes are hung neatly and shoes and other objects are neatly arranged. If something you have stored away hasn't been worn or used in the last year, chances are it never will be. Give it away, sell it, or pack it neatly in a box and store it in the garage.

☐ Have a garage sale! Not only will you be reducing clutter, but you can use the money you earn to finance your touch-ups.

☐ Straighten bookshelves and remove unnecessary papers from coffee tables.

☐ In children's rooms, straighten or store extra toys and remove distracting posters. Arrange toys to look fun and inviting, open a book on a night stand, add a flowering plant and arrange decorative pillows or shams on the bed.

☐ If you have a spare room or storage area, turn it into an area with a purpose. If it's too small to be a bedroom, turn it into a hobby center, study or office.

☐ Again, consider renting storage space to move out items you won't need before you move.

CLEANING TIPS

When a house is clean, it gives the impression that it has been well cared for. Some fresh paint and a one-time professional cleaning service can make your house look like new.

Be sure every room smells as good as it looks, paying special attention to pet areas, children's nurseries and bathrooms.

- ☐ Polish all brass and chrome fixtures.
- ☐ Polish mirrors so they sparkle.
- ☐ Scrub and wax floors.
- ☐ Have carpets professionally cleaned and deodorized.
- ☐ Clean and deodorize garbage areas.
- ☐ Clean sliding door track so that the door moves quietly and smoothly.

REPAIRING TIPS

Making little repairs can make a big difference. Although many families learn to live with a broken doorknob or a cracked window—all of these little things should be fixed when selling your house. The savvy homeowner concentrates his efforts on cosmetic repairs that cost relatively little but return a lot on the investment (don't forget those first impressions!).

- ☐ Repair leaking faucets, running toilets, grout, and caulking as needed.
- ☐ Replace any cracked windows and torn screens.
- ☐ Patch and paint wall and ceiling cracks.
- ☐ Repair or replace loose doorknobs, drawer pulls, sticking doors and windows, warped drawers, cabinet handles, towel racks, switch plates and outlet covers.
- ☐ Tack down any loose molding and glue down any lifted wallpaper.

NEUTRALIZING

Try to create an appearance that allows the buyers to picture themselves living there. Neutral paint, décor and carpeting create a home for any lifestyle.

- ☐ Eliminate distracting colors and accessories so that buyers can concentrate on positive impressions.

- [ ] Brighten things with fresh paint. White, off-white, or beige walls make a room look bigger and lighter. Interior painting costs very little and it can make a big difference in a buyer's perception—so go ahead and do it.

DON'T OVER IMPROVE

- [ ] Preparing your house for sale doesn't need to be expensive or time-consuming as long as you keep up with normal maintenance. In the event you do not have the time to do the cleaning or repair work, consider hiring a professional; it could save you time and money later. And a few hundred dollars well spent can be the best investment you'll ever make. *Remember, you need to think like a buyer now and have a critical eye.*

- [ ] Use caution in planning any major improvements that you think will enable you to get more for the house. Most people shopping for a house would rather plan their own major changes, and you are usually wiser to sell them the *potential* at a price they can afford.

- [ ] Just before placing it on the market make sure that the homeowner prep is complete. Do another walk-through of the house making sure that everything is in 'show-ready' condition.

Step 14: Set Up the Property

Once the property is ready to begin marketing, it's time to do the *property setup*. Property setup includes placement of the sign and lockbox and taking the property photos.

We use an electronic lockbox because it tracks each agent that goes into the house. This tracking is essential for collecting *showing feedback*. I also recommend you use a large sign with your photo and/or logo prominently displayed. Remember we are branding and marketing here so each sign is making an impression. Your well-placed sign is branding you to the neighborhood and surrounding area and can help generate more listings for you.

Step 15: Order Professional Photography

I learned about the importance of hiring a professional photographer when I hired my first team Listing Specialist, Susan Pray *(yes, her real name)*. At the time I had already taken hundreds of listings, but was doing all the photography myself. Susan encouraged me to consider hiring a pro. At first I thought the suggestion didn't make sense because my photos looked all right, and I couldn't understand spending money on hiring a professional when I already had a cool digital camera. But I decided to give it a try, and boy, was I impressed.

If you've ever wondered how top agents get those crystal clear listing photos with fantastic lighting and angles, it's typically because they hire a pro. Likewise, I highly recommend that you order professional photography on your listings (unless you are an exceptional photographer and have really good equipment). A professional photo shoot will cost roughly $80-$150.

Aside from price, I am convinced that great photos can do more to drive traffic through a listing than anything else.

I consider bad photos (or a lack of photos) as one of the top reasons why homes don't sell. I recommend that you include 25 to 40 great looking photos. If the house is small, have your photographer take pictures of the larger rooms from multiple angles, so that you can end up with a larger collection of good photos.

If the house is a *fixer-upper, short sale, as-is sale* or a *distress sale* with below-market pricing, then you can save the photography fee and take the photos yourself because your aggressive pricing will drive traffic through the listing.

A nice 60-second video walkthrough is also a good idea and you can do this yourself or better yet, you can partner with a professional videographer. A nice collection of great property videos will also help to establish you as the neighborhood expert in your farm.

Sample Listing Video Script

You: Hi there, Sandy Jones here at The Jones Team - your Brushy Creek area expert! I'm back with another fantastic listing ... let's take a quick look around...

[Meanwhile walk through the listing pointing out some of the key features]

Step 16: Write the Property Description

In the marketing business we call the property description *ad copy*. If you are not skilled at writing great property descriptions you can work on getting better at it or simply delegate the task to someone else.

When writing the property description it is important to remember that you are not just providing basic information, you are trying to *SELL* the property. Many of the property descriptions that you find on MLS are sorely lacking. They are not creative at all and they don't pique the buyer's interest.

If you want to maximize the number of showings you get on your listings you will want to make sure that your properties have these three ingredients: 1) the right price, 2) great photos and 3) a compelling property description.

When writing your property description be sure to use the Seller's Homework (chapter 5) as a guide to the features, amenities and benefits of the property and the area.

Sample of a Standard Property Description:

3 BR, 2 BA home - 1703 square feet. Tile and wood floors with granite countertops. Stainless appliances and big master bedroom. Nice backyard with lots of plants.

Sample of an *Improved* Property Description:

This is an immaculate and impressive home nestled on a quiet cul-de-sac lot. There are three large bedrooms and two full baths. Home has designer-grade porcelain tile and hand-scraped seven-inch hickory hardwood flooring throughout. The chef's kitchen boasts a stainless appliance package, cherry wood cabinets and beautiful exotic granite. The oversized master suite has 11 foot ceilings, a gigantic walk-in closet and a luxurious master bath that must be seen to be appreciated. You can linger for hours in the English style garden. This home offers comfort and relaxation. Come see!

Property Directions

The property directions that you include on MLS should be clear, concise, straightforward and without error.

Sample Property Directions:

From IH-35: E on Palm Valley (exit 253) > travel approx 2 miles > left at Provident Lane > left at Yorkshire > home is on the right.

Send the Seller a Copy of the Listing Docs

Be sure to send the seller a complete copy of all the documents they signed as soon as possible. You can scan and send them via email as a PDF attachment or you can provide a downloadable link to the docs in your transaction management system. At the Knolly Team we use the *Transaction Manager* in our MoreSolds.com CRM to simply upload the documents and provide our sellers with login access.

You also need to turn these documents in to your broker through whatever preferred method your office uses.

Step 17: Input the Listing to MLS

When having your Admin input the property into the MLS system be sure they take their time and include as many of the features and benefits of the home as possible. Your Admin will use the *Property Information Sheet* from the Seller's Homework in your prelisting package (chapter 5). Be sure to peruse the document to insure that it is accurate.

Step 18: Upload Docs to MLS

If your MLS allows you to upload documents, you should upload all important docs like the property survey, available home inspection reports, floor plans, property reports, any required disclosures, etc. These documents will be available for buyer's agents and will greatly reduce the amount of time that your Admin will need to spend manually sending requested documentation or answering questions.

Step 19: Upload Photos to MLS

Add as many property photos as you are allowed to in your MLS. Also – be sure to add the property photos at the same time you place the property *Active* on MLS. Most of the large and popular search sites (REALTOR.com, Zillow, Trulia, etc) have a linked data feed to your MLS. If you wait even a few hours to add the photos to MLS it may take some time for the listing to update and for the photos to populate to some third party sites.

Step 20: Review the Listing and Make it Active (GO LIVE!)

One of the key benefits of the Seller Homework packet is that it contains a checklist of all the features and benefits of the house, so that nothing is overlooked. Double check all of the details before making your listing Active.

Check the square footage

One critical detail is square footage. It is quite possible that some of the information listed in the tax record is not current. I've had many instances where the square footage of the house was several hundred feet more than tax record showed. This can especially be true for newly-built homes because the builder will generally submit an *approximate* square footage when the building plans are drafted up but may end up with a larger square footage after the construction is complete. Ask the seller for a copy of their most recent appraisal, as this may contain a more accurate and current square footage. If the seller has done any additions to the property (added heated and cooled space), be sure the additions are also included in the square footage as well.

Handling Showings

It is important for your sellers to make the house as convenient and easy to show as possible. If the house is vacant, this will obviously be stress-free, since buyers can view the house without notice and your sellers don't have to prep for every showing. If the house is occupied, providing buyers with a hassle-free showing process will be a bit more challenging.

Be sure that your sellers understand how important it is to try and accommodate any potential showings (within reason).

You: Tim and Karen, please keep in mind that when buyers are out looking at properties, they may be viewing several houses that particular day. That's because most buyers view houses in *"batches"* (3 today in your area and 4 tomorrow in another area). If they are asking to view your house at a particular time it usually means that they will be in your area within that timeframe. If you do not allow your house to be one of the properties viewed, it may be eliminated from their list.

This is why I always recommend that although it may be inconvenient, you should allow your house to be viewed (and be prepped for viewings) whenever possible and within reason.

If your sellers have circumstances that do not allow them to leave their house quickly (disability, work from home, take care of an elderly parent or small children, etc), you can place special instructions under private remarks on MLS like: *"Seller requests 2 hour notice prior to showing."*

Showing with Renters

I have found that properties currently rented create a unique set of challenges when it comes to showing. Tenants are often uncomfortable about the idea of allowing the property to be shown and they can make the showing process more arduous. If buyers are having a difficult time getting in to see the property, you will have a difficult time getting it sold.

My advice is to enlist the cooperation of the tenants. Ask the seller to offer the tenant some kind of incentive for cooperating during the showing process. Perhaps the seller can give them $20 off their rent for every showing, or something creative like that.

Another challenge to showing a tenant-occupied property is that the tenants will likely not have the house in *"show"* condition because they are not personally vested in the successful sale of the property. In some cases they could even be working against you if selling the home has a negative impact on their moving timeframe. Again, my advice is to ask the seller to seek the cooperation of their tenant. Have your seller give the tenants your checklist of tips for showing the house and offer them an incentive for their cooperation.

You Can Use the Following
Showing Checklist for Your Sellers...

Top Tips on Showing
Your House

When it's time for a buyer's agent to show your house, all your preparations will be worth the effort. Here are a few tips that can add that extra touch.

☐ Send children and pets outdoors to play. This will eliminate confusion and keep the prospect's attention focused on your house.

☐ The television and radio should be turned off. Let the buyer's agent and buyer talk free of disturbances.

☐ Be absent during showings. Many prospects feel like intruders when owners/occupants are present. They tend to hurry away or fail to ask their agent the questions they'd really like to ask. Your absence will put buyers at ease and give them a chance to spend more time looking at your house and absorbing its advantages.

☐ Leave drapes open for light and airiness. If it's evening, all lights should be turned on to give the rooms a larger appearance and a cheerful effect.

☐ Be sure the kitchen sink is free of dishes and rooms are uncluttered. Make sure trash baskets are empty.

☐ Make sure rugs are clean and straight. Set a comfortable temperature. Do a "once-over" cleaning—vacuum, sweep, and dust. Final check every room.

☐ If you are at home during the showing, be courteous but don't force conversation with the potential buyer. They want to inspect your house not pay a social call.

☐ Open windows to freshen rooms. Set tables with flowers and linens.

☐ Never apologize for the appearance of your home— after all, it has been lived in.

☐ The buyer's agent knows the buyer's requirements and can better emphasize the features of your house when you don't follow along. You will be called if needed.

☐ Let me discuss price, terms, possession and other factors with the customer. I am better qualified to bring negotiations to a favorable conclusion.

☐ If buyers just drop by and aren't accompanied by a real estate agent, it's best not to show your home. Ask for their names and phone number, and provide it to us for follow-up. (Most agents screen clients so you don't waste time showing to someone who isn't qualified or worse, a potential burglar).

☐ I use an electronic key box system that agents must access in order to obtain the key. This key box records which agent showed your house (and the exact time and date), so that I can track all showings and request feedback.

Chapter 14 Homework

☐ Role Play the Scripts in this chapter.

☐ Set up a test transaction in MoreSolds or your preferred CRM.

☐ Find a great local photographer and videographer to partner with.

Chapter 15

Systematize and Automate Your Listing for Success

Those who know me best know that I am absolutely in love with systems and automation. It appears to me that God loves systems and automation too. Every day God uses systems and automation to run the universe. Every day the sun rises, flowers bloom, the stars illuminate the night sky and the world turns. All of this happens through systems and automation. God set up the system once, and it continues to run in perpetuity.

To become a highly successful Listing Specialist you will need to utilize systems and automation in your business. Systems and automation will allow you to run a larger operation more efficiently than you ever thought possible with much less effort.

In the old days, most of the tasks associated with servicing a real estate listing had to be done manually. Thankfully, today's technology allows us to do many of the redundant tasks involved in a transaction through automation.

In this chapter I will show you how to systematize and automate the majority of the tasks associated with the servicing of your listing.

Step 21: Set Up the Listing in Your Database and Start the Transaction

You previously added your seller to your database (step 4). Now you simply need to enter the listing into your database under the contact record of your seller.

When inputting the listing you will be adding all of its pertinent details (property address, MLS number, listing photo, prospect details, etc).

Once you have added the listing to your CRM you will initiate the online transaction for the listing.

Step 22: Initiate and Invite Seller to the Online Transaction

I'm a big fan of keeping an open line of communication with the seller throughout the entire listing process. This is why I recommend that you set up a *Transaction* file in your CRM as soon as you take the listing rather than waiting until the property goes under contract. Be sure that you use an online CRM that has *transaction management* with a built in client login portal. That way you can invite your client to log in and see the progress of the transaction from the very beginning. Your seller will never be in the dark! Plus, by using a virtual system you will save hours of time that would otherwise be spent on the phone or emailing a client with status updates.

The *Transactions* section of MoreSolds will allows you to invite your seller to a transaction. Once invited, the seller receives an email with their login credentials (user name and password).

All you have to do is direct your sellers to use your online system. Once they begin using it regularly they will love it – because they can login any time of day or night and see the progress of their home sale in *real time*, without having to contact you or your team. In this age where we *Google* everything, more and more sellers want access to tools that allow them to quickly receive information without having to contact anyone directly.

Forcing your clients to manually go through you or someone on your team for information is terribly inefficient and it makes you a cog in the wheel. You become the *bottleneck* in the process. Clients love having a system where they can simply login and obtain the information they need, whenever they want.

You can add notes, upload documents, add tasks, add important dates and assign complete action plans to a transaction. Once the property goes under contract you can assign additional closing parties (buyer's agent, escrow officer, attorneys, etc) each with their own unique login access. We will discuss more about this in chapter 18.

As you can see, the old days of calling or emailing sellers to *try* and keep them up-to-date on what's happening throughout the life of a transaction are long gone. That system is outdated. Sellers want instant information and giving them access to the transaction from the very beginning is a win-win.

Sample Email – Invitation to View a Transaction

Subject: Knolly Williams has invited you to view a Transaction

Dear Simon,

I would like to invite you to view an online Transaction. Simply click on this link and login using the following information:

Login: knolly2

Password: starfish108

NOTE: Please save this login and password information so that you can follow the progress of this transaction. If you want to change the password for this login, please reply to this email with a request to change.

Step 23: Set Up an Action Plan for Your Listing

An action plan is a recurring set of tasks or activities. In your CRM you can assign an action plan to a transaction and it will serve as a *virtual checklist*. The system will even track your percentage of completion!

321

Whenever you set up a new listing or perform contract-to-close on a property you are often performing the same set of tasks each time. You can create an action plan to serve as a checklist for the series of tasks you need to perform. MoreSolds and many popular CRMs have this feature built in. The action plan serves as a virtual to-do list. Another cool feature about using an online CRM is that each task within an action plan can be assigned to a different team member.

Your client should be able to login and see the status of the various tasks that have been completed on their behalf and which tasks are upcoming or outstanding. By logging into their client portal of your CRM your sellers can easily see that you are working hard on getting their property sold. This eliminates any questions about what you are doing and also eradicates any doubt in the seller's mind that you are "on the case."

Once you set up the transaction in your CRM you want to initiate your New Listing action plan.

Sample New Listing Action Plan

Type	Task	Delay Days	Assigned To
To Do	Verify that all listing docs are signed	0	Barbara Riordan
To Do	Review Seller Homework	1	Linda Smith
Email	Obtain Survey from Seller	2	Barbara Riordan
Travel Required	Place Sign and Lockbox	2	Linda Smith
Call	Order Professional Photography	3	Barbara Riordan
To Do	Write Property Description	3	Knolly Williams
To Do	Input Property to MLS	3	Barbara Riordan

To Do	Upload Docs to MLS	3	Barbara Riordan
To Do	Upload Photos to MLS	3	Barbara Riordan
Important	Review the Listing and Make it ACTIVE	3	Barbara Riordan
To Do	Initiate Marketing Plan	3	Knolly Williams
To Do	Setup Listing in MoreSolds and Begin Transaction	2	Barbara Riordan
To Do	Setup Electronic Showing Feedback	3	Barbara Riordan
To Do	Invite Seller to Transaction	3	Barbara Riordan
To Do	Assign New Listing Email Campaign	3	Barbara Riordan

Step 24. Initiate Marketing Plan for Your Listing

Now it's time to go ahead and initiate the marketing plan for your listing. To systematize the process, your Marketing Plan will need to be converted into an Action Plan. Your marketing action plan will keep you on track with all of the marketing items that need to be done so that nothing is overlooked.

In chapter 13 I outlined the marketing plan that we use at The Knolly Team. You can either adopt my marketing plan verbatim or make whatever tweaks you want to it, thereby creating your own tweaked and unique version. Once your marketing plan is complete, it will also become part of your pre-listing package (Chapter 5).

To convert your current marketing plan into a *marketing* action plan, you will now simply take the individual items in your marketing plan and place them into an action plan that you can initiate in your CRM. Once you have created a *New Listing Marketing Action Plan,* you can assign the plan to a transaction with just a few key strokes.

As your sellers log into their client portal they will absolutely love seeing that you are following through on your promise to effectively market their property. Don't let technology fool you. Although it may appear slightly complex and complicated, once in place your system will be surprisingly easy to implement and use on a daily basis.

Sample New Listing Marketing Action Plan			
Type	**Task**	**Delay Days**	**Assigned To**
Field	Sign Placed and Verified	0	Linda Smith
To Do	Add Direct Dial Number Sign Rider	1	Linda Smith
To Do	Assign 24 Hour Text Code	2	Barbara Riordan
To Do	Full Color Virtual Flyers	2	Barbara Riordan
To Do	Add to Brokerage Websites	3	Barbara Riordan
To Do	Add to National Channel Partners	3	Barbara Riordan
To Do	Add to Affiliate Channel Partners	3	Barbara Riordan
To Do	Add to Regional Channel Partners	3	Barbara Riordan
To Do	Add to Craigslist	4	Noemi De La Cruz
To Do	Search Engine Optimization (SEO)	4	Noemi De La Cruz
To Do	Add to all Social Media	4	Meylan Evangelio
To Do	Send Just Listed Cards	4	Barbara Riordan
To Do	Place Real Estate Magazine Ad	4	Barbara Riordan
To Do	Database Mailing	7	Barbara Riordan
To Do	Private Client Login Portal Assigned	3	Barbara Riordan
To Do	'Featured Listing' Exposure	3	Knolly Williams
Call	Professional Photographs Taken	4	David Lemons

To Do	Virtual/Video Tour	4	David Lemons
Email	Monthly eNewsletter Sent	7	Chris Capistrano
To Do	Added to Electronic Feedback System	3	Barbara Riordan
To Do	Brokerage Marketing	2	Noemi De La Cruz
To Do	MLS Marketing	2	Noemi De La Cruz

Step 25: Set up Electronic Showing Feedback

Providing your seller clients with actionable feedback on their property showings is essential to gaining and maintaining a good reputation, and to generating referrals. In fact, one of the biggest complaints that sellers have is that they don't hear from the listing agent *regularly*. By providing showing feedback *your sellers will automatically hear from you every time the property is shown.*

Your clients expect and deserve to know what potential buyers are saying about their house. Using a showing feedback system shows your clients that you are working hard to sell their house, resulting in better communication, much greater customer satisfaction and easier price adjustments. The more information you and your client have, the faster you will get their house sold and the more referrals you will receive as a result.

To solicit feedback from the showing agent I recommend that you use an electronic showing feedback survey system. In my experience *calling* a showing agent on the phone is *not* an effective method because most agents are too busy to call you back and many of the ones that do answer will not remember exactly which house you are talking about – especially if they showed several houses that afternoon. Using an electronic feedback system allows the showing agent to preview a photo of the house to jog their memory. The system emails the showing agent a showing survey with up to 10 questions that are all multiple-choice. The showing survey only takes the showing agent about 20 to 30 seconds to complete online and a copy of the showing results are emailed to you and your client immediately.

There are several good showing feedback software products out there. Again, we created and use MoreSolds CRM which has showing feedback built in.

Showing Survey Request Sent to Showing Agent

Knolly Williams
The Knolly Team
512-206-0060
THE
KN♦LLY
TEAM

Hi Ronald,

Thank you for showing the property at 108 Acapulco Ct., Austin, TX.

Please fill out this simple showing survey. It will take less than 30 seconds and my seller and I appreciate you doing this and I will gladly return the favor. Be as honest and straight forward as possible!

110 Acapulco Circle
Austin, TX 78746
MLS#: 8576648
Click Here to View
Virtual Tour

Powered by

moresolds.com

Did your buyers like the home?
- Yes
- Somewhat
- No

What did you think of the price?
- Priced Correctly
- Should be 5% lower
- Should be 10% lower

Is your buyer considering making an offer?
- Yes
- Possibly
- No

Are they considering a second showing?
- Yes
- Possibly
- No

Rate the exterior
- Good
- Average
- Poor

Rate the interior
- Good
- Average
- Poor

How is the buyer's search progressing?
- Still looking
- Buyer found a comparable home for less
- Finding lots of homes in the area for less
- This one is at the top of our list

Completed Showing Survey Sent to Seller

Knolly Williams
The Knolly Team
512-206-0060

Hi Nancy,

Below is a new showing survey from Ronald Jones regarding your property at 108 Acapulco Ct.

110 Acapulco Circle
Austin, TX 78746
MLS#: 8576648

Click Here to View
Virtual Tour

Powered by
moresolds.com

Your Showing Survey Results:

Q. Did your buyers like the home?
A. Somewhat

Q. What do you think of the price?
A. Should be 5% lower

Q. Are they considering a second showing?
A. Possibly

Q. Are they considering making an offer?
A. Possibly

Q. Rate the exterior
A. Good

Q. Rate the interior
A. Good

Q. How is buyer's search progressing?
A. This one is at the top of our list

Comment
Nice house! Carpet needs a little updating. It's at the top of my buyer's list and we may be making an offer!

Step 26: Set Up "Weekly Update" Email Drip Campaign to Seller with Link to Your CRM

Drip email campaigns are an absolute Godsend. Drip email allows you to send automated emails to your clients and prospects on a pre-specified timetable. Let's face it – becoming a successful Listing Specialist means you will be busy. Sometimes being busy leads to extended periods of time when you don't talk with your clients. When clients don't hear from you they assume that you are not working hard on their behalf. By utilizing email drip campaigns in your business your clients will never again complain about your lack of communication. You simply assign them to the automated email campaign and you're done.

Automation helps to streamline, leverage and systematize your business. When utilizing automated email drip campaigns – it is important to make your messages short, relevant and somewhat informal. The message should appear as if you sat down and quickly typed it up at that moment.

I recommend that you assign an email campaign to your seller clients as soon as you take the listing or as soon as you place it on the market.

Here is the email campaign we use:

Email #	Email Subject/Template	Send After (days)
	New Listing Email Campaign	
1	Thanks for Listing With Us	0
2	Some Seller Tips to Improve Our Sales Odds	4
3	Selling Your House – 1 Week Update	7
4	Selling Your House – 2 Week Update	14
5	Selling Your House – 3 Week Update	21
6	Selling Your House – 30 Day Update	30
7	Selling Your House – 6 Week Update	42
8	Selling Your House – 60 Day Update	60
9	Selling Your House – 10 Week Update	70
10	Selling Your House – 11 Week Update	77
11	Selling Your House – 12 Week Update	84
12	Selling Your House – 90 Day Update	90

Email #1 – Send as soon as the house is on MLS

Subject: Thanks for Listing with Us

Dear Nancy,

I am writing to express my sincere gratitude to you for allowing The Knolly Team to represent you in the sale of your house. I am certainly aware that you have many choices available to you and I am delighted that you decided to go with us. As you know, we are one of the top 10 real estate teams in Central Texas and we hope to continue that tradition with your listing.

This letter serves as my commitment to you. I pledge that we will do everything within our power to accomplish your objectives during the sale of your house. As you know, we have many resources in our arsenal, and we are going to use them all.

I personally handle the marketing of your house using our comprehensive marketing plan. From time to time, I will be sending you emails to update you on the progress of your property sale. You also will be getting feedback emails from agents who show your house.

If you have any questions or suggestions, please do not hesitate to call or email me.

Additionally you can login to access the status of your transaction 24/7 through my online Transaction Management System. Your login credentials were sent in a separate email.

Thanks again Nancy,

Email #2 – Send after 4 days

Subject: Some Seller Tips to Improve Our Sales Odds

Hi Nancy,

I hope all is well. Things are really busy around here! Seems like we've been working late almost every day this week! Houses are selling...and I can't wait to sell yours! :-)

I came across this article some time ago and thought it may be of interest to you...

- - - - - -

10 Home Seller Tips (ARTICLE)

There are, of course, many items which influence a sale. Look upon the following as a checklist of items which will bring you closer to a sale. Every item on which you are unwilling or unable to make a concession moves you further away from a sale.

1. Price the property to SELL. Overpricing your house will not help it compete against similar houses priced at market value. Be willing to consider ANY offer at any time. Remember, you are always the final judge of what's accepted and what's not!

2. Clear the clutter. Make sure your house shows its wide open spaces, free of clutter. This will allow the buyer to better visualize the possibilities. Eliminate any barrier to the free flow of traffic in the property. Such items as bulky or extra furniture; house plants that stick out into traffic paths; toys or clothes not put away; and beds not made, etc., slow down traffic and make rooms look smaller and darker.

3. Keep it clean. Keeping the appearance of your house neat and clean is a must. Remember, you are not only competing against other resale houses on the market, but you may also be competing against new builder properties. Showing your house in its best light will allow you to compete and win!

4. Show it now. If possible, allow the property to be shown with or without an appointment! That's a nuisance, but it's not as bad as being on the market for 6 months!

5. Keep Away. Please be gone whenever a prospective buyer wants to see the house, and

STAY gone until they're gone! Buyers need to "try it on for size," but they can't do that as long as you are there.

6. Mind the Pets. Watchdogs that provide so much security that no one can see the property without a death wish are a problem. Keep pets from disturbing potential buyers by restricting them to the backyard or an alternate location, such as a friend's house, while the house is being shown.

7. Heed your agent's advice. Your real estate agent is on your side and won't get paid until YOU GET RESULTS. Advice from a professional is useless unless you take it!

8. Curb Appeal. Look at the front of your house. Size it up objectively and critically (that's asking a LOT of any home owner!). Ask yourself this question: if a buyer pulled up in front, would the appearance pull them inside?

9. Do basic improvements. Make any and all recommended improvements with an eye toward neutrals—be aware of unusual colors or styles which might clash with a prospective buyer's taste. Minor things like touching up paint, cleaning the carpet, and doing a deep clean, don't cost much—but can go a long way toward getting your house sold.

10. Leave the negotiations to your agent. Let your agent discuss the selling price, terms and other factors with the customer. Never apologize for the appearance of your house. Should any objections or derogatory comments be offered, let your agent answer them. Let your agent emphasize the virtues of your house to potential buyers. If you can help with any questions, your agent will call you.

- - - - - -

Hope this article helps! Call or email us with any questions.

Email #3 – Send after 7 days

Subject: Selling Your House – 1 Week Update

Hey Nancy,

I'm just checking in with you to let you know we are deeply engrossed in the task of getting your house sold. At this point, all of our marketing objectives have already been initiated. You can rest assured that all of the agents in our market are aware of your property.

Many of these agents have already notified the buyers they are working with about your property. That's good, because Linda and I appreciate whatever help we can get in getting your house sold.

Also, it's good for you to know that we use the very latest marketing tools and techniques, particularly the Internet. Since your house hit the MLS, it has been updated to hundreds of Web sites worldwide.

As always, I'll keep you posted along the way.

Email #4 – Send after 14 days

Subject: Selling Your House – 2 Week Update

Hey there Nancy,

We've been on the market for almost two weeks. Of course, I wish I was writing to say

"Congratulations, it's SOLD!" But that's not the case—at least, not yet!

You can rest assured that we are making use of the very best tools and techniques in the real estate industry to help us promote your property. We've already done some initial market testing, and we are confident that folks know about your property.

The two key tools that sell houses are 1) *marketing* (also known as *creating awareness*), and 2) *price*. Of course, marketing is what we have control over, and price is controlled by the market. I want you to get every dollar coming to you! However, we've noticed that several houses like yours have sold since we took your listing, and some of these were more competitively priced.

Let us know your thoughts. We'll keep plugging away!

Thanks again Nancy,

Email #5 – Send after 21 days

Subject: Selling Your House – 3 Week Update

Hi Nancy,

How is everything on your end? I was going through my daily routine of reviewing our "Active Homes" inventory today and I noticed that it has now been right about 21 days since your house went on the market.

At this point, we would love to be moving toward a closing date with a solid contract on your property.

Remember when I mentioned to you that there were TWO things that sell houses: 1)

Marketing and 2) Price? Well, I'm going to keep marketing your house like crazy in order to get it SOLD! But remember, the market dictates the price.

I have found that when our listings have been on the market for this long without selling, they usually fall into one of two categories:

1. Getting no or very few showings: this can indicate that the agents in our market believe the house is overpriced and are not bringing their clients out to see it.

2. Getting showings, but no offers: this can indicate that the home is catching the buyer's eye, but after viewing, they believe it is overpriced – or they are finding similar homes for less.

This is just something to consider. As experts in this market, we pride ourselves in getting our client's houses SOLD quickly and at a competitive market price. You can rest assured that we am doing everything within our power to add yours to our list of SOLDs.

Please don't hesitate to contact us if you have any questions or suggestions.

Thanks again Nancy,

Email #6 – Send after 30 days

Subject: Selling Your House– 30 Day Update

Hi Nancy,

As promised, I am just checking in to assure you that my team is actively on the job of selling your house. The good thing for both of us is that we don't tire easily. We will press on until the mission is accomplished.

I take very seriously the mandate you first gave us – "get it SOLD!" – and we are doing everything we can to do just that. We sure wish we had more control over this market! I also wish that I could once and for all "convince" buyers that your house is the one they've been looking for!

Your house has been marketed vigorously and I have cast it in the best light possible. But alas, we are at the mercy of the market...and it seems buyers have a lot of houses to choose from in the Austin area.

You know how it is when you go to buy something important and you are presented with a lot of choices. Some buyers simply gridlock and don't make a decision at all (they wait). Others look for the best price. Still others look for a combination of price and features, etc. In every case, price is usually a factor.

And even though there are lots of houses to pick from, a buyer can only choose one! It makes me sad when ours is not the one they choose, but I still remain confident that there is a buyer out there who will bite! And my job, of course, is to make our product (your house) as appealing as possible. We do this through marketing the property and offering a competitive price.

We'll get in touch with you as soon as I have something more to report. Let us know if you have any suggestions.

Thanks Nancy,

Email #7 – Send after 42 days

Subject: Selling Your House – 6 Week Update

Hi Nancy,

After reviewing your file recently, I noticed that we have now been on the market for 42 days. I'm sure you are as anxious as we are to get your house sold.

After being in this business for a while, I've noticed that it's not at all unusual for our clients to want to blame *someone* for the lack of interest or acceptable offers on their house. They blame the market, they blame potential buyers, and sometimes they even blame me or my team. I can certainly understand that. And of course, we are always willing to accept responsibility, if we've done a lousy job.

But the facts are that I don't know any other agent in town that does more to market their listings than I do. In fact, we are confident that there is no one who could do a better job. I am in charge of the marketing for the Knolly Team and we use the best techniques and tools to get our listings sold; and we have sold several listings since putting yours on the market.

Having said that, if there is anything you think we should be doing, please don't hesitate to let us know.

If you would like a new market analysis, we would be happy to provide you one.

Thanks again. I know we need to make things happen soon.

Email #8 – Send after 60 days

Subject: Selling Your House – 60 Day Update

Hey Nancy,

I hope all is well.

We are continually pressing forward on your property sale. I still have visions of the "SOLD" sign on your property, and our team is doing everything we can to make that a reality.

Sometimes I wish buyers weren't so picky or wouldn't mind paying a little more. But I guess that's how buyers are. They want the lowest price possible, while we want to get the highest. And it seems like some sellers are willing to price their houses more aggressively, and they are blowing us out. We noticed some of that when reviewing the market recently.

Maybe I just think too much! In any case, we know we don't get paid until we get your house sold, so we are working hard to earn our paycheck (and your confidence).

I'll update you again soon.

Email #9 – Send after 70 days

Subject: Selling Your House – 10 Week Update

Hi Nancy,

I thought I'd better check in with you again. We've been on the market now for over 2 months. It's very rare that we have to write and inform a seller that it has been that long.

Well, I just wanted to write and let you know that we are still burning the midnight oil and trying to come up with a sale on your property. Rest assured that whatever can be done has been. I know it sometimes feels like we are in a waiting pattern.

The fact remains that we are on the same team – and we don't win until you do. We know that houses are selling. We've had many closings since taking your listing; and each time we're pulling up our "For Sale" sign from these listings, we find ourselves wishing it was your house that had just SOLD.

I have been spending lots of time reviewing the market and comparing the recent SOLDs. Let us know if you'd like a new market analysis, or if you want to try a new price. As always, we are here to serve.

Thanks Nancy,

Email #10 – Send after 77 days

Subject: Selling Your House – 11 Week Update

Hi there Nancy,

Just checking in with you again. We are continuing to do what we can to get your house SOLD. Don't give up! It CAN happen and I believe it WILL. But it will take our utmost effort at this point.

If you are ready to pull out all the stops, let's go for it! My advice is to take a painful look at anything you could possibly do to make the house more attractive to potential buyers. And keep in mind that pricing is certainly the main attraction. What's your rock bottom price? At this point, I think we should consider going with 'rock bottom' and await an acceptable offer. Let's price it to sell!

Email #11 – Send after 84 days

Subject: Selling Your House – 12 Week Update

Hi Nancy,

I'm sorry to still have to be writing you at such a late stage in our listing relationship. It REALLY concerns me when one of our listings isn't selling and I feel really bad about this. We've been at it for almost 3 months, and we've continued to question ourselves about anything else we could possibly do to make this happen for you.

After reviewing our comprehensive marketing plan, we are at a loss to know what else we could be doing to make the sale of your house a reality for us. But I promise to continue our aggressive marketing approach in generating an offer.

We'll keep you posted.

Email #12 – Send after 90 Days

Subject: Selling Your House – 90 Day Update

Hi Nancy,

We have now hit 3 months on the market. It's obvious that what we are doing hasn't worked and we need to try a fresh approach.

We need to ask ourselves the tough question: "Why has this property not sold?" You can rest assured that we've done all that we promised; yet our marketing efforts have not produced a buyer willing to pay our asking price.

If possible, I would like to discuss what we've done so far, and see if there is anything else we can do...or perhaps a new approach you think might be best.

Let me know your thoughts.

Keep in mind that the series of emails will go out automatically, at your pre-determined intervals by using the *Email Campaigns* feature. There are a variety of CRMs on the market that feature *automated drip email* (Email Campaigns). Research the market and find the one that's right for you. Again, we use and recommend MoreSolds.com for your automated email campaigns.

Step 27: Make Periodic Price Adjustments

I am confident that by following the strategies I've already outlined, your listings will sell within 30 days! If the market in your area is sluggish right now, be sure to implement your Pricing Strategy (Chapter 13) by adjusting the MLS price at the agreed-upon intervals. You can use your CRM to alert you on the specific dates when price adjustments need to be made on your properties so that they won't be forgotten. When you begin to command a sizable inventory you will appreciate the time that this type of simple systemization will save you.

Although your client previously agreed upon the adjusted price, you will still want to notify and remind the seller that you are making the pre-agreed price adjustment on their listing. You can do this quite simply by adding a

Price Adjustment Action Plan and drip email campaign to the seller contact record in your CRM. The action plan can be set with a series of tasks which serves to remind you to make the price adjustment at 14, 30 and 45 days (or whatever interval you agreed upon). Once assigned, your CRM will automatically add the task to your virtual list at the appointed time, so you won't ever forget! This is a great example of automation at work. Once created it only takes five seconds to select the action plan and this gives you peace of mind that nothing will fall through the cracks.

Pricing Strategy Action Plan			
Type	Task	Delay Days	Assigned To
To Do	Price Adjustment	14	Barbara Riordan
To Do	Price Adjustment	30	Barbara Riordan
To Do	Price Adjustment	45	Barbara Riordan

Additionally you can have a corresponding automated email campaign set for 14, 30 and 45 days with a simple email notifying the seller that the price adjustment has been made.

Price Adjustment Email Campaign

Dear Tim and Gretchen,

Thanks again for allowing me to represent you in the successful sale of your house. I just wanted to send you a quick email to let you know that the list price on you house has been adjusted as we previously agreed in our listing agreement.

> We are working diligently on our end and
> we look forward to getting your house SOLD
> soon.
>
> Thanks!

When working with email campaigns just be sure to *halt* the current campaign as soon as the property goes under contract. Halting the campaign will stop any remaining emails in the campaign from being sent.

Final Note

As you can see, systems and automation allow you to run your real estate practice more professionally and more efficiently. While it may take a little time to set up and learn a good database CRM, having the systemization in place will save you tons of time and money, create a better customer service experience, and will lead to much happier clients and team members!

Chapter 15 Homework

☐ Role Play the Scripts in this chapter.

☐ Set up your *New Listing Email Campaign* in MoreSolds or your preferred CRM.

☐ Set up your *Showing Survey Feedback System* in MoreSolds or your preferred CRM.

Chapter 16

Receiving Offers and Negotiating a Contract

Step 28: Receive and Negotiate Offers

You've come a long way. You've mastered the art of lead generation, you've generated a seller prospect and converted that prospect into a client, placed the property on the market, initiated your automated listing servicing system, and now your hard work has been rewarded with an offer! Great job!

The ability to successfully negotiate offers to solid contracts is where top Listing Specialists really earn their fee. Becoming a *master negotiator* takes time, training and experience. Both the buyer and the seller are running on adrenaline and their emotions can fluctuate rapidly. A deal can easily go south if you let your seller's or your own emotions dictate the outcome. It is your job to remain objective, practical and give good, grounded counsel to your client.

Sometimes the seller can have the mistaken notion that the buyer is the *adversary* in the negotiating process. After all, the buyer wants to acquire the listing for the *lowest* price possible and the seller wants to get the *highest* price, right? Well, while the foregoing may be true, you will want to teach your seller to think at a higher level.

You: You know Cindy; I believe that the buyer and seller should work *as allies* in the transaction; since you both have the same end-goal. You want to *sell* the house and the buyer wants to *acquire* it. This means that a successful sale achieves the goals of both the buyer and seller. Does that make sense?

If the property has been on the market for more than a month, you should run a revised CMA so that you can see exactly what the market is saying at the time the offer is received.

After reviewing the CMA thoroughly I recommend that you call the buyer's agent to get a little *back-story* on the buyer and the buyer's situation. When you get ahold of the buyer's agent, always thank them for their client's offer (no matter how low the offer is).

You: Hi John - it's _____ - how are you?

Buyer Agent: I'm fine, how are you.

You: John, I'm calling to thank you for your client's offer on 101 Hackberry. Thanks for the offer. I'll be presenting it to my clients this afternoon.

Buyer Agent: That's great!

You: John, I'd like to be able to put our best foot forward when I present your client's offer. What can you tell me about your buyers?"

Let the buyer's agent speak freely. Listen to the agent closely and carefully. Take notes and don't interrupt their flow or interject your thoughts on what they are saying. Oftentimes the buyer agent will reveal clues and details that can help you see a bigger picture and could prove useful to you during the negotiating process. Let them talk. After the agent has given you sufficient backstory, use the appropriate follow-up script below.

Follow-up Scripts

Script (if offer is priced well)

Well, thanks again, John. I really appreciate that additional information which will help me when presenting this offer to my client. I'll let you know as soon as I am able to speak with my client and get a response

Script (if the offer is quite a bit lower than market)

You: Well, thanks again, John. I really appreciate that additional information which will help me when presenting this offer to my client.

John - I just ran an updated CMA on the listing which I planned to present with the offer. Unfortunately my CMA is pointing to a much higher market price. Go ahead and send me your CMA so I'll have something to work with when I meet my clients today at 2pm"

[This script forces the buyer agent to come to terms with reality and properly educate their client.].

Script (if the offer is just a little lower than market)

Well, thanks again, John. I really appreciate that additional information which will help me when presenting the offer to my client.

John... how did your buyer arrive at their offer price?"

[This script gives the buyer's agent the job of trying to explain and justify the offer - an often futile task]

Script (if you previously received a similar offer the seller didn't accept)

Well, thanks again, John. I really appreciate that additional information which will help me when presenting this offer to my client.

John, I just wanted to give you a heads up that the seller has already turned down an offer that was a bit more than the price your buyer is offering. I'm hoping we can make a deal here. Do you think your buyer really wants this house?

Don't try to do too much *pre-negotiating* at this point. At this critical juncture, your primary goal is to obtain information that will get you inside the head of the buyer as much as possible, which will help in the negotiating process.

Draft a Seller's Estimated Net Sheet

When you took the listing you presented the seller with an Estimated Net Sheet based on the list price. Now that you have an offer in hand, you will want to draft a revised Estimated Net Sheet containing the terms of the offer received.

Sellers always want to know how much the offer is, the proposed closing date and how much they will walk away with (their net). The Estimated Net sheet will actually answer all of these questions.

What Your Seller Wants to Know:

1. How much is the offer price (or the net price)?
2. How soon do they want to close?
3. How much will I walk away with (after all expenses)?

SELLER'S ESTIMATED NET PROCEEDS SHEET

The figures below are estimates. Actual costs and proceeds will vary. Estimates are not guaranteed.

Seller: Charles Metcalf, Lisa Metcalf

Address: 200 Winding Brook Dr, Austin, TX 78746

Anticipated Closing Date: August 22, 2013

Estimated Annual Property Taxes: 2.670 % of sales price = $ 12,950.00

Estimated Annual Maintenance Fees: $ 320.00

Buyer's Anticipated Financing: ☒ Conventional ☐ VA ☐ FHA ☐ Assumption ☐ Owner ☐ CASH

Estimated Costs		Estimated Proceeds to Seller:	
Attorney's Fees / Doc. Prep.	125.00	Sales Price	485,000.00
Brokers' Fees 6.000 %	29,100.00	Less Estimated Costs	38,221.00
Condo. Transfer Fee		Less Estimated Loan Payoff	322,000.00
Courier & Express Mail Fees	50.00		
Escrow Fee (one-half)	80.00		
Prorations*:			
Taxes *Prorated for 200 days	8,267.00	Estimated Net Proceeds	124,779.00
Interest (Assumptions)**			
Maintenance Fees	204.00		
Assessments		**After Closing Refunds**	
Rents			
Recording Fees	25.00	Estimated Unused Insurance	
Repairs Required by Buyer		Estimated Escrow Balance	
Repairs Required by Lender			
Residential Service Contract	350.00		
Seller Allowances or FHA/VA			
Nonallowables (Para. 12)		Total Estimated Refunds	
Survey Fee			
Tax Certificate Fee	20.00		
Title Policy - Owner's			
Wiring Fees			
Total Estimated Costs	$38,221.00		

Note: Seller may be required to pay some costs directly to the service providers before closing.

Prepared by: Knolly Williams

(TAR-1935) 1-2-03 Seller's Initials to acknowledge receipt: _____ Page 1 of 1

Presenting the Offer to the Seller

When you are new to the listings game it is best to present offers in person (face-to-face) whenever possible. Also, it is best to have all decision-makers present when presenting the offer.

As you become more advanced in your listing skills, you can move to presenting your seller offers over the phone.

Because I rely heavily on systems and efficiency, I switched my offer presentation process to *phone-based* many years ago. This system has been a huge time saver.

I basically present all of my offers over the phone. I then email the offer to my clients and ask my clients to review Chapter 7 of my Seller Book along with the offer.

Here's my 2 step offer presentation system:

Step 1: Call the client about the offer. When calling congratulate them on receiving an offer on their house. Tell them the offer amount and closing date and let them know you will be emailing the offer to them. Also make sure that they read Chapter 7 (Working with Offers) of your book while reviewing the offer and that they then call you back with any questions.

Presenting the offer over the phone and having them read this chapter before you speak will greatly leverage your time.

Step 2: Discuss the offer with the client only after they have reviewed the offer and read Chapter 7 of your book.

Time Savings:

- ✓ Eliminates driving to and from the client's house (1 hour).

- ✓ Eliminates explaining the various terms and clauses of the offer (30 minutes - 1 hour).

This system shaves at least 1-2 hours off every offer presented. With this leveraged system, your phone conversation should take only about 20 minutes or less, while a sit-down meeting (including your travel time to and from the listing) could take up to 1-2 hours. If you sell 60 listings a year this two-step system will save you at least 100 hours each year!

You: Hey there, Paul! I've got good news for you. We received an offer on your house! Now... it's not exactly what you are looking for, so we may have some work to do... but I think the buyers really want your house.

The offer is $380,000 and the buyers can close on June 7th. Now this is very important, Paul - I'm going to email you the offer right now. I need you guys to go back and read Chapter 7 of my book along with the offer and then call me with any questions.

Sample Follow-up Email Template

Hi Paul!

It was great talking to you this afternoon. Good News. We received an offer! Now I know it's not exactly what you are want but it's a start.

As we discussed, the offer is $380,000 and the buyers can close on June 7th.

IMPORTANT: In addition to the offer I have attached an updated market analysis and estimated net sheet. **Please read Chapter 7 of my book along with the offer and then call me so we can discuss any questions you have.**

Thanks again, Paul. I look forward to hearing from you and Betty once you have reviewed the offer and Chapter 7 of my book.

Talk to you soon,

Receiving Multiple Offers

Receiving multiple offers can be a blessing, but must be handled masterfully. When you receive more than one offer on a listing I recommend that you contact the agents and let them know that you have received multiple offers and invite their clients to present their highest and best offer. Give them a firm deadline on when to submit their revised offer. This strategy can sometimes generate offers that are above your list price! However, as previously mentioned, if your client accepts an offer that is outside the range of what the house will appraise for the buyer may have difficulty getting financing.

Always bear in mind that multiple-offer situations can backfire and send skittish buyers heading for the hills. You will have to treat the situation very professionally and you may have to coach the buyer's agent through the process.

Also, whenever you find yourself in a multiple-offer situation you have to educate the seller as to their options regarding the various ways to handle multiple-offer situations and then let the seller, with your guidance, make a decision on the course of action that's best for them. The seller could decide to just counter one of the offers and ignore the others. They could also instruct you to counter all buyers for their "highest and best offer". If you are new to handling multiple offer situations, be sure to seek the advice of your broker and/or a good real estate attorney so that you feel comfortable with your strategy.

Sample Email to Agents Who Presented Offers:

Hi there Charlotte,

Thanks again for your client's offer on 151 Logan Way.

As much as I dislike multiple offer situations - this is where we find ourselves with this property.

The seller has received three offers. The seller has instructed me to apprise you of the situation so that we can treat all parties fairly, which is why I am emailing you.

In the interest of full disclosure, the offers we have received are $274,500, 280,000 and $287,500.

Please have your buyer submit their highest and best offer by Tuesday, May 22 at 3pm - so that we can move forward with escrow on this property.

Thanks so much!

Lowball Offers

Oftentimes (and quite understandably) sellers get offended when they receive a *lowball* offer. This is a very emotional time for them and if they have not yet been able to emotionally detach themselves from the property the entire sales process can be a difficult one. It's your job to keep your seller well grounded.

Even if the offer seems impossible to work with, always encourage your seller to counter.

You: Susan, it is perfectly normal and common to become emotionally upset when you receive an offer that is far below what you consider to be acceptable. However my advice is to take a step back and reassess the situation. Don't be upset with the buyer who made an offer. Instead be upset with all the people who have looked at your house and didn't even bother to make an offer. A low offer is simply an *invitation to negotiate*.

Negotiation Is an Art Form

Master negotiators work to achieve a win-win. Likewise you can achieve the goals of your seller while also making the buyer feel that they got a fair shake.

Negotiations will sometimes involve getting the buyer to see beyond dollars and cents. If the deal is not coming together as expected, it is quite possible that the buyer's agent did a poor job of advising the buyer of the listing's true value. For this reason I recommend that you craft a custom letter reemphasizing the features, benefits and upgrades, and your pricing strategy - proving that your listing is worth what the seller is asking. Most of the time the buyer's agent will simply forward your communiqué directly to the buyers so be sure to word it professionally. This strategy often reignites the fire in the buyer by helping them to see how they will also win by accepting the seller's counteroffer. A proper understanding of the facts helps the buyer to move forward with the home they want at the price your seller wants.

Sample Negotiation Letter:

Dear Jim,

I want to once again thank your clients for their offer on 101 Winners Circle. I had a long discussion with my sellers Jim and Patty Duncan and they requested that I pass this information on to you and your buyers Tim and Susie Smith. Please feel free to forward them this communiqué.

The Duncan's are asking $475,000 for their house. They originally wanted to list their house for $490,000 - but after meeting with me they decided to price it to sell.

The Smiths made an offer of $445,000 and then agreed to come up to $450,000. The Duncan's are willing to go as low as $465,000 -- so at this point we are only $15,000 away from a deal.

Based on the comparable sales which I have attached here, 3 similar homes recently sold for $470,000, 482,000 and $490,000. *If you look at the neighborhood historically, you will see that the property values on similar homes are increasing at an average rate of about $32,000 per year.*

I have also attached a list of this home's upgrades which are valued at $28,000. As you can see the Duncans have meticulously kept up this property, and with these additional upgrades we believe the property could appraise for around $490,000. If the Smiths found a similar home for $450,000 they would likely have to add nearly $30,000 in upgrades to bring it up to this home's current standard.

As mentioned earlier, we are only $15,000 away from a deal. Based on the interest rate the Smiths were pre-approved for - financing an additional $15K would only cost them about $79 per month.

In conclusion, the Duncan's have already agreed to knock off $25,000 (from their original requested list price). They have also added $28,000 in upgrades. This translates to an additional $53,000 in value for the Smiths. Add to that the fact that home values in the area have historically increased at a rate of $32,000 per year.

The Duncan's are hopeful that the Smiths will see the value they are receiving and realize that $465,000 is a win-win. If the Smiths sign off on the deal today, they could be enjoying their new home by October 28.

Let's move forward.

Humbly & Respectfully Submitted,

Skillful and artful communication can mitigate most conflicts as long as all parties remain *reasonable* and *rational*. Again, when you are putting together a negotiation email bear in mind that you will be using this as a tool *to speak directly to the buyers*, since the letter will often be forwarded to them from the buyer's agent. This is a good thing because it removes the buyer's agent as the middleman. *Don't rely on the buyer's agent to simply communicate what you told them verbally to their buyers. Many things can get lost in*

*translation or misconstrued, and oftentimes your message will
not be articulated correctly which could blow the deal.*

The Biggest "Deal Killer"

Now let's talk about the biggest *deal killer* of any real estate transaction. Do you know what the biggest deal killer of a real estate negotiations is? If you guessed *the real estate agent* you are right. I have witnessed real estate agents do more to kill a deal than most anything else. Real estate agents oftentimes act as if they are negotiating their own property. Negotiations can often become rife with emotion, competition, ego and attitude. Some agents take it personally when a lowball offer is received or when the other agent makes a snide remark. Agents oftentimes fancy themselves as superheroes who are out to fight for their clients at all costs. In actuality, our job is simply to be a *fiduciary* for our client and to carry out their wishes in humility. *It is not about us.*

We are here to serve our clients. We must remove all emotion from our side of the ledger. Building adversarial tensions with another agent can lead to them poisoning the mind of their client, which can lead to your seller losing out on a sale. If such an event occurs and you had a part to play in it, then you have failed your client and failed in your fiduciary responsibility.

Negotiating a real estate transaction has nothing to do with you. As a professional Listing Specialist, a real estate transaction has nothing to do with your status, your rank, your ego, your notoriety or anything else. It simply has to do with achieving the objectives of your client whom you are a servant of. Always bear this in mind and you will do well as a negotiator.

Correctly Priced Properties Require Little Negotiation

Over and over again you will see that *price* has more to do with getting your listings sold than any other factor. I encourage you to review Chapter 13 and become adept at pricing your listings and at including a *pricing strategy* with every listing you take. Your primary concern is pricing your properties *correctly*. If you do this, your listings will not require a huge amount of negotiation. Properties that are priced correctly, marketed effectively and prepped for sale, practically sell themselves.

Finalize Your Negotiations

During the negotiation process you may find it necessary to go back-and-forth. Remember that you are a consultant and trusted adviser to your client. Give them sound advice. If the offer is good, let them know. Avoid the temptation to try and fight for every last cent just to make yourself look good. When you feel that the negotiations have reached the point where they are at a win-win, let the seller know and try to wrap up the deal with a signed contract.

Throughout the process strive to cultivate a good rapport with the buyer's agent. Treat them the way you would want to be treated. Be nice, courteous, respectful, objective and thoughtful. Earn their trust and gain their confidence.

Always seek to put a deal together within 24 hours if possible. Don't allow huge delays in relaying information, as this can also trim the sails and take the steam out of a negotiation, and can allow the buyer to cool off. I've seen buyers cycle from red hot to ice cold in less than 48 hours. Letting too much time fly before you have a signed contract is usually not a good thing. Don't rush through the negotiations, but do try to keep them on track, in the right direction and moving steadily forward.

Once the buyer and seller have agreed to all points, move for signatures. Get a firm contract in place and move forward to closing.

Chapter 16 Homework

- ☐ Role Play the Scripts in this chapter.
- ☐ Learn more about working with, negotiating and presenting multiple offers. Discuss best practices with your broker and other trusted agents.
- ☐ Review my *Sample Negotiation Letter* and develop your own template from this model.

Chapter 17
Contract to Close

Now that your listing is under contract, it's time to move on to *closing*. During this period, there are numerous items that must be done in order for the property to close. Thankfully, on the listing side there isn't nearly as much to do as there is on the buyer's side. The seller will essentially be waiting for the closing date while most buyers will need to get their financing finalized, schedule inspections and a host of other transactional tasks.

In this chapter I am going to share with you the main items that must be done in your camp in order for your listing to close in a timely fashion.

While I believe that every Listing Specialist should have a thorough working knowledge of the contract-to-close process, I want to make it very clear that *I do not expect you to do contract-to-close yourself.* It should be outsourced. Practically all the top Listing Specialists I know outsource their contract to close. I will teach you how to do this in Chapter 19.

As a Listing Specialist you should be focused on generating new listing appointments, going on appointments and converting those appointments to active listings. Go back and review *A Day in the Life of a Successful Listing Specialist* (Chapter 1). You will see that no provision is made for anything outside of the most dollar productive activities. *All administrative tasks associated with a listing should be handled by your Admin.*

Think about it this way. There are 46 steps in my listing system. Of those 46 steps, 42 of them can be readily handled by your Admin. Go back and review the steps listed in Chapter 1. You will see that only steps 1, 6, 11 and 28 are the BIG dollar productive activities. *This means that once you fully implement my system 91.3% of the activities that occur on every listing you take will be handled by others.* That's great news for you and your family! You can further eliminate steps 6, 11 and 28 once you hire a *Listing Specialist* to your team (Chapter 21). At that point you will be focusing on just one thing – *Lead Generation* (using the 4 Stage Lead Lifecycle). 98.7% of all the duties involved in your listing business will be handled by others and you can work a 3 hour day and go home. Yippee!

Step 29. Update MLS Status to *Pending*

As soon as a contract is executed by all parties, you should log into the MLS and change the status from *Active* to *Pending* (or *Pending Taking Backups*, if your seller will be accepting backup offers).

Again, once your listing is under contract you should update the status on the MLS immediately.

Step 30. Initiate *Closing* Action Plan

In your CRM you will want to initiate your *Closing Action Plan* and halt any drip campaigns you currently have running. The Closing Action Plan is a checklist of tasks that must be accomplished before the property is closed.

Once you begin to have multiple properties closing each month you will begin to see the enormous benefit of having an online Transaction Manager with Action Plans. Once you assign the Action Plan each team member will receive their list of specific tasks and due dates. Your client will also be able to log in and see exactly what is happening.

Your Admin will upload any documents to the transaction (executed contract, addendums, etc). This way your client will be able to log in to their client portal for years to come and download any docs they need.

You can read more about the transaction manager, action plans and how they work in Chapter 15. Real estate CRMs have been an absolute Godsend for both us and our clients, by allowing us to systemize our listing business while operating nearly paperless.

Sample Closing Action Plan *(for Contract-to-Close)*			
Type	**Task**	**Delay Days**	**Assigned To**
To Do	Insure that Contract has all pages and addendums	0	Barbara Riordan
To Do	Change status on MLS to Pending		Barbara Riordan
To Do	Obtain signed Seller's Disclosure	1	Barbara Riordan
Email	Request Receipted Contract from title company	1	Barbara Riordan
Email	Get inspection time and date from buyer's agent	1	Barbara Riordan
Email	Contact seller with inspection time and date	2	Barbara Riordan
Email	Send copy of signed contract to seller	2	Barbara Riordan
Email	Send email to buyer's agent with a copy of the contract and requesting information needed	3	Barbara Riordan
Email	Email seller's information form to title company	3	Barbara Riordan
To Do	Do DA and DI	4	Barbara Riordan
Email	Confirm appraisal is completed	12	Barbara Riordan
Email	Confirm Survey and HOA information is received by title company	12	Barbara Riordan
To Do	Obtain all addendums needed after inspection	12	Barbara Riordan
Email	Confirm that repairs are done if required (per inspection and addendum)		Eunice Garza
Email	Forward DA and DI to Title Company	15	Barbara Riordan
Phone Call	Confirm Closing Date	20	Barbara Riordan
Email	Obtain preliminary HUD-1 from Title Company	22	Barbara Riordan
Email	Send sellers the address and directions to Title Company	22	Barbara Riordan
Email	Remind sellers to bring keys, garage door openers, etc to closing	22	Barbara Riordan
To Do	Pick up sign and lockbox	30	Eunice Garza

Step 31. Congratulatory Call and Email to Seller

Now is the time to congratulate your seller! Even if you have already expressed your congratulations, this simple follow-up call and email will go a long way toward conveying your team's professionalism, building deeper client loyalty and generating more referrals.

You: Hi Carolyn! I just wanted to call and congratulate you once again on getting a contract on your house! We are on our way!

Client: Thank you! We couldn't have done it without you!

You: You know Carolyn, we continue getting calls on your property and we have several buyers who are interested in your area. So I was wondering - who else in your neighborhood needs to sell?

Client: You know, I'm not sure. I'll have to think about it.

You: I understand, Carolyn. Just keep us in mind as you are talking with your neighbors. Since we will still be getting lots of buyers contacting us over the next 30 days, now is the best time for any of your neighbors to list with us.

Client: I sure will!

Follow up Email

Hi Carolyn,

Once again I would like to congratulate you on the sale of your house. I know we've already congratulated you a few times but this is a momentous occasion!

Of course, we are still not out of the woods. There's a lot of due diligence that my team has to do in order to get us all the way to the closing table. The great news is we are up to the task! Don't forget to check in to our online portal at www.SellerStatusReport.com for the latest updates.

By the way... over the next 30 days I am looking to help 4 more families with their real estate needs. You can help by keeping us in mind as you or talking with your neighbors! Since we will still be getting lots of buyers contacting us over the next 30 days, now is the best time for any of your neighbors to LIST WITH ME. Be sure to give them a copy of my book!

Thanks Again Carolyn for trusting us with your sale!

Step 32. Send Executed Contract to Seller

Make sure that the seller receives a copy of the fully executed contract as quickly as possible. You can do this by simply uploading the contract to the *Transactions* section of your CRM, making it convenient for your seller to access and download at their convenience. Otherwise you or your escrow company can email or snail mail a copy to the seller.

Step 33. Negotiate any Post-Inspection Items

Most contracts have a rescission clause which will allow the buyer to cancel the transaction within a specified number of days from the execution date. Often called an *option period* or an *inspection period*, this time period is usually anywhere from 7 to 10 days and allows the buyer to do their due diligence and inspections on the property. During this window of time, the buyer will typically order a home inspection. It is the inspector's job to check out the major and minor systems of the house. No matter what condition your listing is in, the home inspector will almost always find a list of issues.

If not handled masterfully a contract can easily unravel during this volatile time period. That is why it is so important for you to educate your seller and properly set their expectations.

Educational Email to Your Sellers:

Hi John and Kathy,

I hope you are both well. As we move toward closing on your house, I wanted to take a moment to remind you to read Chapter 8 of my book so you can better understand the entire closing process.

At this point the buyer has 7 days to order any inspections they want completed. My business partner Barbara Riordan will be available for any questions you may have from now through closing and beyond.

As you will read in Chapter 8, once the buyer receives their home inspection report, they will generally review it with their agent and seek advice from their agent. Oftentimes the buyer will seek to have some of the issues on the report addressed by the seller. It is important for you guys to understand that you are not contractually obligated to fix anything that is found in the inspection report. At the same time, if the buyer finds issues that they cannot live with and you don't agree to address them in any way, the buyer can terminate the transaction (within the agreed upon time period).

If we do receive an amendment requesting additional repairs, I will call you to discuss your options and guide you in the decision-making process.

Generally speaking, you can either 1) agree to fix some or all of the items, 2) agree to provide a cash allowance so that the buyer can address these issues after closing, or 3) decide not to provide anything at all.

I always advise my clients to mentally set aside 1% of the sale price to address any repairs that come up during the option/inspection period. Since we sold your house for $315,000, count on about $3,000 set aside (usually payable at closing) for inspection related issues, just in case they come up.

I want you to rest assured that I will diligently negotiate and seek to minimize any potential expenses. At the same time I don't want to blow the deal at this stage in the game. This is a very emotional time for the buyer, as they are in the midst of the largest financial decision of their life. Minor repair issues can easily be blown out of proportion if not addressed in a fashion that mentally satisfies the buyer.

Again, I'm just sharing with you what to expect at this point, based on my vast experience. In any case I will work to achieve a win-win as always.

Thanks again to you both. Please email or call Barbara with any questions during the closing process.

Step 34. Send *Client Information Sheet* to Escrow Office

If the seller is carrying a mortgage on the property the escrow company closing the transaction will have to order the seller's payoff balance from their mortgage lender so that the mortgage liens can be paid off through the settlement. Be sure that the escrow officer has the seller's information as soon as possible so that there will be no closing delays.

Here is the basic information needed:

☐ Name and contact information of Seller

☐ Name and contact information of Mortgage Lender

☐ Property Address

Step 35. Weekly Contact and Updates to Seller

Once the house is under contract endeavor to have your Admin and/or Escrow Officer maintain at least weekly contact with your client. While there won't be much for you to do, the seller should be apprised of exactly what is happening so that they won't feel left in the dark.

Again, you can task this job to the Escrow Officer closing the transaction or your Admin. They should make weekly calls or send a weekly email to the seller to keep them posted and encourage them to log in to your CRM portal.

Sample email template to your sellers *(sent from your Admin):*

Hello Devin and Cindy,

Congratulations on the contract! We are excited for you both.

As you know, I am the one of the business partners here at the team. I will be working with you all the way through the closing of your property. My job is to ensure that we have a smooth and stress-free closing.

At this point there isn't much for you guys to do except wait for the closing date to approach and finish packing! In the meantime I want to make sure that you are kept in the loop on the latest happenings. Therefore I will be updating the information on your transaction every Tuesday, so you will know where things stand. All you have to do is login weekly and see the status.

To login to your transaction simply go to www.SellerStatusReport.

Right now we have your closing scheduled for on or before May 28. Please be sure to read Chapter 8 of our Seller Book to become better aware of the closing process.

Once again Congratulations! We look forward to working hard for you until your property closes and funds.

Thanks again!

Step 36. Submit All Documents to Your Compliance Department

Your office or brokerage will have a checklist of the items that you need to turn in for compliance.

Making sure that all of your documents are in compliance is a great thing because it helps to keep you out of trouble. It's great to know that someone is helping you cross your "t's" and dot your "i's" while you are super busy, out there making deals happen.

Typically your office will want copies of the listing paperwork, executed contract, and any addendums for their files, and to ensure that the transaction is covered by their E&O (Errors and Omissions) insurance company.

It may seem like a hassle to have to gather up all of these docs – but don't sweat it – your Admin will handle this for you! Remember – you are supposed to be focused on the most dollar productive activities, right?

Step 37. Send DA and DI to Escrow Office

Once all of your documents are cleared through your office's compliance department, you will receive a Disbursement Authorization form which breaks down the amount you are getting paid.

At The Knolly Team we take the Disbursement Authorization from our brokerage and send it along with our own Disbursement Instructions document which shows how we want the money wired (which bank accounts and the amounts to each account).

Step 38. Handle All Closing Details

There are many tasks that must be completed during the contract-to-close phase. Below is the contract to close checklist that we use at The Knolly Team. Again, as I mentioned earlier, due to the tedious and administrative nature of these tasks I always coach and advise that you delegate this phase of the transaction so that you can focus on the most dollar productive activities. This is essential, even if you aren't super busy and feel like you can currently handle the workload. Again, go back and review *A Day in the Life of a Successful Listing Specialist* in Chapter 1. As your Success Coach, I want you to focus solely on the things on that schedule. In Chapter 19 I share with you some great ways you can delegate *all* of your administrative activities to your Admin.

Sample Contract-to-Close Checklist:

Initiate File:
- ☐ Contract has all pages including 3rd Party Addendum.
- ☐ HOA Addendum (if necessary).
- ☐ Lead Paint Addendum (if necessary).
- ☐ Non-Realty Items Addendum to Contract.
- ☐ Seller's Disclosure Notice.
- ☐ Option Period Begins on:_____ for _____ days
- ☐ Option Period End on: _____

Contract:
- ☐ Request receipted copy of contract from Title Co.
- ☐ Contract received.
- ☐ Special Provisions: _____

Amendments:
- ☐ Regarding changing of price.
- ☐ Regarding change of Title Company.
- ☐ Regarding change of option period.
- ☐ Regarding change of closing date (1st).

- ☐ Regarding change of closing date (2nd).
- ☐ *Addendum of Sale for Other Property* by Buyer.
- ☐ Amendment(s) sent to Office, Title Company, Buyer Agent.

Referring Agent: ______________________________

- ☐ Signed Referral.
- ☐ W-9.

Send Email to Buyer Agent Including:

- ☐ Copy of Executed Contract.
- ☐ Title Co. directions.
- ☐ Copy of Survey.
- ☐ Requesting SD.
- ☐ Requesting Lender Info.
- ☐ Requesting time & date & who will do inspection.

Send Email to Seller Including:

- ☐ Receipted Contract, etc.
- ☐ Title Co. directions.
- ☐ Advise of inspection date – will buyers be present.
- ☐ Remind sellers to bring keys, garage door openers, etc. to closing.
- ☐ Remind sellers to bring original survey, if needed.
- ☐ T-47 Affidavit.

Forward to Title Company:

- ☐ Copy of Executed Contract.

CONTRACT TO CLOSE

- ☐ Survey.
- ☐ Client info including phone #'s, email addresses.
- ☐ Buyer Lender pre-approval letter and contact info.
- ☐ Amendments.

Inspection:

- ☐ Name of Inspector: _____
- ☐ Company Name: _____
- ☐ Phone #: _____
- ☐ Email Address: _____
- ☐ Date & time of inspection: _____

Appraisal:

- ☐ Name of Appraiser: _____
- ☐ Company Name: _____
- ☐ Phone #: _____
- ☐ Email Address: _____
- ☐ Date & time of appraisal: _____

Foundation Inspection:

- ☐ Company name: _____
- ☐ Phone #: _____
- ☐ Email Address: _____
- ☐ Date & time of inspection: _____

Termination of Contract and Release of Earnest Money:

- ☐ Send Release to Seller.

- [ ] Send Termination & Release to:
    - Title Company
    - Office
    - Buyer Agent
- [ ] Place back as Active on market.

Forward DA & DI to Approval:
- [ ] Forward DA & DI to Title Company.
- [ ] Forward final HUD to Buyer/Seller.

File Wrap Up:
- [ ] Call buyer agent & ask if he/she wants us to leave key at the house or wants to pick it up prior to closing.
    - [ ] Confirm in writing and cc team Listing Specialist.
- [ ] Have team Listing Specialist pick up sign & lock box
- [ ] Remind team Listing Specialist what to do with key or if agent picked up.

Send Email to Seller Including:
- [ ] Title Co. directions.
- [ ] Remind sellers to bring keys, garage door openers, etc. to closing.
- [ ] Remind sellers to bring original survey (if needed).

Step 39. Review *HUD-1 Settlement Statement* with Seller

The HUD-1 Settlement Statement is an official review of all of the settlement charges being assessed to the seller and buyer, and shows what the seller will net. It's a really good idea to review the HUD-1 Settlement Statement 24-72 hours prior to closing. With our clients, we have the title company send us a copy of the HUD-1 first (before sending it to the seller), so that my team can review and make sure that there are no mistakes. Once we are convinced that it looks good, my Admin will send the settlement statement to the seller and we will review the statement with them.

On the HUD-1 Settlement Statement, the right side of the form is the seller's side. It only takes about five minutes to review the statement with the seller over the phone. This assures you that there will be no surprises at the closing table.

Another thing to keep in mind is that the escrow company can generate an *Estimated* Settlement Statement for the seller even a week or more in advance of the closing. Once the Escrow Officer has received the amounts due (loan payoff, taxes and any other liens) they can go ahead and complete the statement for the seller. The *buyer side* of this statement on the other hand may take more time. That's because there is a lot of information that the title company must receive from the buyer's lender in order to accurately spread those numbers into the statement. Your seller is not concerned about the buyer's side, so the escrow company should be able to send you a statement reflecting the seller's side far in advance of closing (even if the buyer's side of the transaction is not complete). If the escrow company is telling you that they don't have a final settlement statement to send to you yet, it is generally because they don't have the buyer's side completed yet (typically because they have not yet received the final documents from the buyer's lender). If you run into this, simply ask the Escrow Officer to go ahead and send you a settlement statement *that just reflects the seller's side* so you can review it with your client.

Step 40. Attend Closing

Now it's time to attend the closing! Hooray! You've already completed steps 1 through 39 and you are almost at the finish line!

I always request to close my sellers separately from the buyers. I want my sellers to be able to get in and out as quickly as possible. It can sometimes be a bit awkward for both the buyer and the seller to be at the same closing table. The buyer is usually excited about their new home, while the seller has mixed feelings. *The closing is typically a much happier occasion for the buyer than it is for the seller.*

When closing a buyer transaction the closing will typically take about an hour due to the many forms that need to be signed. Closing the seller on the other hand usually takes less than half that time. This is because there aren't nearly as many documents for the seller to sign and most sellers don't require a thorough review of every document. Sellers mainly want to make sure that the Settlement charges are correct (step 39). Sellers realize that *once they sign all the docs they are one step closer to getting their money*, which also helps to speed up the process.

This is your chance to make a final impression. *When you are at the closing table you should also ask the seller for more referrals and ask the seller for a testimonial.*

Ask for more referrals at the closing table

You: Thanks again guys for letting me represent you in the successful sale of your house. Are you satisfied with the job I did?

Seller: You bet we are! You got it sold!

You: Awesome! Well right now what I need most is *more inventory*. Remember we still have lots of buyers looking for houses, not only in your area but all over town. I'm going to give you five copies of my book. Feel free to pass them out to anyone you run into who is thinking about selling their house."

[Hand them an envelope or small box containing copies of your book]

Seller: You bet we will!

You: And by the way, I'll be calling you from time to time, just to check on you and of course to see if you need any more copies, or know someone looking to buy or sell. Would that be OK?

Seller: Of course!

This system is much more effective than giving your client five or ten of your business cards at closing. Guess what will happen to those cards? *Nobody knows.* Your stack of books however will be readily handy for your sellers to pass out at a moment's notice.

Get a Testimonial

Again, once closing is concluded ask your sellers to stick around to do a quick one minute video. Simply whip out your video camera and ask your sellers to recommend you in one minute or less.

 You: Thanks again Patrick and Sheila for allowing me to represent you in the successful sale of your house. I love to share my success stories with my other clients. One of the best ways I have found to do that is with a quick one-minute video.

It's nothing super professional or scripted. Just talk about the experience you had working with me and my team and how we were able to achieve success for you.

Then simply point the camera and let them talk!

Be sure to send your clients the video clip and be sure to tag the sellers, the escrow officer and the referral source (if applicable) when you post it on your Facebook page and on other social media. You can also tag anyone else who was a part of the transaction.

Should You Attend Closing?

Okay… So I just finished telling you about all the great things you can do at the closing table like getting a testimonial video and recruiting your clients into action by giving them copies of your book to pass out. Yet there is a growing trend where agents are considering skipping out on the closing altogether.

Truthfully, not attending the closing could be a tremendous timesaver for you if you are running a high-volume business. Let's assume it takes approximately 30 minutes to drive to the escrow office, 30 minutes to close and 30 minutes to drive back to your office. Add another 30 minutes for incidentals. That means at least two hours per closing. Multiply that by 60 closings and that's 120 hours of your life spent in a closing room (or in traffic) each year!

Truthfully, since you have already reviewed the settlement statement with your client (step 39), there isn't much for you to do and there typically isn't anything for you to sign at the closing. Your closings can easily be attended by your Admin (Chapter 19) or your Listing Specialist (Chapter 21). You can also teach these staff members the aforementioned script so that any one of them can attend the closing on your behalf.

If you will not be attending the closing all you have to do is let your client know after you review the HUD-1 with them (during step 39).

You: Thanks again Sheila for reviewing the Settlement Statement with me. It looks like we are all set for closing!

Client: Yes! Thanks so much!

You: Now Sheila, I just wanted to give you a heads up that as my business partner, Barbara will be attending the closing on our team's behalf. There really isn't anything that our team does during the closing, since the title company handles everything at that point, but I wanted to make sure that you have an advocate there with you, just in case.

Client: Oh, OK. Sounds good.

> You: Again, I will not *personally* be there but you will be in good hands with Barbara. I may be at an appointment during the time of your closing, however I will be on call for you. If anything comes up, or you need me for any reason, be sure to ask Barbara to contact me on my cell phone and I will step out of my appointment.
>
> Client: OK - sounds good!

So, you may be wondering *what about making a last-minute impression at closing? Doesn't that help lead to more referrals?* Well, yes, it does. Keep in mind that you can train your Admin or Listing Specialist to make this important impression on behalf of the team. And since you will be employing my *"Client for Life"* method (Chapter 18), your clients will absolutely *never* forget you, and they *will* send you referrals!

To make a final impression you can always offer a congratulatory call to your client after the closing is completed. This can be a simple 3 minute congratulatory call.

> You: Hi Sheila! Congratulations! I heard the closing went very well?
>
> Client: Yes, it sure did! Thank you!
>
> You: You bet Sheila! And we will be sure to forward you your video so that you can add it to your Facebook page!
>
> Client: Awesome!
>
> You: Thanks again, Sheila! If there's anything that I can do in the future for you or your

friends and family, please do not hesitate to call!

Client: Will do!

With this method, you can spend just a few minutes of your personal time on each closing while your team handles everything else. Again, whether or not you personally attend the closing will be a personal decision for you.

Well, now that the transaction is closed and you have achieved success for both you and your client, let's move on to converting them into a *Client for Life!*

Chapter 17 Homework

- ☐ Review and Role Play the Scripts in this chapter.
- ☐ Create your *Closing Action Plan* in your CRM
- ☐ Practice reviewing the *HUD-1 Settlement Statement*

Chapter 18
Creating a Client
for Life

Being truly successful in real estate means seeing past the current transaction. Creating a client for life is not something that happens by accident. You have to be purposeful. While you may be *currently* conducting a transaction with newlyweds Jim and Julie Smith, your ultimate goal is to be the agent of choice for their children and *ultimately* their grandchildren. You want to be their *agent for life*.

Too many real estate agents completely drop the ball when it comes to managing an ongoing flourishing relationship with their past clients. We talked about this in Chapter 7.

Steps 41 through 46, coupled with the SOI marketing techniques you learned in Chapter 7 will allow you to put a system in place that creates a client for life.

Step 41. Send Post-Closing Gifts to the Seller and Buyer

Now that the transaction has successfully concluded, you want to dispense your closing gifts. Of course you will want to give a closing gift to the seller but why not also give one to the buyer of your listing?

In Chapter 7 we talked about how most buyers are completely orphaned after the closing. Since you will be adopting the buyer and adding them to your database, why not begin the relationship with a thoughtful closing gift?

There are perhaps hundreds of different options you can choose from when it comes to an appropriate closing gift. I believe that the best closing gifts are those that are useful (everyday functionality) and have a long shelf life. In other words, pick something that they will use often and something that they will use for a long time.

For the buyer, you can simply leave the gift at the house, mail it, or drop it off in person.

For the seller, you can give them their gift at the closing table, or, for added affect (and flair), you can have it *delivered* to their workplace with balloons! Depending on where they work, this can serve as a great conversation starter with their fellow employees. If you send it to their workplace, be sure to send the gift with extra copies of your book so that they can immediately pass them out while talking about how wonderful an agent you are.

Step 42. Send the *Homeowner's Tip Guide* to Buyer

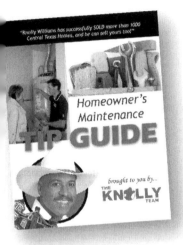

It's a great idea to send the buyer a copy of your *Homeowner's Tip Guide.* This handy guide will share with the buyer everything they need to know about the basic everyday care and maintenance of their house (plumbing emergencies, roof maintenance, exterior caulking, garage doors, refrigerator and freezer tips, etc.). You can mail a copy your guide to the buyer or leave a copy in a kitchen drawer. Your Homeowner's Tip Guide should be custom branded with your information, giving you top of mind awareness with the new homeowners.

Buyers (even second or third time homeowners) absolutely love this invaluable resource. You can find many samples of a Homeowner Tip Guide on the Internet.

Step 43. Update the Transaction in Your CRM

Now that the transaction has closed, it's time to close out the transaction in your CRM and complete any action plans. You also want to halt any pre-closing email campaigns that are currently running.

Be sure that all of the final closing documents are uploaded to the Transaction in your CRM so that your clients can readily access any documents they need in the future. Clients will sometimes contact you two or three years after the closing for a copy of their HUD-1 Settlement Statement or some other document from the transaction. Having all of the documents in your cloud-based CRM where your sellers can readily login and download anything they need is super handy for them, and it makes you look like the ultra-professional that you are.

Step 44. Add Buyer to Your CRM

Now that the transaction is closed I recommend that you add the buyer of your listing to your database. We talked about this in Chapter 2 (reason #9). It's pretty easy to add them because you already have their mailing address!

Some of my coaching students do not *feel* that it is right to add the buyer (whom they did not represent) to their database. They don't think it is *right* to *steal* another agent's client. I can certainly appreciate that. Let me ask you a question. Once the transaction closes whose client is the buyer? Nobody's. They are completely up for grabs, and statistics tell us that about 90% of the buyers that you add to your database will be abandoned by their former agent. So if *you* don't form a relationship with them, *someone else will.* From my point of view you are the most likely candidate for election as their next agent, since you've already sold their house before!

Just recently Derek called me up and asked me to list his house. After looking up his contact information in MoreSolds, I realized it was a house that I had recently sold where he was the buyer on the transaction. Listing these properties is almost too easy. I literally called him up with the following script:

Me: Hey Derek it's Knolly over at the Knolly Team how are you?

Derek: Great Knolly!

Me: Thanks Derek for calling me about listing your house.

Derek: You bet.

Me: Hey Derek... I sold that house before, *didn't I?*

Derek: Yes, you did.

Me: And you know I can sell it again *don't you, Derek?*

Derek: Yes, I'm sure you can.

Me: Great Derek. I'd be happy to help you get it sold!

Working with past buyers of your listings is about as easy as working with a past client. You don't have to sell yourself, because they already believe you can get the job done.

Just this past weekend Sam contacted me because he was getting a job transfer and needed to sell his house. It turns out he had been offered a fantastic job opportunity in Carlsbad, California and was moving from Austin to his company's corporate headquarters. Guess how Sam heard about me? You guessed it. He had purchased the house from my seller nearly 9 years ago. Where was his former agent? I don't know and I surely didn't ask. I was more than happy to help. Sam had been receiving my monthly email newsletter for the past 9 years so I was the one he thought about when it came time to list.

Now for those of you who think that soliciting another agent's former client is akin to stealing their clients, let me assure you that you are mistaken. I am actually *adopting* a client who was *abandoned* and *orphaned*. They never heard from their former agent again, meanwhile they continually receive my postcards and newsletters. It's no wonder they vote for me when it comes time to elect their next agent.

The truth is, neither Sam nor Derek would have contacted me if I had *not* stayed in touch with them. *Likewise, neither Sam nor Derek would have contacted me if their previous agent had stayed in touch with them.*

It helps to think of your selection as your client's *Listing Agent* like you would think of a *political election*. When a seller or buyer signs with you, it's akin to you getting their *vote* and being *elected* for the *office* of LISTING AGENT for that property. Once the transaction is consummated, your term *automatically terminates* and you must be *reelected* whenever it comes time for them to buy or sell again.

Truthfully, I don't believe that a client can be stolen. Even if I gave you the login credentials to my MoreSolds database account, *you could not steal my clients from me*. It would almost be comical to watch another agent cold call my list of past clients whom I have cultivated for many years and try to win them over. People do business with people they know, like and trust. If you stay in touch with your SOI they will be loyal to you and untouchable.

Step 45. Send the Seller Your Post-Closing Seller Satisfaction Survey via Email

Now that the dust has settled it's a good idea to send the seller your *Post-Closing Survey*. This survey helps you assess what you are doing right and what areas could use a little improvement.

Becoming a legendary agent requires a phenomenal system. There is no one better qualified to help you fine-tune your system than your past clients. Your past clients are walking, talking *case studies* for your real estate practice. Tap into their insight.

Sample Seller Satisfaction Survey

Thank You for allowing us to sell your house. Can you do us a HUGE favor and fill out our Seller Satisfaction Survey. It only takes 3 minutes! We take our job very seriously and we continually strive to be better at what we do. We feel that we become more informed with each transaction we complete, and we rely on your valuable input to help us become the best we can possibly be. Please circle the most applicable answer and be honest!

Please rate us on a scale of 1-10
(10 = Strongly Agree | 1` = Strongly Disagree)

1. We delivered on what we promised.

   1   2   3   4   5   6   7   8   9   10

2. We effectively marketed your listing.

   1   2   3   4   5   6   7   8   9   10

3. Our Team's communication was superb throughout the process.

   1   2   3   4   5   6   7   8   9   10

4. I am satisfied with the sales price I received.

   1   2   3   4   5   6   7   8   9   10

5. I am satisfied with the number of days my house was on the market.

   1   2   3   4   5   6   7   8   9   10

6. We were accessible when you needed to reach us.

   1   2   3   4   5   6   7   8   9   10

7. We listened and were attentive to your needs.

   1   2   3   4   5   6   7   8   9   10

8. We did a great job educating you on what was to be expected during the home selling process.

1   2   3   4   5   6   7   8   9   10

9. You are very likely to refer our team to a friend or family member.

1   2   3   4   5   6   7   8   9   10

10. You will definitely use us again in the future, once the need arises.

1   2   3   4   5   6   7   8   9   10

11. If you owned our real estate business, what would you do differently? _____

12. Who do you know that is interested in buying or selling real estate? _____

13. Please leave additional comments on how we can create a more pleasant experience for our home sellers. We take customer service very seriously and we truly appreciate honest feedback. _____

Step 46. Pick Up Your Sign and Lockbox

Now we come to the final step in my 46 step listing system. It's time to go and pick up your toys.

During your visit to the house you can drop off the buyer's closing gift (step 41).

You can also go one step further and offer them your *Love It or Leave It Guarantee.* At The Knolly Team, the way our Love It or Leave It guarantee works is simple. If a buyer doesn't absolutely love their new home, we will offer to sell it for free within the first 12 months of escrow. After 12 months the offer converts to a *"$1000 OFF"* coupon for the future sale of that property. Buyers absolutely love this guarantee! Although they would surely almost never need to sell within 12 months, they like the *assurance* of knowing that they aren't stuck in a house that they don't love. In my career, I have only had two buyers who have had to sell their house within a year of escrow. And with the $1,000 coupon, the buyer has an incentive to call YOU when it comes time to list!

Script to use when picking up your sign and lockbox:

You: Hi there, I'm _____ and I was the listing agent on the house.

Buyer: Oh, Hi.

You: Congratulations on your home purchase!

Buyer: Thanks!

You: Listen, I didn't mean to disturb you. I'm just here to pick up my sign and lockbox.

Buyer: Oh, sure.

You: By the way, I wanted to make sure that you know about our *Love It or Leave It Guarantee?*

Buyer: No, what's that?

You: Well, I brought a copy of it with me. Basically, we stand behind every home we sell and we want you to rest assured that you made the best decision in purchasing this home. If you don't absolutely LOVE your new home we will sell it for free anytime within the next 12 months. It's our *Love It or Leave It Guarantee.*

Buyer: Wow! That's great!

You: Congratulations once again and I wish you guys all the best.

If you have your Admin, a team member or your Listing Specialist pick up the sign, simply teach them the script and have them use it whenever they pick up the sign and lockbox behind your sold listings. Your *Love It or Leave It Guarantee* is a powerful tool to help you get that house back into your inventory at some point in the future. Even if you did have to list it within 12 months for free (which will almost never happen) remember that each properly marketed listing should result in another listing and two buyers.

Congratulations! You have successfully completed the 46 step process! Don't skip a step! You can tweak the system to better suit you, but only after you have mastered it and are using it consistently with great skill.

Now let's move on to the next section where I will show you how to grow your listing business and how to build your real estate power team!

Chapter 18 Homework

- ☐ Create your *Homeowner's Tip Guide*
- ☐ Create your Seller Satisfaction Survey.
- ☐ Create your *Love It or Leave It Guarantee.*

Section

V

Growing Your
Listing Business

Chapter 19
Building Your Power Team

As I travel and speak across the country and meet agents in large and small cities alike, I ask them this question: *"Do you have a team?"* Most solo practitioners say they do not. But the truth is *Nobody Succeeds Alone.*

We all understand what a traditional real estate team looks like – multiple Administrators, Buyer Specialists and Listing Specialists all working as a unit to achieve maximum results. But the truth is – every real estate agent – even the solo practitioner *already has a team*. Right now, *today even,* you should begin to think like and operate like a team. In your everyday speech, you must replace your *"I"* with *"We"*.

The Critical Members of Your Current Team:

I am going to show you that you really and truly do already have a team. It's true. Let's review the critical team members of your current team.

YOU

As the CEO of your team you are the *visionary* and *leader* responsible for ensuring that all goals are set and that these goals are either met or exceeded. As a leader you are also primarily a *servant*. Your job is to *serve* your teammates and your clients.

If you think about your business from a biblical perspective, you see it more as a *ministry* than simply a moneymaking enterprise. Like Jesus, you serve a small group of team members (disciples) as well as your clients.

Office Broker/Team Leader

Your office broker and/or team leader acts as your guide, counselor and business consultant. They are there to serve you as needed, and can help with your business planning.

Your Coach/Mentor

Your coach will assist you in reaching your highest potential by helping you discover what you truly want and holding you accountable as you pursue your goals. A great coach can help you achieve your highest possible potential by pushing you on to greatness, when you would otherwise stop short of your personal best. Jesus personally coached a small group of disciples and he taught each of those disciples to go out and coach/mentor their own group.

Mortgage Lender

Your preferred mortgage lender is responsible for staying on top of the latest trends, products and programs in the mortgage/banking industry. On the buyer side they will service and provide sound counsel to your team's buyer clients. With your listings, your lender partner will be able to look over the pre-approval of any would-be buyer and give your sellers the peace of mind that everything looks as it should.

Escrow Officer

Having a great Escrow Officer is a must for a Listing Specialist. You need someone you can count on to pick up the slack, talk with your sellers, and ensure – insomuch as possible – that your deals close timely. They may have to perform additional duties for you like help clear up liens, perform preliminary title searches on properties, etc.

Attorney

A fantastic (and available) real estate attorney is an absolute must. Since you cannot give legal advice, having a reputable attorney who will get back with your clients quickly will give your sellers the confidence that you are *on top of your game* because you have surrounded yourself with the best people.

Tax Consultant

An expert who understands the tax implications of various types of real estate transactions is absolutely indispensable. Savvy sellers want to know how the sale of their property (especially probate and investment property) will affect them. A great tax consultant will be able to advise them on the best strategy to employ when it comes to selling.

Handyman/Contractor

Having a reputable, honest and fast handyman or contractor is also essential. This professional will be able to walk through your listing and give your sellers a reasonable bid on work that may need to be done. Your contractor will also be able to quickly get minor repairs completed should the need arise after an inspection.

Home Inspector

More and more Listing Specialists are recommending that the houses they list (especially those that are 10 or more years old), have a pre-inspection. A good inspector may be able to give you a *frequency discount* and help you resolve issues prior to placing the house on the market. Since inspection-related issues are a huge deal killer, having a pre-inspection can help avoid surprises and disappointment.

Other Team Members

Other key team members may include a home warranty company, a house cleaning company, painter, electrician, plumber, roofer, HVAC contractor, landscaper and carpet cleaner.

All of these individuals should know you on a first name basis and they should be trained to speak highly of you when they meet with your seller. Plus... they should always reciprocate the referral gesture on your part by asking this simple script: *"Knolly asked me to check and see who else you might know of that needs to buy or sell?"* Then train them to get the contact information of any prospects they dig up, and *call you* with their information. Your team members should be trained to bring you those leads on a regular basis, thereby perpetuating their own business.

I recommend that you type up a list of your "team members" and make it available on each listing appointment you conduct. You can also make it part of your pre-listing package. When you give your sellers a list of your team members, they will gain a whole new level of confidence when it comes to hiring you.

Using Leverage in Your Business

Every one of us will need *leverage* to succeed. Leverage is made up of 3 key ingredients known as P-S-T. People, Systems and Tools.

P-S-T

- **People** - who will do it?
- **Systems** - how will they do it?
- **Tools** - what will they do it with?

Leadership

When you hear about companies that are *succeeding* and others that are *failing* make no mistake about it, companies do not succeed or fail, *people do.*

By aligning yourself with good talent, you can go much further. Still, at the head of every great company is great leadership. *You have to be an outstanding leader.*

No person in history has ever personified in better detail what true leadership looks like than Jesus Christ. Jesus demonstrated that a true leader is first a servant.

If you haven't already, over time you will definitely come to understand how being a leader means being a servant. Your job is to train and equip. Once you have the right people in place, and they are trained and equipped, your role will primarily be to share with them the *vision* and *hand them the ball.* Then you will provide them with *support* and *hold them accountable.*

Here is the Jesus Method:

1) Teach and Train your people well.
2) Send them out to learn *and fail* in the real world.
3) Hold them accountable.

Steps 1-3 are continually repeated and throughout the entire time you are sharing with them your long term vision and providing your people with all the support they need to succeed. As they take the reins and move the ball forward, *you become their servant.*

Your people are on the front lines of the battlefield. You are back at base command overseeing the mission. *Your primary concern is to find out what your people need and serve it up to them.*

The Required Skills of a Top Listing Specialist

To be a Top Listing Specialist, here are the attributes you will need:

- ☐ Amazing Lead Generator;
- ☐ Incredible Presenter;
- ☐ Marketing Wizard;
- ☐ Excellent Leadership Skills;
- ☐ Fantastic Counselor;
- ☐ Administrative and Organizational Genius;
- ☐ Expert Negotiation Skills;
- ☐ Dynamic Consultant;
- ☐ Must Have Tons of Patience and Tenacity.

If you possess all or most of these attributes then you are off to a great start! But beware! Those who excel in many of these areas often feel that they don't need help or that they can do a better job than anyone else. While it may be true that you *are* superior to many in several areas, remember that *perfection is the enemy of progress.*

Look back through the list again. How many of these skills and attributes do you possess? Where do you fall short?

A BIG TRAP:
Thinking You Can Do It All

A lot of the top agents that I train have a *big problem with delegating*. They believe the old adage: *If you want something done right, you have to do it yourself.* For the Type A/High D (the personality profile of most top agents), this misnomer falls flat. The more appropriate truth is: *If you want something done at all then you must hire others to do it!*

You need to understand where you are weak and partner with others who are strong in those areas.

Read the preceding sentence a few times. It is essential to your success that you understand this. I've had coaching clients tell me that this one concept alone is responsible for more than *doubling* their business.

So how do you *understand where you are weak?* Usually your weaknesses will manifest themselves as the things you are *avoiding*, the things you *aren't particularly good at* or the things you simply *don't enjoy doing*. However, a simpler and more accurate way to understand where you are weak is through the *DISC Personality Profile* test or the *Strengths Finder* test as we discussed in Chapter 3. By taking these simple online assessments you will quickly see where your strengths are and where your weaknesses lie. If you simply partner with others who are strong in the areas where you are weak, you will enjoy your greatest potential for success. For a free online assessment go to my website at www.SuccessWithListings.com where I provide links to my favorite free sites.

Working On Your Weaknesses

I come across agents all the time who talk about how they are working on their weaknesses. *"Well, Knolly, I'm not very organized, but I've been working on it!"*

Why?

Do you think the President of the United States is very organized? If not do you think the President is working on becoming *better* at being organized? *Probably not.*

Rather than waste your time working on the areas where you are not naturally strong, why not just build upon your strengths and partner with others who are strong in the areas where you are weak?

Don't get me wrong. You already know that I am a *lifelong learner*. I am huge on encouraging my Success with Listings Academy members to become more self-aware, to constantly improve and become better. I'm an advocate for learning and improving and I want you to be the best you can be. However, once you have proven without a shadow of a doubt that you absolutely *stink* in a particular area, why not gracefully move on? Why not focus your energy on becoming even better in the areas where you already excel?

For example, in my own life I love to write. Not only do I enjoy writing, it comes naturally to me and I am constantly working to improve my writing skills. Yet, even if I didn't like to write, I could still be an author. All I would have to do is partner with someone who is a writer and simply share with them all of my ideas, letting them articulate them in written form.

God created all of us with different gifts. I believe He did this so that we would seek to *work together. We need each other.*

I like to think of our relationship to others like an old western town. You had one barber, one schoolteacher, one blacksmith, a shopkeeper who ran the general store, a druggist, one or two small hotels and one or two saloons, etc. In town everyone had their own unique and individual trade. Outside of town you had the farmers and ranchers, each with their own unique crops and livestock. People would often barter with each other and trade the goods that they had. In this way, everyone had everything and no one lacked anything.

If you are not a great public speaker, then sure you should work on becoming better at it. If you are not a great writer, then sure you should work on becoming a bit better. But I don't recommend that you work on *mastering* something that is outside of your natural personality profile. Work on mastering the areas where you are already good, and turn good to great and then even greater. Realize that not everyone is meant to be gifted in all areas. God set us up to rely on one another. *People need people.*

For example, if you are really good with people then you should probably be spending a lot of time with people. *Forget about the paperwork, being organized or data entry.* Just fill up your social calendar with events, lunches and meetups; and fill up your business calendar with listing appointments. Get in front of as many people as you possibly can each week and watch your business flourish. Then, simply hire others to handle the tidal wave of new business while you are out *playing*.

If you are a wiz with spreadsheets and paperwork but don't really enjoyed being around people, then spend your time in the office running a revolutionary real estate practice with you in the control room pushing the buttons. While you are behind the scenes overseeing the organization, you can simply hire someone with a nice smile and a great attitude, who can go out and do all your listing presentations. You'll be raking in the business!

I recently had a conversation with Chris Rios. At the time we spoke, Chris had been an agent with our office for less than six months. In his former life, Chris was a master *Telemarketer* at the very top of his game. Chris decided from the very beginning that he would be a Listing Specialist and he began making his calls in the mornings and going on listing appointments in the afternoons. He spent his mornings prospecting and his afternoons doing listing appointments. But Chris quickly figured out that he could actually *get more listings* if he did not have to go out on appointments. Since he is great on the phone, he wanted to spend his *entire day* doing nothing but *prospecting*. His solution? He simply has partnered with someone who loves going out and doing presentations, but doesn't want to be bothered with prospecting. It's a win-win relationship.

No matter where your strengths lie, you can succeed as a top Listing Specialist, but you must partner with others who are strong in the areas where you are weak.

The 3 Stages of a Business

Every business goes from I *to* We *to* They.

- **I Do It** - this is *you* as a solo practitioner working alone.
- **We do it** - this is *your team* working together.
- **They do it** - you become the owner and work *on* the business and not *in* it.

If your business is not moving along this trajectory then you have an *unnatural* business. Many agents actually curtail their own growth because they are afraid of success or they are afraid to grow too large, for fear that a larger business will create a larger workload. The truth is, the *larger* your business grows, *the less you personally have to do*.

Let's say you figured out a way to build a better computer. You tinkered around and started your business out of your college dorm room. Orders are starting to come in and you are keeping up with the demand all by yourself. Soon, however, you are getting more orders than you can handle. You have to hire some of your buddies to help out. Now there are two or three of you in your dorm making computers. Soon afterward, the demand is so large that you have to expand further. This is the story of almost all the computer startups in the early days. Do you think that Michael Dell still *personally* builds any of the computers that Dell manufactures? Of course not. His business went from I to We to They.

The bigger your business becomes the *easier* it should be to run. Many have a hard time understanding this simple concept. Just imagine for a moment that you opened a McDonald's restaurant. You have ONE location and you are new to the restaurant business. *How much time do you think you will need to spend at your McDonald's?* Probably *all* of it!! You will probably feel as though you were living there.

Now fast forward 7 years. You have mastered all the company's franchise systems and you have expanded. You now own fourteen McDonald's locations across the state. How much time do you suppose you would spend at each location? Very little to none. You now have 14 general managers (one over each store), 3 regional managers who oversee the 14 and one person who oversees the entire operation. Just as with your smaller operation, you still have just a few people who report to you. Your days are filled with *growing* your organization and/or *play time* (i.e. doing whatever you want to do). You are simply articulating the vision and holding your people accountable by reviewing the results alongside the expectations.

If your organization is structured *correctly* and you are leading *effectively*, the larger you allow your organization to grow the easier your job will be. Many of the agents that I coach in my academy have come to realize that they are subconsciously stifling their own growth. As your *Listing Success Coach*, I urge you to stop setting limitations on yourself! Allow your organization to grow as big as it wants to be!

Chapter 19 Homework

☐ Remember – you already have a team. Develop your list of Critical Team Members.

☐ Determine which steps in my *46 Step Listing System* that you will perform yourself and which ones you will delegate.

☐ Determine where you are strong and where you are weak by completing and/or reviewing your assessment tests from Chapter 3.

Chapter 20

Your First Hire: An Administrative Assistant

Trust me, if you don't already have help you need it. Better yet, you need it *NOW*!

Go back to Chapter 1 and take a good look at *A Day in the Life of a Successful Listing Specialist*. You will see that a Successful Listing Specialist doesn't have time for *paperwork*. Your mornings are filled with prospecting and your afternoons with appointments.

91.3% of the steps outlined in my 46 step Success with Listings System are administrative in nature. *Therefore, your focus will be on less than 10%.* Your Admin(s) can handle the rest.

Many agents don't hire an Admin because they feel that they cannot *afford* one. The truth is, you cannot afford *not* to have a good Admin person. With your first hire you are now able to provide your clients with superior service on every listing you take. Nothing falls through the cracks. This will result in higher client satisfaction and more referrals.

Ideally, you will hire Admin help at the very *beginning* of your listing career. Sure, you may want to handle a half dozen or so transactions on your own, so that you can get the feel of it. After that it's time to hand it off!

Your very first hire should be *Administrative help* – that is, an *Administrative Assistant* (Admin) who can handle all of the administrative tasks associated with each transaction. Your Admin can also be trained to double as a *Lead Coordinator* handling all sign and marketing calls from buyer and seller prospects, and assist with marketing activities, social media and inside sales.

Ultimately, by hiring your Admin, you should be able to take the listing and throw the listing over your shoulder. Your Admin should be able to "catch it" and take the file all the way to the pay window.

Partnering with an Admin

Your objective when partnering with an Admin is to build a fantastic duo. You do the front end work and your Admin does the back end.

Here are the 5 Steps you will be doing:

✓ Generate the seller prospect (step 1);

✓ Research the property (step 5);

✓ Conduct a phone consultation and set the listing appointment (step 6);

✓ Obtain the listing (step 11);

✓ Negotiate a contract (step 28)

Here is what your Admin will be doing:

✓ Everything else.

Compensation Options

There are a variety of ways that you can compensate your Admin. Here are the most popular options according to best industry practices.

Option 1: Pay an Admin per Transaction

The fastest option for you to begin handing off the administrative duties is to simply hire a *Transaction Coordinator* or *Contract-to-Close Coordinator* on a per contract basis. In other words you will partner with an Admin who is an independent contractor and use them only when you have a transaction for them to work.

Partnering with someone who already has a business that handles real estate transactions is great because you don't have to spend any time training them. You simply need to spend a few hours with them to go over your system.

Your Duties and Theirs

If you hire a company that simply does contract to close, they will be handling steps 29 - 40. For an additional fee they may also be willing to handle some of the pre-listing duties in steps 10-29 as well, like adding the property to MLS, uploading photos, managing your CRM, etc.

Screening a Contract-to-Close Contractor

The most important thing to look for when hiring a third-party Admin is not their fees, but their *experience* and *their track record for success.*

Here are some questions and requests for any individual or company you are considering hiring:

> ➤ How many listings have you closed? (preferably more than 100)

> ➤ How long have you been closing real estate transactions? (preferably more than 2 years)

> ➤ Send me a list of 3-5 agents you are working with right now.

> ➤ Send me a list of several agents you've done more than 10 transactions with.

Be sure to check out their website for a complete list of services they offer; and follow up with the agent references they provide you.

Option 2: Hire a Part-time or Full-time Admin

When hiring a person on staff, you can choose from either a person who works from your office location or you can hire a virtual assistant (VA). At this point I am sold on the latter.

For years I had been apprehensive about the idea of hiring a VA. You know, someone who works from home, and could be hundreds or even thousands of miles away. I've always felt like I needed someone that I could communicate with face-to-face. But times are changing.

After reading *The Four Day Workweek* by Timothy Ferris several years ago, my mind opened up to the *idea* of working with VAs. In 2009 I shut down my office and sent my three Admins home to work for me *virtually*. The idea was difficult for me to embrace, however my Admins loved it. There are obvious pros and cons to this approach, however for me the pros have far outweighed the cons.

Finally, my good friend Daniel Ramsey convinced me to bite the bullet and hire my first *Overseas VA*. Daniel owns and operates MyOutdesk, the largest virtual assistant company for real estate agents. Currently MyOutdesk employs more than 2000 virtual assistants. I've known Daniel since before he and his brother Jason started the company and we reconnected at a convention where his company had a booth. I begin sharing with him what I was doing as far as my speaking engagements, touring etc. I also told him we needed to hire a *Director of Support* for our MoreSolds CRM, since my current Director had recently retired. *"Dude, you need to hire one of our VAs,"* Daniel told me quite convincingly. I fed Daniel a few lines about why I needed to have someone local, yada yada. After patiently listening to all my self-limiting beliefs, Daniel sat me down in front of a computer registration screen in their booth and said, *"Dude. Hire one of our VAs and let's get you on to success."* After a little additional coaxing from my wife, I apprehensively signed up. Hiring someone to work virtually, from the Philippines was something I had never done before or seriously considered, and I've hired lots of people over the past 20 years. I decided to give it a try. *"After all,"* I thought, *"it's month-to-month and I can cancel anytime. I might as well give it a shot."*

Partnering with MyOutdesk for my staffing needs has been a *game changer* for me. Truthfully it has been the best leverage move I have ever made, and it has completely freed me up to flourish because I am able to focus on what I love doing (teaching, writing, developing, training, mentoring, traveling, etc). In fact within 6 months of hiring my first VA, I had a team of 3 full time VAs!

As far as hiring a either a VA or an in-house Admin to handle your administrative duties, as a rule of thumb, I don't recommend that you hire one until you are getting a steady stream of at least three or more listings per month. MyOutDesk offers the option of a part time VA (20 hours a week) or a full time one (40 hours a week). They also have a rigorous training program so your VA comes to you already pre-trained in the core business of real estate.

Your Duties and Theirs

Your VA will be handling *all of the administrative duties* that are involved in both your listing and buyer transactions.

The sooner you can hire an administrative assistant the better, however you will need to have a steady volume of business in order to provide (and justify) a secure job.

Cost of a VA

You can hire an Advanced Real Estate Virtual Assistant for around $8.60/hour. If you hire a part-time VA the cost would be roughly $688/mo. A VA can also double as a marketing assistant, helping with your social media posting, calling on your database, contacting *Expireds* and *For Sale by Owners*, setting appointments and much more. *Be sure to check with your broker as to the specific duties that an unlicensed assistant can perform on your behalf as this varies from city to city and state to state.*

As a person who has had to administrate payroll for over 20 years I love the fact that I don't have to pay any payroll taxes, matching federal tax or provide health insurance (which MOD provides to their VAs).

If you choose not to go the overseas VA route, you will likely pay a stateside VA $12 - $30/hour, plus payroll taxes, withholding and health insurance if the law requires it.

Below is a sample job description (JD) for the Administrative Assistant role.

Administrative Assistant Job Description

About the Position

Our Team Administrative Assistant will be responsible for ensuring that all administrative aspects of the team are completed timely and per our system.

Administrative Duties:

- Compile, edit and use the Team Operations Manual that documents all systems and standards.
- Develop and implement systems for sellers, buyers, lead generation, contact database management and front and back office support. Ensure that all systems and processes run efficiently, making revisions as needed.
- Answer and route all phone calls.
- Coordinate the purchase, installation and maintenance of all office equipment.
- Develop and maintain the team filing systems (listings, contracts, legal, correspondence, etc) and computer databases.
- Complete weekly and monthly reports.
- Serve as first point of contact in handling customer inquiries and complaints.
- Responsible for all financial systems. This includes maintaining the books, paying the bills, handling payroll, assuring the collection of commissions, maintaining the budget and generating financial reports. Responsible for the accuracy and timelines of all financial information.
- Receive DAs and draft DIs.

Transaction Duties for Listings:

- Serve as key relationship for all sellers.
- Conduct initial phone consultation with intake sheet.
- Complete seller market analysis (per SWL method).
- Preview seller properties and write up preview report.

- Responsible for timely and consistent follow up on all seller leads.
- Draft listing documents.
- Schedule in-office meeting with potential sellers.
- Order photos (for new listings).
- Input and maintain properties on MLS.
- Set up showing feedback and transaction in our MoreSolds database CRM per our checklist.
- Make weekly calls to sellers with recommended price improvements.
- Review any pre-option period requests with seller.
- Review inventory weekly and reevaluate pricing as needed.
- Contract-to-close
- Send post-closing gifts.

Transaction Duties for Buyers:
- Responsible for timely and consistent follow-up with all buyer leads.
- Conduct initial phone consultation and follow-up email.
- Set up search portal for each prospect via our MLS system.
- Connect prospective buyers with our preferred lenders.
- Draw up Buyer Representation agreements.
- Serve as key relationship for all buyers.
- Conduct initial phone consultation with intake sheet.
- Draw up buyer contracts.

Knowledge, Skills, Experience needed and Attributes desired:

- Proficient computer skills.
- Excellent phone skills.
- Experience in the real estate industry.
- Good people skills.
- Friendly personality.
- Attention to detail.
- Ability to manage and lead others.
- Ability to design and implement efficient systems.
- Work well with little to no supervision.
- Trustworthy.
- Task oriented.
- Results driven.
- Ability to prioritize.
- Excellent written and verbal communication skills.
- Internet savvy.

Proficient skills in the following are highly desired:

- MLS System.
- Zip Forms.
- Docusign.
- Excel, Word, PowerPoint, Publisher.
- Excellent and fast computer navigating skills.
- Great management skills.

Term:

- We will begin with a 100 day initial evaluation term. At the end of the 100 days, we will mutually evaluate each other and decide if we can continue.

5 Compensation Models for Your Admin

You can compensate your Admin in one of five ways. There are other models for how to pay, however these are the most widely used. If you are not working with an independent contractor, you will need to factor an additional 15% to these rates to the cover your employer's portion of federal income taxes plus additional expenses if health insurance is required.

1) **Outsourced VA through *MyOutDesk*:** Pay $8.60 per hour; $688 for a part-time VA (20 hours/wk) or $1,376 for full-time (40 hours/wk).

2) **Hourly:** $12 to $30 per hour or more depending on your market area. No compensation per transaction, just an hourly wage.

3) **Salary Only:** Monthly salary of $1,200 to $2,000 (part time) to $2,400 to $4,000 (full time), depending on the hours they work and the going rate in your area.

4) **Salary Plus Bonus:** Pay an Admin a flat monthly fee, say $1,200 per month (full time) PLUS $300 to $500 per transaction.

5) **Fee per Transaction:** Pay an Admin a per-transaction fee of $300 to $400 or more per closed transaction, depending on the volume of transactions you are closing

per month and the specific duties they will be performing.

Conclusion:

It is important to remember that as you begin to take on more listings, you will need to hire someone to handle the administrative tasks and other tasks associated with successfully servicing and closing your mounting supply of listings.

The most important initial hires to your team will not be other real estate agents – they will be Administrative people. Because real estate transactions are so heavily administrative, your Admin staff can perform more than 91% of the tasks associated with each listing.

In the next chapter we will discuss your second critical hire – a Team Buyer's Specialist.

Chapter 20 Homework

☐ Research local contract-to-close companies

☐ Take a look at MyOutDesk.com for a list of VA options. I've negotiated a special discount for my readers ($250 off the initial setup fee). Just mention that "Knolly" sent you

☐ Develop your Job Description for you Admin person by tweaking my template

Chapter 21
Your Second Hire: Team Buyer Specialist

I have witnessed many agents grow a successful listing business while completely neglecting the buyer side of their business. Every well-marketed property you list has the potential to generate another listing and at least two qualified buyers who will buy.

Once you have a steady stream of listings and a well-oiled operation with solid Admin(s) in place, you will want to hire a team Buyer Specialist. A well trained Buyer Specialist who has a good understanding of your current and upcoming inventory will be able to educate prospects and should be able to convert many buyer prospects to *clients*.

A great Buyer Specialist should have a *field day* when snapped into a team that has a good inventory of listings.

Since you are providing the leads – a typical split with a buyer's agent is 50/50. If you carry a decent listing inventory (even as few as 5 or more listings) and you do not have a

Buyer Specialist on your team, you are foregoing a good amount of potential income.

Keep in mind that once you begin to focus on listings the way you should, buyers will become a complete distraction for you and your business. With rare exception, they should be serviced by your team Buyer Specialist(s).

You can also assign your Buyer Specialists additional tasks such as setting up your listings, placing your signs and lockboxes, runner duties, implementing marketing, making prospecting calls and much more.

Below is a sample job description (JD) for the Team Buyer Specialist role.

Team Buyer Specialist Job Description:

About the Position:

Through our various marketing efforts, our team generates buyer leads and buyer showing requests. Our Team Buyer Specialist is responsible for going on all showing appointments and successfully securing buyer listings from these leads.

Main Responsibilities for this position include:

- Responsible for timely and consistent follow-up with all leads.
- Conduct initial phone consultation and send follow-up email.
- Set up a search portal for each prospect via Matrix.
- Conduct face-to-face meetings with buyers
- Serve as the key relationship for all buyers.

- Develop expert knowledge regarding mortgage financing, neighborhoods, schools and all home ownership issues.
- Provide high level fiduciary advice to all clients.
- Consult with clients to ensure fiduciary service of the real estate transaction from initial contact through contract to close.
- Effectively negotiate for all buyers.
- Set up leads on a drip email campaign using MoreSolds.
- Work directly with Office Admin on any issues that require resolution.

Job Context:
- Opportunity to work from home or from our main office.
- Opportunity for career growth within the team.

Knowledge, Skills, Experience needed and Attributes desired:
- Excellent presentation skills.
- Excellent time management.
- Excellent negotiating skills.
- Excellent phone skills.
- Experience in the real estate industry.
- Good computer skills.
- Friendly personality.
- Good people skills.
- Attention to detail.
- Work well with little to no supervision.

- Trustworthy.
- Task oriented.
- Results driven.
- Ability to prioritize.
- Excellent written and verbal communication skills.
- Internet savvy.

Proficient skills in the following are highly desired:
- MLS System.
- Microsoft Word.
- Excel.
- Excellent computer navigating skills.

Goal/Expectation:
- Place 3 buyers per month into escrow.

Compensation:

Based on the listing and closing goals we project, this position can earn $60,000 to $90,000 per year. Buyer Specialist split is 50/50.

Initial Term:

We will begin with a 100 day initial evaluation term. At the end of the 100 days, we will mutually evaluate each other and decide if we can continue.

Next let's try and scrape your plate even further by hiring a Team Listing Specialist.

Chapter 22
Your Third Hire: Team Listing Specialist

Your operation is buzzing. You already have one or more Admins handling all of your administrative duties. You also have one or more Buyer Specialists handling all of the buyer inquiries and the buyer side of the business.

Once you are getting a significant amount of listings you may choose to hire a team *Listing Specialist* to take over the majority of your remaining duties. Your team Listing Specialist will handle all of the duties involved in setting up a listing, including putting together a CMA, handling the listing appointment, receiving and negotiating offers and managing your listing inventory. This hire frees you up to be the *rainmaker* – allowing you to focus your time and attention to building your database and generating more leads for your team.

It's important to note that by the time you need this person you may already have multiple Admins and Buyer Specialists. The fact that this is your *third hire* does not mean that it is the third *person* you bring on to your team. It simply means that this is the third *category* of talent. For example you could already have two administrators and five Buyer Specialists, and be closing 200 transactions a year before you need to bring on this 3rd spoke in your wheel. Make sense?

This individual will be conducting your listing presentations, therefore, it is important that you hire someone who is pleasant, likable, impressionable, dependable, and can be easily trusted. Since you already have the machine in place, this person is essentially a *presenter* and a *consultant.*

In my own practice, I took a schoolteacher who was earning roughly $22,000 per year and groomed her for this role, where she earned more than $100,000 a year. She already had the personality for the job, she just had to be trained and licensed. Today, using the principles outlined in this book she and her husband consistently earn more than $300,000 per year by *focusing on listings.*

Document and Cross Train

Make sure that your systems are well documented. You should have step-by-step instructions and checklists for every task and duty performed by the members of your team. This training guide serves as the foundation for your system. As your listing business progresses, you can tweak and adjust your system as necessary. Once your well-oiled machine is operating at maximum capacity, you may find it necessary to add even more talent. If so, you may simply add an administrative assistant or two and bring them to assist your already trained *Power Team*. In fact, make sure that each of your team members is *cross-trained* (trained to do other team member's duties) in case a team member is out sick, on vacation or quits. Building a great team can be very rewarding once they are all properly trained and feeding the machine.

Your third hire can essentially help scrape your plate.

Compensation Options:

Remember that your team Listing Specialist is primarily consulting with clients and doing live presentations. They will be compensated in one of several ways. Here are a few ideas:

➢ **Hourly:** Pay your Listing Specialist an hourly wage (perhaps $18-25 per hour or more), depending on your market area. No compensation per transaction, just an hourly wage.

➢ **Salary only:** Pay a Listing Specialist a monthly salary of $3,000 to $4,000 (full time) or so, depending on the hours they work and the going rate in your area.

➢ **Salary plus bonus:** Pay a flat monthly fee, say $2,000 per month (full time) PLUS $300 to $500 per transaction.

➢ **Per transaction percentage only:** Pay a Listing Specialist a per-transaction split of 20% to 30% per closed transaction, depending on the volume of transactions you are closing per month.

Below is a sample job description (JD) for the Team Listing Specialist role.

Listing Specialist Job Description

About the Position:

Through our various marketing efforts, our team generates seller listing leads and listing appointments. Our Team Listing Specialist is responsible for going on all listing appointments (with equity sellers) and successfully securing listings from these leads.

Main Responsibilities for this position include:

- Serve as the key relationship for all equity sellers.
- Go on listing appointments and successfully convert leads to listings.
- Provide high level fiduciary advice on pricing strategies and staging houses for sale.
- Follow up with leads from *Expireds, Geographical Farms, Past Clients*, etc.
- Consult with clients to ensure fiduciary service of the Real Estate transaction from initial contact through contract to close.
- Evaluate Showing Survey feedback and re-evaluate pricing as needed.
- Effectively negotiate for all sellers.
- Maintain the transaction and client information in our MoreSolds online contact and transaction management system.

- Responsible for timely and consistent follow-up with all leads.
- Set up leads on a drip email campaign using MoreSolds.
- Work directly with our Admin team on any issues that require resolution.

Knowledge, Skills, Experience needed and Attributes desired:
- Excellent presentation skills.
- Excellent listing skills.
- Excellent negotiating skills.
- Excellent phone skills.
- Experience in the real estate industry.
- Proficient computer skills.
- Friendly personality.
- Good people skills.
- Attention to detail.
- Work well with little to no supervision.
- Trustworthy.
- Task oriented.
- Results driven.
- Ability to prioritize.
- Excellent written and verbal communication skills.
- Internet savvy.

Proficient skills in the following are highly desired:
- MLS System.
- Microsoft Word.
- Excel (not required).

- Excellent computer navigating skills.

Goal/Expectation:

Maintain a 70%+ conversion rate at converting listing leads to appointments, and maintain an 80%+ success rate at converting appointments to signed listings agreements. Of your listings taken, you will be expected to maintain a closings average of 90%+.

Compensation:

This is a 1099 contractor position and it pays commission only. Commission paid to you is 30% on listings closed. We will provide you with our independent contractor's agreement.

Initial Term:

We will begin with a 100 day initial evaluation term. At the end of the 100 days, we will mutually evaluate each other and decide if we can continue.

Chapter 23
Replacing Yourself

As your business grows you may eventually decide to *fire yourself* and hire someone to run your operation.

Here are some of the situations that may lead you to find a replacement:

➤ You are highly entrepreneurial and therefore too busy with other endeavors to properly manage and oversee your team on a daily basis.

➤ You want to focus all of your energy on the most dollar productive activity (lead generation) and let others handle everything else.

➤ You are ready to retire or semi-retired from the business and need someone to take over your duties and your database.

➤ You need someone to oversee your business while you focus on a new niche, division or department of your operation.

I've coached some agents who are just plain *bored with success*. They've reached all of their goals and the business is no longer *fun* for them. *They feel called to do something else.* Rather than just *abandon* the empire that they have built, they feel that it makes more sense to keep the vision running through others.

Others find that they have reached a *ceiling of achievement* and need to bring on fresh talent to take the business to the next level.

As you would expect, finding the right person to take over your real estate operation may not be easy. You need someone who can uphold your high standards and move your operation forward.

As far as job duties are concerned, *your Operations Manager* may do any of the job duties that the Listing Specialist does, or they can simply oversee the operation filling in wherever needed.

Your compensation for this person can be a set monthly salary, monthly salary plus a bonus per closing, or just a percentage of each transaction closed (i.e. a percentage of the operation).

About the Position

This person will operate as the Team CEO and could be responsible for lead generation, company vision, team member performance review, hiring, firing and training of team members, etc. They can also dually serve as the team's Lead Listing Specialist (see job description in Chapter 22).

Note that this person will do all of the duties that you are currently doing, thus they will effectively become your replacement. If you want, you can hold on to *lead generation*, time blocking your daily 3 or so hours to be the rainmaker while this person oversees everything else.

You will need to have weekly accountability/coaching meetings with your Team CEO/Operations Manager to review your numbers *(Productivity Meeting)* and hold every team member accountable to the team goals. Don't wait to have these meetings monthly – as that is too long a time span to correctly calibrate when you are off course. Hold weekly meetings (they can be phone based) to review your numeric goals (see Chapter 4).

Although you are now retired, *or semi-retired*, you can *never take your eyes off the ball*. Remember that you may be called upon to step back into the operation at any time, and at a moment's notice – *so stay sharp!* Continue to hold your replacement accountable and take time to enjoy your life – YOU'VE EARNED IT!

About Knolly Williams

Knolly Williams is an Author, Trainer and National Speaker, and has been featured on ABC, NBC, FOX, CBS, Newsweek and in over 300 newspapers worldwide. Knolly has coached tens of thousands of new and seasoned real estate agents on how to effectively list and close more real estate transactions by modeling the best practices of the nation's top listing agents.

Since he obtained his real estate license, Knolly's focus has been on LISTINGS. He took 21 listings during his first 74 days in the business and went on to take more than 1000 listings during his first 10 years as an agent.

Knolly provides tools and resources that help real estate agents succeed and excel at finding, securing and closing more seller listings. Through **SuccessWithListings.com**, Knolly helps agents generate more leads, more listings and grow their business while mastering the best tactics that are working today.

Knolly also serves as the CEO of **MoreSolds.com** – America's fastest growing free online cloud-based contact and transaction management software for real estate agents.

In his personal life, Knolly's biggest joy is his Christian faith and relationship with the Lord, his relationship with his wife Josefina (they married in 1992), and his weekly Bible classes, which he has been teaching since 1989. His mission and purpose in life is to connect with others and help them fulfill their goals and aspirations.

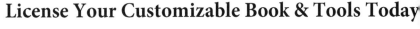

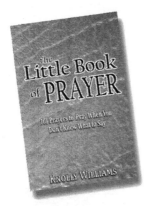

This is <u>Your Special Invitation</u>:

Hey there! Are you ready to really <u>EXPLODE</u> your listing business?

I mean, are you ready to REALLY succeed at the highest level possible? YES? Then my Success with Listings Academy is for YOU!

I've helped thousands of agents double, triple or quadruple their production. <u>YOU'RE NEXT</u>!

Take a LOOK at What You Get...

Monthly Group Coaching Call with Me! Connect directly with me and learn the best new listing tactics, get advice, ask questions and grow your business!

Monthly Training Video! NEW Video Trainings designed to help you blow up your listing business. Learn the best tips, tricks and tactics for Success!

Private Facebook Group Page! Continue the conversation and get up-to-the-minute advice and your questions answered through our private community!

Library of Scripts! Access the best listing scripts that are working in today's market. New scripts are added monthly!

Library of Coaching Calls! All calls are recorded and archived! If you can't make a call - no worries. It's saved in our online library forever!

Library of Videos! Access the entire library of monthly video trainings. New videos are added monthly!

Nationwide Referral Network. Network with and receive referrals from other Listing Specialists around the country.

Support Hotline. Direct telephone access to my Support Team; 5 days a week Monday - Friday! **JOIN TODAY!**

www.SuccessWithListings.com